SUPERTUBE

SUPERTUBE

THE RISE OF TELEVISION SPORTS

RON POWERS

COWARD-McCANN, INC.

NEW YORK

The author gratefully acknowledges permission from The New York Times
Company to reprint a column by Arthur Daley, © 1955 by The New York
Times Company.

Designed by Richard Oriolo

Library of Congress Cataloging in Publication Data

Powers, Ron.
Supertube: the rise of television sports.

Bibliography: p.
Includes index.
1. Television and sports—United States. I. Title.
GV742.3.P68   1984   070.4′49796   83-7425
ISBN 0-698-11253-9

ACKNOWLEDGMENTS

The memories, the personal records and the informed analyses of nearly 100 sources, both active in and retired from network television, advertising, public relations and financial research, form the journalisic spine of this book.

From the many whose generosity and patience were unwavering, I would like to particularly salute a few who provided an especially significant yield of data and support:

For their historical and statistical contributions, I thank Albert S. Leonard, the retired public relations director of Gillette Co.'s safety razor division; Joel Nixon, public relations director of the National Hockey League; Irving Brodsky, director of sports information for ABC Television, and the members of Brodsky's staff; Kevin Monahan of NBC Sports publicity; and Doug Richardson of CBS Sports publicity.

ABC Sports executives whose cooperation proved extremely helpful included Roone Arledge, president; Chuck Howard, vice president for program productions; James Spence, senior vice president; Julius Barnathan, president of broadcast operations and engineering. My thanks also to broadcasters Howard Cosell, Jim McKay and Chris Schenkel.

At NBC Sports, special help came from Mike Weisman, NBC Sports' executive producer; Harry Coyle, director; and Linda Jonsson, coordinating producer of SportsWorld. Don Ohlmeyer, the former executive producer of NBC Sports and currently president of Ohlmeyer Communications, was also helpful.

At CBS Sports, I am particularly grateful to Neal Pilson, president; Van Gordon Sauter, the former Sports president and later president of CBS News; to vice president Carl Lindemann, Jr.; to producer Terry O'Neil; to Mort Sharnik and Perry Smith; and to broadcaster Lindsey Nelson.

I am grateful, too, for the additional reminiscences of these men, whose stories unfold in the ensuing chapters: Edgar J. Scherick, Tom

Villante, Mel Allen, Reuven Frank, Jack Buck, Tom Gallery, Dick Ebersol, Tom Moore, William C. MacPhail, Don Dunphy, and Barry Frank.

Louis A. Guth, senior vice president of National Economic Research Associates, Inc., supplied many useful insights into the economic realities that underlie the world of televised sports.

I am grateful for the research assistance that was provided by Mary Bruno and by John Freeman.

Finally, I want to express my gratitude for the friendship, guidance and criticism of several close friends who are themselves writers and editors: to John Walsh, the brilliant editor of the late, exquisite *Inside Sports* magazine, who helped me conceive a sports-media column for that publication; and to *I. S.* editors Jay Lovinger and Larry Schwartz, whose thoughts about the cultural impact of televised sports formed the early momentum for this book. And to David Haward Bain, Bob Riess and Ambrose Clancy, companions and fellow adventurers in the craft of writing, whose talent and devotion to excellence define the scope of my own ambition.

For Joyce

CONTENTS

I

THE ULTIMATE GAMES

What would Zeus have made of Los Angeles in 1984?

Zeus, who won the first Olympics by wresting the earth from Kronos—how would he begin to comprehend this latest homage to his splendor?

He would need a brochure. He would need to reorient himself to the updated iconography. The very year belongs, not to Janus, the god of good beginnings, but to Orwell, the god of bad ends. The city, not to Athena, but to some weird consortium of Evelyn Waugh, Walt Disney and the William Morris agency.

And the Games . . . well, the Games. The Games of the XXXIII Olympiad are symbolized not so much by an Eternal Flame or by the interlocking Circles of Brotherhood as by a fifty-pound fiberglass animated Disney eagle named Sam.

These Games, clearly, would beggar the imagination of Zeus, this god who never contemplated his own image on videotape replay, nor got to proclaim his greatness to Howard Cosell. These will be the Ultimate Games of Television, a Promethean force that will hurl the electronic images of the gladiator-gods and -goddesses before the eyes of two and a half billion mortals on every inhabited surface of the planet. (The other billion and a half, presumably, prefer old movies or reruns of *Lucy*.)

It is almost universally agreed that there will never again be an exclusive network sporting event on the scale of the Los Angeles Games. Already some experts predict that the winning bid for the 1988 Games in Korea will approach $1 billion. This begins to get into real money. No network can unilaterally absorb that kind of cost, expecting to offset it with advertising revenues. What may happen, many people believe, is that after 1984, a network will share its telecast rights—and its expenses—with a pay-cable distributor such as Home Box Office, somewhat on the model of the United States Football League telecasts, shared by ABC and the cable system ESPN.

Thus the notion that the LA telecast will mark the last, best spectacle of its kind—an Ultimate Games of television.

One hundred forty miles separate the northernmost perimeter of LA Olympic competition (Lake Casitas near Santa Barbara, site of the rowing) from the southernmost (the pentathalon venue in Cota de Caza, south of Long Beach). That is six times the distance that Pheidippides ran between Marathon and Athens to bring news of the Athenian victory over the Persians—after which Pheidippides dropped dead. From the weightlifting at Loyola Marymount University to the handball in Pomona a god would have to schlep thirty-five miles. Which would render him some twenty-eight miles from the cycling, back at California State University in Dominguez Hills.

In fact, adding up the distances along the perimeter of the various venues in Los Angeles—from soccer at the Rose Bowl to equestrian events at Santa Anita Park to handball at California State University-Fullerton to fencing and volleyball and yachting in Long Beach to the Olympic Villages on the campuses of USC and UCLA, one arrives at an unsettling realization: these Olympics will encompass more than one thousand square miles.

But mere mileage, of course, is hardly the *point* of the 1984 Games. Mileage is of moment only to the twenty-five hundred ABC employees and the fourteen thousand competitors (a number equal to General Pickett's force at Gettysburg, before the charge) and the few hundred thousand spectators who will actually be *there*. The real setting of the Los Angeles Olympics is no earthly one. It is the television screen. And on the screen, there is no distance, no separation, no sense of *transit*—only phenomena, unremitting and immediate.

The most olympian competition at the 1984 Summer Olympics will not be between any two star athletes, nor even between any two rival nations. It will be between two abstractions—*television* and *distance*. And if ABC flawlessly performs its herculean agenda of intricate switchings and dissolves and remote pickups, if the dense electronic web of microwave circuits holds and the aural interlacing of intercom voices prevails without dissolving into chaos and if the directors can maintain their air-traffic-controller's concentration over endless hours without breaking down; if nothing breaks—then the highest goal of this competition will be realized: it will remain invisible to the audience.

There are no guarantees that the system will hold. On the contrary, Los Angeles' very infrastructure seems to throw itself against success. ABC broadcasting to the nation—that is no problem. ABC broadcasting to itself—that will be something else. Since great swatches of distance will separate the dozens of network production crews, a fail-safe internal communications system will be indispensable. But Los Angeles is nothing if not a communications hive. The over-air frequencies are saturated with users, and the area's hills and canyons defy long-range, line-of-sight transmission in any event.

A solution appeared to present itself in the form of Pacific Telephone & Telegraph. By one of those coincidences that normally materialize only in West Coast spy-caper films, the phone company just happened to be in the process of installing a fiber-optics network linking most of the various Olympic venues. Fiber optics are flat, thin ribbons of pure glass—just hundredths of an inch in diameter—capable of transmitting data in the form of light. Even aural information can be encoded at one end, transferred to light, and decoded at the other. Pacific Telephone & Telegraph invited ABC to tap into its three hundred miles of fiber-optic network at what PT&T considered a nominal cost. Just $15 million above ABC's projected budget for internal communications.

The Los Angeles Games will be the most protean pageant in the history of sport, wedded to the most leviathan deployment of circuitry, audio and video hardware, rolling (and airborne) stock, engineering, production, on-air and managerial manpower for any self-contained event short of a shooting war in the forty-year history of television—indeed, in mankind's first century of broadcasting.

—TV cameras numbering 207; or 157 more cameras than needed to telecast the Winter Olympics at Sarajevo;

—Videotape machines numbering 279 of the one-inch variety and 117 of the three-quarter-inch variety;

—Character generators (those keyboard devices for flashing up names, statistics and bulletin information on the screen) numbering 23, including some with capabilities so revolutionary that ABC classified them as Top Secret before they were unveiled;

—Mobile units (mostly studio-equipped vans, but also some helicopters and a blimp or two) numbering at least 25, with a collective retail value of $100 million—nearly every major mobile unit in the United States;

—Five "Flash Units," a sort of Rapid Deployment Force—mobile vans and helicopters capable of telecasting live or recording on tape from point of origin by means of microwave relay, plus additional units from ABC News—that will be kept on twenty-four-hour alert, ready to rush to cover something that both ABC and Olympic officials pray will never materialize: a breaking news event, which (given the pattern of past

Olympics "breaking news") would likely mean a defection, a gesture of class or nationalistic protest, or an act of terrorism;

—A vehicle (still on the drawing boards as late as spring of 1983) capable of propelling itself along a thoroughfare for as long as two and a half hours, supporting heavy cameras, mikes and power supplies for telecasting a marathon race, without discharging gasoline fumes into the runners' faces;

—And perhaps most prodigious of all, a self-contained complex (known to ABC insiders as "the Little Olympic Village") of studio control rooms, complete with camera-switching consoles, monitor screens, microphones and telephones for communicating with producers in the field, and also containing the principal studio set for the Olympics' ABC host, Jim McKay—a complex that was constructed in Los Angeles, then taken apart and shipped to New York, where it was reassembled for testing, later to be torn down again for shipping to Sarajevo for use in covering the Winter Games, after which it will be disassembled again and shipped back to Los Angeles for Summer 1984.

The 1984 Games will be in many ways the supreme handiwork of a modern-day Zeus: a television deity named Roone Arledge. Arledge, the dual president of ABC News and Sports, will personally supervise nearly half the total telecast. His presence at the controls will mark the denouement of a forty-year romance between American television and American sports. RCA-owned cameras actually transmitted two baseball games as far back as 1939—Columbia-Princeton and Brooklyn-Cincinnati—but World War II deferred the real beginning of the Television Age until late 1944. It has been an erratic romance. Contrary to popular assumptions, television has been a highly unwilling suitor through most of it.

Before Arledge stepped into the picture in 1960 as a smart, unterrified twenty-eight-year-old, sports were something the networks covered virtually with fingers held to their corporate nostrils. Sports weren't Jack Benny. They weren't Edward R. Murrow. They weren't any of the things that had made radio so fashionable. Clearly, sports held little promise as mainline TV fare.

It took a succession of visionary but anonymous advertising men to force-feed the first generation of prepackaged sports telecasts to the network airwaves. Arledge was the first network regular to appreciate the power inherent in TV sports, and he created a wholly original idiom that brilliantly released that power. His underdog network, ABC, gambled on his vision and won; ABC rode TV sports to parity with its richer, complacent rivals over a dramatic sixteen-year haul that climaxed in 1976. In that year, buoyed partly by its triumphant telecasts of the Montreal Olympics, ABC leaped from last place to first among the Big Three for the first time in its history.

Arledge's coup was astonishing. More astonishing still was that CBS and NBC were nearly fifteen years in taking the hint. Indisputably, CBS was the ancient network of the NFL and NBC had its blue-chip bowl games and World Series. But they had *inherited* these events, and covered them mainly as though they were breaking news stories; sports at those networks were a generally scorned appendage of the news divisions. Not until the early 1970s did the older networks begin to copy ABC Sports' prototype in earnest. By then, a new surge of post-Watergate, post-Vietnam public appetite for pleasure and self-fulfillment had catapulted games, and athletes, into the forefront of the pop culture. Billie Jean King and Bobby Riggs, Evel Knievel, Muhammed Ali, Sugar Ray Leonard, Joe Namath, John McEnroe, Jim Palmer—all these stars, and others, became part of America's video household, as famous as prime-time sitcom characters or anchormen. Sports salaries exploded, domed stadiums sprouted like metallic mushrooms upon the landscape, and telecast rights soared in value.

Looming over all the scrambling frenzy was the one supreme event, through which Arledge had honed and perfected his idiom. The event that had come to be associated with his name. His event. The Olympics.

America on the eve of the 1984 Olympics is a nation seemingly stupefied on sports.

Consider a random survey of the figures: a $2-billion contract between the three major networks and the National Football League (with the resulting advent of the $345,000 NFL commercial minute); network TV-radio revenues of $2 million for each of the twenty-six (!) major-league baseball clubs, plus a total of $65 million in various local broadcasting rights; a six-year contract worth $1,722,000 signed by a head coach—Jackie Sherrill at Texas A&M University—to help ensure the school's chance at premium TV revenues for football telecasts; a combined $260-million football rights package signed by CBS, ABC and the National Collegiate Athletic Association; an average salary for professional basketball players of $246,000 (an increase of one hundred percent from the mid-1970s); product-endorsement fees totaling $2 million a year for TV-tennis superstar Bjorn Borg . . . One could go on.

By 1982 ABC Sports' total billings had climbed to nearly $350 million a year. NBC Sports was at around $300 million and CBS Sports at $250 million. Each of these budgets indicates capital assets that would rank its network's sports division alone within the country's leading six hundred corporations. In terms of monetary power, these three sports divisions rival the dozens of leagues and franchises they cover: the aggregate revenues of all professional sports clubs, as compiled by the 1977 United States Census, equal only $937 million.

As a final insight into TV sports' imperial status, consider this incident that took place in 1978. A man named Mickey Holman, then the executive director of the Missouri Valley Conference, telephoned the ABC Sports division headquarters in New York with a plea as outlandish as it was urgent. "Can you get one of our conference games on your telecast schedule?" Holmes implored an ABC executive. "Because if you can't, we're going to have to close our doors. Fold the conference." *Fold the conference.* The economic benefits of just one network telecast would spell the difference between survival and oblivion—not for just one school, but for an entire collegiate conference. ABC complied.

This ultimate Television Olympics may prove to be more than the sum of its micro-electric and competitive parts. It may stand as an archive, a sixteen-day summing-up of a certain moment in American time. This moment spans the decades between the end of industrial America—a demise triggered by the consequences of World War II—and the onset of the Data Age, an age that already has begun to separate a technological elite from the rest of society, with still-unknown consequences for the individual identity. The moment spans an epoch of intense, agnostic, nuclear-addled confusion. Walker Percy has identified this moment in terms of what it lacks; religious faith, community, fidelity, chivalry, an intolerance for the culture's Sodomlike attributes, a will for redemption.

Percy's picture of a spiritually sterile postwar American landscape superimposes quite neatly upon a corresponding development since the end of World War II—an explosion in the popular culture's yearning preoccupation with sports.

The evidence hardly needs recounting: the cultural and political deification of athletes, the tortuous and almost prayerful pressure upon the hundreds of college teams to be "Number One," the compulsive rise in sports gambling, the semireligious significance bestowed upon the Super Bowl, the frenetic construction of mosquelike domed stadiums from New Orleans to Indianapolis to Minneapolis and from Houston to Detroit to Seattle; and, perhaps most telling of all, a citizenry that seems bent on internalizing the sporting gods' grandeur by living out a liturgical style. Americans dress themselves in numeraled team jerseys and team hats; they speak to one another in athletic jargon; they elect former players and professed worshipers of players to high political office. They often seem to see America's place in geopolitics through a prism of athletic revelation. And they emulate the manners and the physical style of the famous athlete-gods—gliding and juking on the worst ghetto basketball courts, swearing and screaming on the best suburban tennis courts. Even their children must conform to the examples of the elect: eight-year-old sons are conscripted into "pro-style" football leagues with playoffs in Honolulu; their sisters enter training under the aegis of Peggy Fleming or Tracy Austin.

Most people, when they think about the relationship of TV to sports, assume that Imperial Television moved aggressively to absorb and "colonize" sports, as television is seen to have colonized nearly everything else in its path. The truth is quite a bit more complex than that. A careful examination of the history of TV and sports since World War II shows that sports, as often as not, colonized television—that they forced their way into the mainstream of TV programing only after decades of indifference and active hostility on the part of the highest network executives. The conduit for this forced access was a succession of professional advertising men, acting as surrogate network programers.

Extended indifference—followed by an era of inept and wholesale exploitation of sports' basest marketing appeal—changed and cheapened a source of video content that many serious critics now regard as the content most naturally suited to television's peculiar capacities. There was one resounding exception to that general pattern, however: the ABC Television Network, particularly in the first several years before and after Roone Arledge assumed control of ABC Sports.

Because of ABC's historic competitive disadvantage in relation to its older, more established rivals, ABC was virtually forced into a series of long-shot gambles in sports programing, gambles that CBS and NBC disdained. Roone Arledge inherited the early, paradoxical success of these gambles, and he also inherited a free-wheeling, almost piratical approach to programing that came to define ABC's corporate style.

A man prodigiously equipped to exploit his particular moment in time, Arledge created a new legitimacy for games on television. He created a complex and far-reaching apparatus for covering those games. More significant still, he created a unified and fundamental theory of television itself, a theory that took into account the ancient principles of dramaturgy as well as the most contemporary sensibilities of a video audience.

The hallmarks of Arledge's style were a high respect for the power of *story* over the human imagination, a probing visual intimacy with the subject matter, a relentless, even obsessive preoccupation with the smallest detail ("I always know when an on-air announcer has just received a call from Roone at home," a former ABC producer said. "I can hear it in the change in his voice"), and—most mystical of all—an abiding sense of ABC itself as an unseen but always involved character in whatever event it is transmitting. That event might be a sporting match, or it might be (as Arledge's idiom spread) a newscast, or a breaking live story, or a documentary, or a morning or late-night discussion show. The self-referential quality of ABC News and Sports—both of which Arledge has headed since 1977—may have been the most important subliminal key to his programing success. Like most of his innovations, it was widely ridiculed by critics and competitors—and, inevitably, imitated, made standard.

By 1984, ABC will have telecast nine of the past fourteen Olympics. Before 1960, there were no Olympics on television. In 1960, CBS telecast filmed highlights and a few live events in the Games from Squaw Valley and from Rome. There was little discernible audience enthusiasm. It became apparent to the network executives of the time that TV audiences were interested only in sporting events that had already implanted themselves in the public consciousness: familiar blue-chip attractions such as the World Series and the Rose Bowl and heavyweight title bouts.

But in 1961, a twenty-nine-year-old Arledge inherited from his mentor, a shrewd if unsung programer named Edgar Scherick, an experimental Saturday-afternoon format, a potpourri of filmed and videotaped events—the sorts of events most people had never bothered to follow: rodeos and demolition derbies and wrist-wrestling matches, plus a few major amateur track meets. The experimental show was cheap. It would give ABC a weekly sports presence on the air *and* save money—if it worked. The show's name was *Wide World of Sports.* Its host was a short, unknown former game-show announcer named Jim McManus, or Jim McKay, as he preferred to be known.

Rival networks sneered at *Wide World of Sports.* NBC made a particular point—which it drove home for years—of being the network of *live* sports coverage. Nevertheless, within a few years, Arledge had crafted *Wide World of Sports* into one of the most popular—and profitable—shows on all of television.

Wide World covered Amateur Athletic Union track and field competitions, which were considered to be utterly without following by TV audiences. The AAU coverage led Arledge and ABC into the Olympics. ABC's Olympics coverage led the network, in 1976, from last place to first in the ratings. In the same year, the United States Olympic Committee officially credited ABC with bringing about "significant increase in contributions for the Olympic movement and in evoking interest on the part of U.S. citizens wanting to become participants" in the next Winter Games. The committee reported that within one month of the telecasts from Innsbruck, Austria, it had received more than thirty-three thousand requests for Olympic patches, plus 250 letters a day requesting information on such matters as how to apply for a position on the bobsled and luge teams.

That curve of interest continued to climb through Montreal and Lake Placid, and into 1984: the People's Republic of China, which had stonily ignored Olympics competition for fifty years, announced that it would send thirty athletes to Mr. Arledge's Los Angeles Games. Then the People's Republic reconsidered. It would send three hundred.

These Ultimate Games of television—which will have a total cost of $500 million and a projected total revenue of $616 million, which will cost $500,000 for a commercial minute and will have a projected audience of 2.5 billion, which will summon Russia and China, England and Argentina and all those other lions and lambs, even as the ancient Olympics were said to have halted wars for their duration—these Olympics will be the logical extension of young Roone Arledge's cost-cutting mandate back in 1961. They will be the ultimate *Wide World of Sports*.

Of course, all of this deployment of money and technology assumes a very basic premise: that when the Eternal Flame is lighted (engulfing the tiny ABC microphone that will be embedded therein to record its "whoosh") and those 207 cameras go hot, *somebody* out there in America will be watching Channel 7.

ABC estimates that 190 million Americans—eighty-six percent of the population—will watch at least part of the telecasts. But unless the audience is gripped, and gripped early, by what it sees, ABC could conceivably have a certain amount of explaining to do to those half-a-million-a-minute sponsors.

What this means is that ABC Sports faces an Orwellian task between now and July 28, the opening day in LA: it must *create* an Olympic audience to consume the tele-sports behemoth that it has also created. In other words, ABC will undertake—has undertaken by the time you read this—a massive on-air conditioning process. Its aim: to instill in the public psyche a strong sense of who the leading competitors are (and not just Americans; ABC must make household words of surnames from all over the globe); which events are crucial and why; how the scoring systems for various events work—in short, a preconditioned system of responses for thousands of personalities and their Olympic aims.

The principal vehicle for this process—completing a historic cycle—will be *Wide World of Sports.* ABC producers are busy jamming the *Wide World* schedules with competitions that look like Olympic events and, whenever possible, involve Olympic athletes. Foremost among these are the United States Olympic trials, which will produce America's competitors. Covering these events serves a dual purpose. Not only does it turn TV audiences into dutifully hip Olympics consumers, but it also allows the camera crews and producers a kind of extended dress rehearsal before the real thing begins.

The matter of creating an audience for an Olympics is not unique to 1984. The most ill-starred example of the technique was launched by NBC in May 1978, when that network still assumed that it would carry the 1980 Games from Moscow. In 1978, the Peacock paid the United States Olympic Committee $7.5 million for rights to telecast the Olympic trials. That was to be the first stage of a massive, coordinated campaign to orchestrate an informed viewership for the Games. NBC even created a weekend showcase for this campaign—*SportsWorld,* a magazine format modeled on *Wide World of Sports.* The head of NBC Sports publicity set out the goals of the strategy in an unusually candid memo to his corporate chieftain. As quoted in *The New York Times* of May 14, 1978, the memo states in part:

> If we plan and execute our activies well, we will have made the Games so familiar and appealing to the viewers that anyone missing so much as a half-hour of coverage will feel deprived. We will have turned the American people into a nation of Olympics addicts. NBC will be hailed as the presenter of the most creative sports coverage ever, and be recognized as the unquestioned leader in network sports.

What nobody knew, of course, was that Russia had some public-opinion-molding designs of its own, chiefly in Afghanistan. The Carter administration's response to the Soviet invasion of Afghanistan was, in its curious way, a testament to the swollen parapolitical sway that modern Videolympics held upon world opinion. You crush a sovereign people under your totalitarian will? All right, then. *We* won't let *you* on our television show.

This, then, is the American context for Arledge's return to his boot-strap days as a hands-on producer of a live sporting event: 187.5 hours of coverage over sixteen days, from 7:30 A.M. in Los Angeles until 2:30 A.M. in New York. Not even Arledge, famous for his feats of sleep-deprivation during these occasions, will be able to oversee every hour of coverage. But he plans to work at least one full shift every broadcast day.

By the summer of 1984, ABC Sports will be at the peak of its influence and prestige. Not only will the network be responsible for the American coverage of the Games, it will also originate the video and some audio signals for transmission to some 130 countries around the world.

This worldwide transmission duty presents untold logistical problems for Arledge's Special Projects people in Los Angeles—the language barriers alone will require a translation system that eclipses that of the United Nations. No less than $70 million of ABC's total $225-million rights payment will go toward financing a worldwide broadcast center, plus cameras, mikes and dozens of commentator booths to be used exclusively by foreign announcers. (Each country will pay for its own telecast rights, but the money will not go to ABC; it will go to the Los Angeles Olympic Organizing Committee, which has set for itself the olympian goal of running the Games without a deficit.)

The reward for this particular expense and these particular headaches lies in the area of raw power. For the first time in human history, a single communications source will exercise control over an information stream influencing the thoughts of more than half the people on the planet.

Each Olympic venue will be double-covered. Cameras transmitting signals to the world broadcast center (from which foreign producers can select and edit their own sequence of images from a vast menu of monitor screens) will mingle with supplemental cameras "Americanizing" each event for the domestic feed. At a basketball game at the Forum, the world *and* the United States will follow the basic flow of the game. Only Americans will glimpse intimate closeups of the United States coach, Bobby Knight, as he crouches in a huddle during a time-out.

Arledge's hands-on presence at the controls of ABC's live coverage may not seem exceptional to a living-room viewer of television sports. Isn't that what executive producers are supposed to do? Produce? Within the television industry, however, such a capacity is tantamount to a suspension of corporate etiquette. Not that either of Arledge's counterparts at CBS or NBC could claim the training or talent to run a sports telecast if he had somehow been seized with the urge. For Arledge is not only the "executive producer" of ABC Sports—something of an honorific, truth to tell, for at least the last decade—he is also the *president* of ABC Sports. And, simultaneously, of ABC News, as well, in which capacity he will be charged with overseeing coverage of the Democratic National Convention, which will occur shortly before the Olympics, and of the Republican National Convention, which will unfold shortly thereafter.

For a television network executive of Arledge's rank to descend into the gritty combat zone of an on-line production is an act roughly comparable to that of a United States President showing up to help lift sandbags at the banks of a flooded river—and not just to lift one or two ceremonial bags, but to oversee their supply of sand, and personally direct the height and the calibration of the wall, and, in the end, transform the floodwaters into a lovely municipal lake.

But that kind of gesture is the essence of Arledge's intervention in the muddled and mismanaged history of network television sports. Arledge's many and intricate layers of contribution to video technique have been reductively pigeonholed by various critics and network rivals as "showmanship," as "electronic razzle-dazzle," as "show-biz hype." There is some truth in these capsule summations, in the persistent argument that Arledge carried many of his techniques to excess—whatever meaning the word "excess" may have in the context of American commercial television. There is even debate whether some of these techniques, transplanted finally to the ABC News division, have advanced or stood in the way of the public interest.

But overlooked in these reductions and ancillary arguments is the elemental fact that Roone Arledge, in the years since 1960 and to a degree not readily apparent from the vantage point of the video-saturated eighties, reinvented television. He did so by calling on impulses gleaned from sources as varied as Lionel Trilling in a Columbia University classroom and his wife's momentary drift of attention in a college football stadium. He augmented the power of these impulses by a willful nature and by his ability to utterly discard the past.

The 1984 Games in Los Angeles will be a testimony to all that Arledge has accomplished. In a manner of speaking, Roone Arledge invented these Ultimate Games, in the same sense that he reinvented television. Small wonder that he wanted to put his fingers, once again, on their controls.

The network TV logic that created an opportunity for Arledge and ABC, and the forces of exploitation and banality in the years since 1970, reveal a great deal about the role TV sports play in America's consciousness—and about what might have been.

II

LUNCH AT THE RITZ

I n the summer of 1939, America's past and future seemed to meet briefly, creating an overlay of premonitory, haunting images before hideous torrents washed them forever apart.

If you had known what to look for in that year, you could have gazed upon any number of these Januslike images and circumstances in theater, books, statecraft and the military, fashion, mass communications and popular technology. And in sports.

Phil Spitalny and his World Famous All-Girl Orchestra were at the Paramount in Times Square that summer; in Germany, Adolf Hitler was at his mountaintop in Berchtesgaden, presumably studying the planets. Television was in its experimental stages. A men's Palm Beach suit at fashionable Weber and Heilbroner cost $15.50. Submarine warfare began in the North Atlantic.

One of the most popular pavilions at the New York World's Fair was the World of Tomorrow. Among the thousands of visitors to the World of Tomorrow were the movie stars Norma Shearer, Charles Boyer and George Raft; and an eight-year-old boy from Long Island named Roone Pinckney Arledge, Jr.

A short, plump and slightly florid young man strode into the Ritz Carlton Hotel in New York for lunch one July day in 1939. Two hours later he re-emerged into the ninety-five-degree sunlight on Madison Avenue. He had just created a business deal that would alter the social habits and articulate the folk values of his country for the last half of the twentieth century.

The young man hardly appreciated that fact at the time. All he knew, strutting along through the straw-hat swarm, was that he had committed $203,000 of his company's limited finances—nearly one-fourth of its entire advertising budget—to exclusive sponsorship of the 1939 World Series on Mutual Radio. The young man had brashly consummated this deal with his luncheon partner, Fred Weber of the Mutual Broadcasting System, without having obtained specific permission from the head of his own company, Gillette.

The World Series was only three months away. There would be almost no time for Gillette even to organize a coordinating promotional campaign. This did not trouble the young man, who styled his name A. Craig Smith. Seven days' worth of coast-to-coast publicity for Gillette Blades, two to three hours of air time each day . . .

Smith reached Pennsylvania Station in a pitch of exhilaration, and boarded a train for the hot pull back to company headquarters in Boston. Already he had begun to picture the awed congratulations from his colleagues, their astonishment over his bold harnessing of seven nationwide days. And then a sickening thought wilted A. Craig Smith: What if he *hadn't* bought seven days? What if the mighty New York Yankees were to crush their probable opponents, the Cincinnati Reds—as they had the Chicago Cubs the autumn before? What if the 1939 World Series were to end in four broadcasts instead of seven?

As he slumped into his pullman seat and folded his damp jacket onto his lap, A. Craig Smith reflected sourly how he never had cared much for the sport of baseball in the first place.

On August 17, 1939, the ancient commissioner of baseball, Judge Kenesaw Mountain Landis, sat down at a table at his office headquarters in Chicago. The table was ornamented with a grand, weighty "salt-shaker" broadcast microphone emplated with the Mutual logo. Judge Landis peered with a mildly puzzled scowl at the visitor from New York on his left, Joseph P. Spang, Jr., the president of Gillette.

Spang, his slick hair parted straight as a razor down the middle, gripped a pen in his right hand. When the photographers stopped popping their flash powder, Spang was going to sign his name to a contract for $100,000, the amount that major-league baseball would receive in return for granting Gillette and Mutual the exclusive coverage rights to the Series. (The balance of Gillette's $203,000 would go toward air time, talent and production costs.)

Spang's thin-lipped smile back at Landis might have betrayed his own puzzlement over what kind of harebrained gamble his young advertising director had gotten the company into. It was not simply that Gillette in 1939 faced its lowest profits since 1915, and thus a fair prospect of extinction. Nor was it that Spang, president of the pioneering razor-blade firm for only eight months, would take the responsibility if Gillette went under.

All of that contributed to Spang's uncertainty, of course. In 1939 Gillette controlled just eighteen percent of the safety-razor market that it had invented at the turn of the century. No fewer than three thousand rival brands of blade now glutted the country's sales counters.

But scarce capital was only one of Joseph Spang's misgivings. There was another. It was sports on the radio. Nobody had ever made a dime on it. Take the Ford Motor Company which had tried sponsoring the World Series three years previously. It was not one of Ford's better ideas. Distressingly few ball fans in this Depression economy had been inspired to run out and order a new Model A because Graham McNamee told them to on NBC. Ford backed out. The company was so discouraged by the results that it didn't even bother to air commercials on the last year of its rights agreement. Since then, radio broadcasts of the Series had been *sustaining*—that is, whoever broadcast the games had to bear the costs, without advertising.

Nor had Ford's fiasco been the worst danger sign. Spang knew that in 1936, the people who ran the Orange Bowl football game in Miami actually had to *entice* CBS to come down and put the contest on the air. The enticement cost the Orange Bowl people five hundred dollars. (In 1982, TV rights to the Rose Bowl would cost NBC $11 million.)

And Spang was distastefully aware of Gillette's last foray into tying up its money with sports.

In 1935, Gillette had made its first venture into sports sponsorship on the radio. The company underwrote the broadcast of the world heavyweight title fight between Max Baer and challenger James Braddock. Baer, the champion, was a vicious, fearless puncher who had destroyed several opponents by knockout. It seemed obvious to everyone that he would rule the heavyweight ranks for years to come.

So obvious did it seem that Gillette got greedy. It tried to follow up its position as fight sponsor with a primitive experiment in total media packaging. It decided to make Max Baer a star. Gillette signed up the accommodating Baer to play the title role in a thirteen-week adventure radio program called *Lucky Smith, Detective*. In a burst of strategic finesse, Gillette timed the series so that six of the installments were scheduled to run *after* Baer's triumphant title defense.

The American public may not have lost its head over Max Baer's new celebrityhood. But Max Baer nearly did. On the night of the fight—no doubt under the spell of his suave "Lucky Smith" radio persona—Baer did not come lumbering and snarling out of his corner in his usual way.

He glided out, prancing and swooping like Fred Astaire in *Top Hat*. Instead of battering Braddock with his brutal hooks and overhand rights, the nation's newest radio darling *danced*. He skipped. He bobbed and dipped. Max Baer was still dancing and skipping and bobbing and dipping fifteen rounds later, while Braddock was thoughtfully tattooing him with enough points to win the decision.

Now Gillette faced a decision of its own. What to do with this egregious has-been? Hold a contest, someone at Gillette muttered, to name a dog. Max Baer had purchased a hound, someone discovered. The brainstormers at Gillette hit on the idea of keeping up the interest in the deposed Baer, and thus *Lucky Smith*, by asking the radio audience to send in suggestions for the animal's name. With proof of a Gillette purchase, of course.

In four weeks, Gillette received what should have been a convincing revelation of radio's power over public response. No fewer than a quarter of a million entries flooded into the company's Boston headquarters. The winner successfully exploited his knowledge that Baer hailed from Livermore, California. He suggested that the dog be christened "Livermore Gay Blade."

In wasn't exactly "Rin Tin Tin," but the Gillette people at that point were not being choosy. The contest was declared over. There is no known record of the dog's ever having answered to his name.

But at least Gillette had stumbled out from its first encounter with radio sports advertising with the company treasury intact. Barely.

In spite of his misgivings, Spang could not help feeling that A. Craig Smith knew what he was about. Smith had that effect on people. He seemed hooked into some light source that no one else could see, this small damp man with the shined shoes, and he churned through his various quests for the company showering optimism like sparks.

Smith had actually descended upon Gillette a couple of years before Spang himself, and so enjoyed a certain informal edge in seniority. He had progressed to Boston from the Maxon Advertising Agency in Detroit, which held the Gillette account.

Smith had startled the celluloid-collar Bostonians with his offbeat qualities of brilliance and aggression. He was high-strung and temperamental, but his ear for the nuances of spoken English was perhaps without equal in the industry. (God knew, Gillette needed such an ear: one of the company's earliest attempts at advertising its blades was a 1910 magazine ad bearing testimonials from baseball stars. To John J. McGraw, the savage manager of the New York Giants, was attributed the statement, "It makes shaving all to the merry.")

In mapping the company's advertising strategies, Smith often drew upon his personal storehouse of eccentric adventures aimed at "self-improvement." Some of these adventures, viewed from more jaded times, are almost touching in their optimism. A University of Michigan man, Smith had worked a stint in Detroit as a police reporter, the better to absorb the patois of the city's fringe classes—or what we have since pigeonholed as "street life." He trudged door-to-door selling brushes in order to experiment with sales pitches and measure the customers' reaction.

"He wanted to learn how to write interesting copy about uninteresting products," recalled a close friend—and if that were indeed his goal, A. Craig Smith succeeded brilliantly. "Craig was an odd duck," recalled the friend. "He had a way of lulling people and then pouncing on them. At sales meetings he was the least attentive person there—he always seemed to be tying his shoelaces. But then, at a critical point, he'd always be the one to interrupt the speaker with something right on the money that would begin, 'Did you ever stop to think—?'"

Spang was counting on another member of Gillette's executive command besides A. Craig Smith: the aloof, intimidating Harvard aristocrat G. Herbert Marcy, the company sales manager. That innocuous title scarcely conveyed his fearsome reputation within Gillette. Marcy had joined the company as a youthful "efficiency expert" out of the Harvard Business School. His mission was to get rid of employees who were not absolutely essential to production. This task Marcy carried out with a relish that struck some associates as frightening. "He used to walk down that carpet," remembered a former colleague, "and look people in the eye and say, 'You, you, you—you're out.'"

Marcy would eventually rise to an executive vice presidency at Gillette. Now, at this pivotal moment in the company's history—with perhaps survival itself at stake in the World Series ad campaign—G. Herbert Marcy found himself called upon to help assess Gillette's chances. At a selective staff meeting in Spang's office a few days before Spang would meet with Judge Landis in Chicago, Spang turned his slick coiffure toward Marcy and put him a blunt question: How many of the hastily assembled "World Series Special" sets of the Tech model razor and five blades, specially priced at forty-nine cents, did Marcy think Gillette could sell as the result of radio commercials?

G. Herbert Marcy stared back at Spang. He produced a notepad. He lowered his head. He scowled. He scribbled for a few minutes, The people in the room waited. Finally Marcy looked up, met Spang's stare again and replied: "We'll sell a million."

A *million*. A million sets of blades would recoup Craig Smith's investment and even turn a modest profit. Spang felt some of his anxiety lessen.

But Joseph P. Spang's ultimate determination to sign that contract was fueled by one additional factor—a quality that even A. Craig Smith lacked. Spang was a sports fan.

On Sunday, October 8, 1939, the New York Yankees completed a four-game sweep of the Cincinnati Reds with a 7-4 victory at Crosley Field. ("It was so hot," *The New York Times* confided to its shocked readers, "that some of the correspondents worked with ties loosened and shirt collars wide open.")

It was even hotter on Monday, October 9, when A. Craig Smith walked into Gillette's offices in the large red-brick building at West First Street and Dorchester in South Boston. More than forty years later, Smith could remember how subdued things seemed inside that building, whose austere windows commanded a spur of the Charles River. He couldn't shake the feeling that some of his fellow workers were eyeing him—*measuring* him, as he'd done his door-to-door customers—as if to memorize the features of the culprit who had finally contrived to foreclose the American dream that King C. Gillette had struggled so hard to launch back in 1901. And all because of a luncheon on a hot July day at the Ritz. "That quaint period," Tennessee Williams wrote of the thirties, "when the huge middle class of America was matriculating in a school for the blind." But not everyone was blind. Certainly not young A. Craig Smith. His vision was not immediately apparent. There were no computers in those days, no Telex inventory systems to measure overnight a product's performance in the marketplace. The Gillette people were obliged to wait for several weeks— nearly until Thanksgiving—before they could be certain that Smith's and Spang's eccentric World Series gamble had not ruined them.

But with each day, the evidence looked better. The mail delivery to South Dorchester brought business receipts from America's drugstores, hardware shops, sporting goods dealers and jewelers, and the accumulation of those receipts showed that something awesome had happened on the American airwaves on those four broadcast days in 1939. American men had done as they were told by the World Series announcers: they went out and bought Gillette razor blades. Some sixty-four minutes of commercial announcements on Mutual Radio had generated sales that even G. Herbert Marcy hardly dared dream of: not one million, but nearly *four* million World Series Special razor sets. Gillette's survival worries were over. And the age of broadcast sports had truly begun.

But in the very end, it wasn't Marcy, nor Smith, nor Spang, nor anyone else at Gillette who controlled the company's hopes. It was the World Series announcer, the radio play-by-play man who finally controlled those hopes, who held the fate of those bold business decisions and fanciful figures in the very tenor of his voice, in his thrilling delivery, his intimate pitch.

And what more prophetic pitchman for a line of razor blades than a fellow named Red Barber?

For his heroic success in recommending Gillette blades to America's millions, A. Craig Smith paid Red Barber $280.

The two men at that Ritz table could not have dreamed that they were sowing the seeds of a national mandate for personal achievement in an age of moon landings and Jupiter probes; for an amateur hockey match as surrogate superpower showdown; for a thirst to taste personal power so compelling that citizens in their Columbus, Ohio, living rooms would one day "vote" on the play-by-play strategies of the local semiprofessional football team by pushing remote-control buttons connected to their cable television systems; for a January football game inside a domed building that would transfix, in silent ritual rapture, nearly as many Americans as then existed in the Republic.

Muhammad Ali owes his global fame and fortunes and symbolic power to that lunch, and it is possible that thousands of less gifted urban blacks and Hispanics have diverted their lives in vain because of it. It triggered an explosion of monetary rewards that opened up certain "upper-class" sports—tennis, golf, swimming, skiing, ice skating—to the aspirations of ethnic Americans and working-class whites. John McEnroe, raging his suburban obscenities into the CBS courtside microphones, can trace his troubled superstardom to that day inside the Ritz Grill. As can Mark Spitz his Olympic gold medals, Jan Stephenson her soft-focus photo layouts, Suzy Chaffee her soothed lips.

Craig Smith's impulsive deal sent its aftershocks into America's universities, widening the already troublesome gulf between academicians and athletic departments as television rights jackpots turned recruiting into an art akin to pyramid-robbing.

It reached into the public morality, as gambling—an illegal practice under federal law—was openly encouraged, even promoted, by network television oddsmakers.

It prefigured a confrontation between middle-class Americans and the emerging New Sexuality: television first "domesticated" the flamboyant heterosexuality of football quarterback Joe Namath, and then, two decades later, it did the same for the homosexual relationship disclosed by the great women's tennis champion and heroine to many families, Billie Jean King.

It sent reverberations into American politics, contributing successful athlete-candidates to the new "telegenic" era of celebrity office seekers, much as Congressman Jack Kemp and Senator Bill Bradley.

Finally, the universe of television sports germinated by Craig Smith's luncheon would eventually provide many millions of fans with a means to observe, and follow, and root for *themselves,* as participants in a new kind of sports-theater: the camera's eye began inevitably to swivel around to include the spectator in the same field of vision as the athlete. Not every child might grow up to become a Yankee, but every child might well grow up to be televised in Yankee Stadium.

Craig Smith had stepped beyond the known universe. Working without a blueprint, he had forged a new broadcasting form, one that made utter logical sense—in hindsight. In a medium controlled even then by mostly cautious, conventional men, he had reached into some chamber of intuition and charged everyone's perception of the possible.

This would set the pattern of discovery as sports and the airwaves continued their erratic but ever-thickening fusion: a combustive burst of one individual's intuition, usually in a period of general quiescence, usually generated by someone with a lot to lose. Smith himself would generate several more such moments over the course of a remarkable career.

III

ELECTRIC NARRATIVE— THE RADIO MAN

The broadcast world was slow to grasp Red Barber's achievement for what it was: the first important welding of sports and the airwaves.

Barber felt that he had already made announcing history that summer. The point would be hard to argue. What was one more World Series radio stint (his fifth, after all) compared with what Barber had pioneered on August 26 of that year at Ebbets Field, during the first game of a Brooklyn-Cinncinnati doubleheader? On that dusty Saturday afternoon, Barber became the first announcer ever to call the play-by-play for a big-league *telecast*.

The TV "network"—if a few dozen primitive receivers scattered around New York might properly be called a network—was NBC. Barber had several friends within that powerful radio empire, and the notion to try a video broadcast had a charming, anyone-for-tennis sort of origin: one of Barber's cronies, Alfred H. "Doc" Morton, an NBC programer, simply called up the Redhead one day and said, in effect, "why not?" (NBC had telecast a Columbia University baseball game that May—the first live sports event ever attempted on American TV.) Barber, who couldn't think of a good reason why not, then telephoned another good friend, Brooklyn general manager Larry MacPhail, and the adventure was on.

But it was not without its annoyances for Barber. Finding a good seat was one of them.

The Brooklyn management not only billed NBC for the honor it received (the price was a receiving set installed in the Dodger pressroom), it also stuck the magisterial Barber up in the second deck, on the third-base side, alongside one of the two cameras—*among the fans*. This, of course, was before the era when an announcer would as soon sit among fans as walk naked through the streets of Beirut. Barber could not have guessed it that day, but he was beginning yet another tradition: it would be years—well into the 1950s—before television announcers and crew were treated as anything more than borderline gate-crashers in the big-league social order.

There were other problems. Barber's earphones did not work, so he could not communicate with his director in the truck outside the park. He could never be certain which camera was on; the one next to him or the second one at ground level near home plate. Not that it mattered to the handful of viewers peering at their five-inch, mirrored screens at home: the NBC cameramen, in a misplaced burst of journalistic zeal, tended to pan their lenses to cover the flight of each pitched or batted ball. The effect undoubtedly resembled the random trajectory of a videogame pellet.

But through it all, Barber managed to improvise a fairly accurate, if rough-edged, prototype for baseball telecasts that has endured ever since. He restrained his commentary so that it supplemented the picture, or at least what he assumed was the picture. He conducted the first pregame TV interviews. (There exists an oddly antique and touching photograph of the fierce Brooklyn manager, Leo Durocher, gripping his cap in his hand as he stares transfixed into the alien lens.) And Barber did commercials. One for Ivory Soap, one for Wheaties, and one for Mobil Gas.

Despite the brisk pace of developments in 1939, sports telecasts would not move beyond the experimental stage for another seven years. Television as an entity was virtually forgotten as the American public absorbed World War II through the radio voices of Edward R. Murrow, Elmer Davis, and of course Franklin D. Roosevelt. Experimental sets disappeared from stores. Many TV stations left the air. But the dominant competitors, RCA and CBS, continued their behind-the-scenes technical development at a furious pace. When television re-emerged in the postwar years, it would be sports programing that established the early beachheads in America's consciousness.

Television is popularly thought of as the latest, and the most unexpected, of all modern electronic communications forms. How eerie it is to consider that the principles of video transmission were vaguely understood as early as 1876—fifty-one years before the first "talking picture"—when Alexander Graham Bell introduced his telephone to the world. Trendy conversationalists of that day soon began flinging about such expert terms as *telephonoscope*. And in 1879, the British magazine *Punch* published a drawing by the artist George du Maurier that had an otherworldly prophetic vision: it depicted a couple seated before a large viewing screen implanted above their living-room mantel. They were watching a live tennis match.

Laboratory experiments began to imitate these artists' visions. The superb broadcast historian Eric Barnouw has noted that the first primitive television technology made its appearance in 1884, in the form of the "Nipkow disk." Named for its inventor, the German Paul Nipkow, the disk would rotate rapidly while beams of light shone through its perforations. The pattern of the pinpoints caused the light to cast patterns that simulated movement, similar to the effect of light on movie film. For several decades, the Nipkow disk remained the last word in television development. *

By 1923, only three years after amateur radio transmitter towers began springing up all across America, TV experiments in the United States and England were generating positive results.

Technicians within the fledgling RCA system, as well as experimenters for General Electric and Westinghouse, pressed for an electronic means of generating the Nipkow "scanning" movement. RCA gave birth to the National Broadcasting Company in September 1926, and the airwaves' close relationship to big business and advertising began to transform the popular culture immediately. In 1927, a magazine called *Television* went on the newsstands in New York. That same year the advent of *The Jazz Singer,* the first motion picture to incorporate sound, thrust the broadcasters and the movies into an open race for technological supremacy.

The events of Black Friday, 1929, brought this race to a premature halt—just as World War II would again arrest the technology a decade later. Television's development slowed as RCA's stock plunged from 114¾ to 20 within a month.

But by 1935, NBC was telecasting regular programs from a studio in Radio City. By 1937, the company had a mobile van; it relayed the telecast of a fire in 1938, thus defining the classic role of TV mobile units for all time. On May 17, 1939, that same mobile unit lumbered out to Columbia University's Baker Field. There, using one ponderous Iconoscope camera mounted on a wooden platform, and featuring a bewildered Bill Stern at the microphone, NBC telecast the first video

---

*Eric Barnouw. *Tube of Plenty*. N.Y.: Oxford University Press, 1975.

sports event ever: that baseball match between Columbia and Princeton.

Anticipating Barber's effort three months later, that telecast fell short of Peabody Award caliber. The self-conscious Stern forgot his toupee en route to the park and insisted on going back for it. He nearly missed the game. As for camera *movement*—years later Stern confessed to William O. Johnson of *Sports Illustrated* that the sweeps and jerks and wobbles got so desperate that he and the crew began to pray for batters to strike out. In its review of the event the next day, *The New York Times* sniffed that the players looked like white flies. The *Times* added, with wicked glee, that "when the age-old hidden ball trick was worked by the third baseman the camera was not fast enough to turn on the quick turn of events."

Even the signs and portents were against the broadcasters. Red Barber wrote to NBC after the Brooklyn-Cincinnati game, requesting a memento of some sort. NBC sent him a silver engraved cigarette box "in grateful appreciation, National Broadcasting Company." Accompanying the box, Barber later wrote, was a bill for thirty-five dollars. The networks had lost no time figuring out ways to make money from sports coverage.

But that was of small comfort to Barber. As far as this proud Southerner was concerned, the networks—and the advertisers—were making money that should have been going into his pocket. The thirty-five dollars for the NBC "memento" he could stomach. After all, he had asked for it. But he was still steamed about Craig Smith's $280 paycheck forty years later, in his autobiography, *The Broadcasters*.

By Barber's account, Smith arrived at the fee by asking a labor man in New York what the compensation to an announcer should be *for each game*. The labor man, using a criterion that is lost to history, informed Smith that the fee should be thirty-five dollars. Smith ended up paying Barber double that amount—because, as Smith's accompanying note assured the announcer, "you did such a good job." (Apparently Smith had earlier tried to soften up the Redhead a bit by pointing out that most announcers would *pay* to have this assignment.)

Barber did not soften easily. "Seventy dollars a game," he wrote later, "for an all-out commercial exclusive of the biggest job in my profession. To this day I wonder who that union man was."

Barber continued:

> I started some serious thinking. The biggest job in my business . . .
> the World Series . . . exclusive to one sponsor, on one network.

After doing four World Series for no extra pay—just as another one of the many jobs covered by my basic salary at [Cincinnati's] WLW—now to do my fifth, and my first all-out commercial Series—and to get two hundred eighty dollars. I began to wonder what was going on. What did it mean to reach the top—the top where there was no higher place to go? Why all the pressure and worry and preparation and concentration and risk? I could hardly eat several days before the Series started. You were doing ad-lib work . . . sticking your neck out every time you took the mike . . . I know I got as many butterflies in my guts before the World Series as Broadway or the Met could deal out. *

It is interesting to note, in light of all this indignation, that Barber continued to broadcast the World Series for Gillette through the 1943 season, never once making so bold as to negotiate his salary beforehand. And yet Barber had put his finger on an important issue, the one business transaction that would retard the full development of sports-casting as a profession in America. Barber failed correctly to interpret this transaction, but did identify the business of an announcer's being compensated by a sponsor. To the listeners and viewers of America, the amount of those paychecks would mean nothing. But their source—an advertiser, and not the broadcast station or network—would mean everything, in terms of editorial freedom.

In consenting to accept his salaries from sponsors, Barber placed himself technically in the category of an entertainer, setting a precedent that would bar sports broadcasters from any claims to journalistic independence during the critical formative years, and for decades beyond.

In fairness to Barber, it isn't likely that his decision was even framed as a moral choice. Adversary journalism, as it is understood today, was not exactly a staple of any mass medium of the 1930s, whether the topic was sports, the rearmament of Germany or starving sharecroppers in the South. Nevertheless, Barber had led his profession across a distinct line. If the nation's newspaper sportswriters had suddenly begun drawing their paychecks from display advertisers, or from the ballclubs themselves rather than from their publishers, the scandal would have been monumental.

But radio was fresh, magical, cheaper than the movies. It was the sweet dreambox in a nightmare economy. The issue of "journalism," at

---

* Red Barber. *The Broadcasters*. N.Y.: Dial Press, 1970.

least as it applied to sports coverage, was never brought up. If Red Barber turned sportscasting away from the strictures of pure journalism, it would be awfully tough to make a case that his listening audiences cared. Hardly anyone thought of broadcast sports as a matter of objectivity. The great radio sportscasters belonged to myth, they ascended quickly into a kind of sublime, semidisembodied *presence* on the airwaves, and became pied pipers of pleasure for America's working class. Who paid them? Who cared? They brought news, yes; but it was news from a crackling realm somewhere above and beyond the pall of duty; beyond the droning purview of federal government or City Hall.

From its very earliest origins, sportscasting on the radio invited, even demanded, distance from workaday concerns.

What kind of secret stuff must Harold Arlin have been made of? To most of the world, for most of his life, Harold Arlin was a cipher, a dot in the census. His job was that of daytime foreman for KDKA in Pittsburgh, generally recognized as the first established radio station in America.

And then one day Harold Arlin invented sportscasting. The day was August 5, 1921. Records of the event are sketchy, but it seems that Harold Arlin simply rounded up a carbon microphone and a power generator of some sort, and wandered over to Forbes Field, where the Pittsburgh Pirates were to play the Philadelphia Phillies. Arlin paid his way into the park, set up a microphone stand behind the wire screen directly in back of home plate—*and began doing the play-by-play*. Harold Arlin was now a sportscaster! Why? Who knows? Because he decided to be. That was the way people did things back at the dawn of broadcasting.

In no other area of broadcasting—not in entertainment, not in fine arts programing, not in news and public affairs, not even in advertising (with its saturation doses of applied behavioral science) would the inventions ever be as pure or influential as in sports. The breakthroughs in sports announcing, as in sports technology and even in sports' characteristically personal point of view, have cross-fertilized the rest of the broadcast universe. To say nothing of the popular culture beyond.

What did Harold Arlin *sound* like on that August afternoon, to those scattered few listeners in Pittsburgh—perhaps including some men not long returned from the battlefields of France? Did he pick up a cadence, assume a rhythm, lapse instinctively into the shorthand phrasing necessary to keep pace with baseball's explosive bursts of action? Or did he call the game in the more leisurely idiom of the ballpark fan, reprising and summarizing each play after the dust had settled? Did he remember to repeat the score? The inning? (Red Barber years later would bring a salt timer to the announcer's booth; when the salt ran out he would give the score and then turn the device upside down again.)

The informational demands of World War I had thrust radio's development forward at quantum speed ("wireless" messages via Morse Code had been a reality only since 1906), and by the early twenties, sports were a fixture on the air.

A month before Harold Arlin's audacious broadcast—on July 2, 1921—David Sarnoff, the founder of RCA, put together a jerry-built relay broadcast of the Jack Dempsey–Georges Carpentier heavyweight title fight at Boyle's Thirty Acres in Jersey City, New Jersey. This was *technically* the first sportscast ever attempted. But owing to some rather quaint logistical problems, the radio voice that listeners heard that day belonged to a man who could not even see the fight: he was holed up in a metal shack several blocks away.

As Red Barber unraveled the story, Sarnoff obtained permission from the promoter, Tex Rickard, to broadcast the fight over station WJZ in Newark. Sarnoff then borrowed a portable transmitter from General Electric and hired the editor of *Wireless Age*, Major J. Andrew White, to call the blow-by-blow from ringside.

Barber recalled:

> Major White and Sarnoff got the Lackawanna Railroad to permit a crew of two electricians to string up an antenna between two of its towers . . . and to have use of an adjacent hut, constructed of galvanized tin sheets, in which to set up the equipment. The Pullman porters kicked up a fuss. That shed was where they changed from their street clothes to their uniforms. The porters were so angry about temporarily losing the use of their dressing hut that one of the technicians, a man named J. O. Smith, slept there the night before the fight to guard the precious equipment . . . .
>
> White was at ringside, Smith stayed in the hut. White spoke into a telephone to Smith. So—White did the blow-by-blow, and Smith wrote down what White said . . . the voice that came over WJZ that July second afternoon, 1921, belonged to J. O. Smith.

Six years after that, in 1927, an eight-year-old boy named Lindsey Nelson sat in his family's living room on South Main Street in Columbia, Tennessee, and listened to a man named Graham McNamee tell him that he was close enough to a boxing ring to *reach out and touch the canvas.* The phrase, and the imagery it suggested, transfixed the small boy.

Graham McNamee was speaking from Chicago. The ring he was talking about contained two boxers named Gene Tunney and Jack Dempsey. The device that brought McNamee's voice to the Nelson family was a rectangular box called an Arbiphone. Tuning it required the exact adjustment of three separate dials. The Arbiphone's speaker rested on top of the box. More than fifty-five years later, Lindsey Nelson could summon its shape to mind. "It looked like a big question mark," Nelson said. "It sometimes sounded," he went on, "like a big question mark."

Bill Stern of NBC and Ted Husing of CBS became the first sportscasters to gain the status of national celebrities. In the 1930s, these two giants frequently found themselves covering the same college football game—because neither network wanted to risk conceding an "exclusive" to its rival.

Stern was a tragicomic figure, a man whose character seemed fated to be expressed cruelly on his physical self. Stern wore more synthetic paraphernalia than a hairpiece to that historic 1939 telecast at Columbia University: he wore a wooden left leg—the result of an amputation in 1935, following an automobile accident. This gifted but compulsive man maintained a lifelong fixation on his personal image—a fixation that matched his temperamental approach to sportscasting as entertainment first, information second.

It was Stern who crystallized the early resentment that newspapermen felt toward their new electronic competitors, a resentment that burned brightly into the time of Cosell and beyond. For Stern, it must be declared, made mistakes on the air. Correctly identifying the ball carrier in a football game was never a skill that came easily to him. That alone was enough to set the typewriter corps' collective teeth on edge. But Stern compounded the shortcoming! He explained to his spotters that if he continually corrected himself on the air, his listening audience would lose confidence in him; moreover, the broadcast would lose its *entertainment* value. So, he told his spotters—among them a young University of Tennessee student named Lindsey Nelson—"if we have a man with the ball on his way to a touchdown and we discover at the five yard line that we have the wrong man, *we will have him lateral to the right man.*"

So notoriously did Stern come to depend on this last-ditch, face-saving technique that he very nearly condemned his entire profession to the status of buffoonery. He also provided the inspiration for one of the most famous put-downs in broadcast history.

The perpetrator was an elderly rasp-voiced broadcaster named Clem McCarthy. Toward the end of his career, McCarthy himself made a glaring on-air mistake; he called the wrong horse as the winner of the Kentucky Derby. Stern turned the incident into a joke at McCarthy's expense, making great capital on the old man's error—but he made a mistake. Told of Stern's public sarcasm, McCarthy turned upon his informer and snarled the classic squelch: "Well—you can't lateral a horse."

Ted Husing was equally theatrical on the air, but his professional standards were more highly regarded by the print press. Lindsey Nelson recalls that it was Husing who made a science of the art of "spotting"— that silent supply line of information from a sharp-eyed observer in the booth to the on-air man. Husing, Nelson remembered, rigged up an electronic spotter's board that had to be operated by two men: one to scribble out the names of players coming into the game, and attach them to the board, the other to illuminate a light beneath the scrap of paper bearing the name of a key player. Such jerry-built systems were essential to the serious-minded radio play-by-play pioneer: there were no reliable numbering systems for players in those days, and no unctuous, obliging, fact-laden public-relations men to spoon-feed information to the broadcaster.

The 1930s were a time of almost surrealistic possibilities in broadcasting. Young, obscure men stumbled into radio booths on the unlikeliest of errands and pretexts; confronted with the magical properties of the microphone, they stayed, and fashioned careers that would make their names—even their *voices,* detached from the name—instantly recognizable to generations of Americans. In that watershed year of 1939, two men who would later help establish the craft of television sportscasting burst into radio in typically oddball style: Nelson, and a fellow Southerner, a cerebral young law student and schoolteacher named Melvin Israel—or Mel Allen, as he would become known.

Lindsey Nelson owed his first break in a distinguished broadcasting career to the vagaries of plumbing. At the University of Tennessee, which he attended from 1937 through 1941, football broadcasters worked from the second deck of a wooden shack atop the west stands. There was no way to reach the wooden shack except by climbing a stepladder—a swaying, unpromising wooden contraption that might have brought out vertigo in a llama. There were no restrooms inside the shack; once ensconced, a broadcaster was more or less there for the duration, relying not only on his strong voice, but on his strong kidneys as well. Besides the fifteen or twenty minutes of awkward air silence that would have resulted from a trip to the gent's, there was that daunting stepladder climb: getting *down* it was scarier than getting *up* it, particularly on a full bladder.

In November of 1939, Jack Harris, of station WSM in Nashville, was calling the play-by-play for the Tennessee-Vanderbilt game. Nelson was the student spotter. At halftime, the supple young Nelson routinely shinnied down the wooden stepladder, fetched the statistics from the Tennessee athletic department, and returned with them to the booth. He found Jack Harris staring wide-eyed at him, a fixed sort of expression on his face. "Here are the stats," said Nelson. "You do them," squeaked Harris, and was gone; a moment later, Nelson heard the unmistakable rattle of a stepladder against hardwood. Lindsey Nelson was into radio sports announcing. "If Jack Harris had denied himself a second cup of coffee at brunch that morning," Nelson mused some thirty-five years later, "my life may have taken another direction."

It was, by any fair reckoning, a *decisive* cup. Nelson went on to perfect a clean, meticulous line of narration that proved ideal for his eventual transition from radio to television. (Both Stern and Husing, among other great radio pioneers, tried to adapt to the visual medium; both failed.) A thoughtful and analytical man inside his outrageous trademark sports jackets, Nelson was among the first TV voices to appreciate the importance of constantly matching the spoken word to what the viewer was seeing on his home screen. ("If a cameraman accidentally tipped his lens down to a chewing-gum wrapper on the floor," an admiring colleague remarked, "Lindsey would figure out something to say about chewing-gum wrappers.") This fidelity to the technical demands of his craft led Nelson to stardom at—by turns—CBS, NBC, ABC, Mutual Radio, the Liberty Broadcasting System and, for seventeen years, the TV networks of the New York Mets and San Francisco Giants. Nelson made college football telecasts his own form; he also called various World Series, All Star Games, Rose Bowls, pro basketball, golf, boxing, bowling—and twenty-two Cotton Bowl games.

"Radio was an announcer's medium," Nelson remarked not long ago, as he tried to explain why so many of the early stars had failed to survive the transition to television. "Sure, there was a producer or director on hand, but their main duty was to signal when a commercial was due; otherwise, they'd just give the announcer a nod, and he was *it*, for better or worse, until sign-off. You can imagine that there was a certain kind of majesty associated with this kind of control of the microphone.

"But what these guys had to accept—and many didn't—was that television was a *director's* medium. Now the announcer has a little speaker stuck in his ear, and it's connected to a powerful director in the remote truck, and this man is giving him orders. The director and the producer are shaping all the diverse visual and audio elements of a game telecast, and the play-by-play man is just one component of that mix. Some of those early guys never came to understand that. Some of them even tried to insist that the *credits* at the end of a telecast refer to the authority in the truck as the *camera* director—so as to imply that he had no control over the announcer."

As the voice of the New York Yankees (and thereby a certified Eminence), as the early TV announcer for Gillette-sponsored World Series and All-Star broadcasts, and as the possessor of one of sportscasting's original "signature" lines *("How a-bout that!"),* Mel Allen burned even more brightly than did Lindsey Nelson in the 1940s and 1950s. But Allen's career, or at least his national reputation, skidded abruptly into oblivion in 1964—for reasons that remained clouded by official silence and unofficial rumor for years afterward.

Melvin Allen Israel—he changed his name legally to "Mel Allen" in 1943, as the entertainment world's unspoken proscription of Jewish names extended well into radio sports—was born of Russian-immigrant parents in Birmingham, Alabama, in 1913. He obtained his law degree at the University of Alabama in 1936, and was teaching speech at the university when the football coach, whose name was Frank Thomas, invited him to announce over the public-address system the details of each game—who carried the ball, who tackled, the substitutions.

This opportunity led Allen quickly to a job at a Birmingham radio station. A CBS executive heard the young man doing the play-by-play of an Alabama-Tulane football game, and Allen joined the network as a disk jockey and news announcer.

Allen's breakthrough into stardom, in 1939, was a good deal more flamboyant than Nelson's; it was certainly more *lyric.* CBS radio had secured the rights to cover a regatta—the art of radio-regatta coverage has since fallen into neglect—on the Hudson River near Poughkeepsie, and had dutifully dispatched a reporter to the scene. But the splendor of the man's narration went for naught: the crafty folk at NBC stole CBS's own story by sending one of its operatives, however uninvited, to report the results from an airplane circling overhead.

The CBS people plotted revenge. On the following weekend, CBS would score a *double* coup: Ted Husing himself would cover the Drake

Relays from a church steeple in Des Moines, Iowa. Meanwhile, the new young fellow, Allen, was going to cover the Vanderbilt Cup auto races on Long Island from an airplane—and God help any aircraft that hove into view bearing the NBC insignia.

Husing's part of the assignment proceeded flawlessly. But it rained on Long Island. The Vanderbilt Cup races were called off. This development might normally have pleased Mel Allen, who has borne a lifelong revulsion toward aircraft of any size. But in 1939, Allen needed steady work. He talked the pilot into taking the CBS craft up anyway—and for the ensuing hour or so, Allen wafted back and forth across Long Island, reporting on *anything* he happened to spy: tennis matches, boat races, any stray form of competition. Allen had gone up there a raw kid from the turntable department. He came back down a star. His manic ad-lib performance had stunned his employers into a kind of arm's-length respect: before the year had ended, Allen was announcing major-league baseball games, and by 1941, he was earning the rarefied sum of thirty thousand dollars a year.

By the time he entered the Army in 1943, Allen had already called three World Series games on radio. He became the Voice of the Yankees upon his discharge in 1946. At the same time, he continued to enjoy national exposure as Craig Smith's announcer of choice for World Series, the Rose Bowl and All Star events. Allen's huge success was due in part to his vibrant speaking style—he let his sense of startled, schoolboy enthusiasm loose on the big plays, and his deep-voweled Southern phrasings seemed to add a natural drama to a crucial moment. His famous catch phrase evolved in 1949, when Joe DiMaggio belted four home runs in a three-game span, after having been sidelined for several weeks with an injured heel. *"How a-bout that!"* Allen began to marvel as the impact of each DiMaggio shot began to sink in on the ballpark crowd; the phrase became a part of his on-air persona.

But something began to happen to Mel Allen in the 1960s. No one who knew him, not even his closest friends, was ever sure what it was. Calling the 1963 Yankee-LA World Series game along with the Dodgers' announcer, Vin Scully, Allen began to emit strange noises in his throat during the late innings. He started to rasp, then made a series of croaking, almost choking sounds. But Allen refused to surrender the microphone voluntarily. The situation was not resolved until NBC's massively built director of sports, Tom Gallery, reached into the broadcast booth and seized Allen with both hands, lifting the Yankees' announcer up and away from the microphone. Scully finished the broadcast alone.

Later that year, doing a routine summary of sports scores on NBC's flagship station in New York, WNBC, Mel Allen suddenly froze on-camera. His face assumed a stricken expression, like that of a speaker who has forgotten his lines. He was unable to finish the show. About that time, producers and directors who had formerly enjoyed working with the warm, ebullient Allen noticed an abrupt change of mood. Now he would lapse into unexplainable fits of surliness; he would refuse to follow routine studio instructions and would snap out sarcastic rebuffs when addressed by members of the production crew.

There were no available clues to the source of his distress. Allen never married; he lived alone in Stamford, Connecticut, and remained devoted to his mother throughout her life. His change of temperament, his lapses, simply yielded to none of the conventional explanations.

Mel Allen's brilliant career ran out—as far as his national image was concerned—in 1964. He was just fifty-one years old; the extraordinary voice was intact (despite the strange lapse in the previous World Series), and he was, if not at the absolute peak of his fame, then at least a bona fide broadcasting institution.

In 1964 the New York Yankees were sold—to, of all corporations, CBS. A CBS-appointed executive in charge of the acquisition, Michael Burke, embarked upon a housecleaning spree. Burke fired the Yankees' general manager and their field manager and released or traded several of the team's aging stars. When the dust from his housecleaning had settled, Mel Allen was among those missing. There were no farewell dinners, no fond ceremonies. CBS did not even bother to issue an explanation, formal or informal, as to why it had consigned one of the most popular play-by-play men in history to oblivion. NBC Sports stopped asking him to do the Rose Bowl game. As far as the larger American public was concerned, Mel Allen simply ceased to exist. And the rumors began, the dark speculations and suspicions.

Allen's life, however, did not deteriorate, at least not to the degree one might have expected, given his erratic behavior and the abrupt blow to his greatest source of personal pride. He harnessed, or contained, the demons that occasionally tormented him. He acquired a soft-drink bottling franchise in Stamford, and assured himself of a comfortable income base. And as the years went on, Mel Allen began to make himself available for play-by-play assignments. He called some games for the Atlanta Braves, and some for the Montreal Expos. He never left the broadcasting business entirely. When cable television began carrying local baseball broadcasts, nearly twenty years later, a New York system hired Allen—then approaching seventy—to do some pregame interviews and scoreboard work. And finally, belatedly, NBC invited the old sportscaster back on the network airwaves to handle some assignments that coincided with its 1982 World Series telecasts.

The assignments were to do voice-over narration for "promo" spots heralding prime-time shows for NBC's new fall season. Some quick-thinking executive at NBC had decided this would provide a whimsical, baseball-oriented touch. Mel Allen handled the assignment with his customary high professionalism and dignity. The voice never sounded better.

IV

"PENCIL-NECKED GEEKS!"

Gorgeous George, the Brooklyn Red Devils, the Demolition Derby, Jersey Joe Walcott, the Pabst Fights, the Yankees, Giants and Chicago Cubs—even a primitive ancestor of *Monday Night Football,* played in prime time on Saturday nights: these were among the first stars and mainline programing attractions in American mass television's postwar formative years.

Television's popular history makes little mention of the Red Devils or Gorgeous George. Popular history usually cites Milton Berle, Arthur Godfrey and Fred Waring, *Your Show of Shows* and *Truth or Consequences* as the stars and shows that ushered in the Age of Television. That is because the Warings and the comedians and the quiz shows were the networks' own ideas of what constituted prototypical television fare: that is, radio with pictures. William Paley at CBS and David Sarnoff at NBC were radio pioneers first and foremost; their first instinct upon finding themselves television barons was to reward their greatest radio stars with exposure on the new video curiosity.

Sports? Paley and Sarnoff weren't interested in sports, unless you counted polo and golf. Sports was so—well, working class, except perhaps for the bowl games and the Derby, and maybe that thing with baseball in the autumn, the Series. Sports, on network television in the early years, with the possible exception of those desperate wogs at DuMont, was filler; a holding action until the next radio crooner could be gentled and soothed and assured and signed. So the networks deigned to carry the odd boxing match, the occasional blue-chip classic championship or ceremonial event from the very beginning: they just did not talk about it any more than necessary.

But the networks were not the only sources of TV programs, even at the outset. From 1944 through the breakthrough year of 1948—and

continuing doggedly into the mid-1950s, in the teeth of mounting industry disdain—there flourished a doughty, scatter-quilt, often semi-
disreputable, almost gypsylike subculture of local and regional TV
sporting attractions. Many of them survive on independent and UHF
stations to this day. Given the enduring popularity of these "fringe"
athletes and the sometimes baroque competitions they engaged in, it
seems even more inescapable that mainstream American television
blundered through most of its first two decades in pompous disregard of
its most natural, diverse and authentic entertainment form.

Television awoke from its enforced wartime hibernation with an intense hunger. It needed to feed on something. It needed *content*. But the
pickings were scarce. For the past quarter-century, the world's foremost
engineers and electronics specialists had been pouring their energies
into conceiving television's anatomy, its central nervous system. Now
that the beast was alive on the operating table, it was suddenly apparent
that no one had thought much about its diet.

Television had been created to consume images; that was its sole and
absolute technical function. Television was technology's great white
shark, a comparison that would gain in accuracy as the years went on
and the cry arose from the vast Hollywood production centers, "There's
not even enough *mediocrity* to go around!"

In 1944, there were not even any Hollywood production centers for
television. With the new medium on the verge of a historic explosion
(there were 7,000 TV receivers nationwide that year; by the beginning
of 1947 there would be 60,000 sets, and by the end of 1947 there would
be 165,000), no one had thought to begin assembling an inventory of
program content.

Videotape was twenty years from perfection. The thought of America's motion picture industry adapting itself to this new competitor's
needs was ludicrous (and less than ten years from reality); even if
William Paley or David Sarnoff had been inclined to call upon the major
studios for product, the major studios doubtless would have recoiled.
The major studios regarded television as a form of smallpox.

Television needed something to eat, something live, something con-
spicuous and established as a field of human interest; something that
could be transmitted from a relatively small, highly defined field of
activity.

Television sank its teeth into sports.

The gypsylike subculture sprang to life on the nation's scattered small
screens. While the big, established networks competed in a desultory

way for the rights to telecast the nation's blue-chip events, and ABC took what was left (usually boxing), the real action was being generated on independent stations by a brash, colorful breed of outside entrepreneurs.

These were the counterparts of the network outsiders—the shrewd advertising professionals—who supplied what little there was of a sports esthetic to CBS and NBC and ABC. These were men who had come of age in vaudeville, in Depression-era "promotions" or in smoky caverns of the fight world.

Dick Lane was a titan amidst this breed. A child actor, an acrobat who hung by his teeth from a rope in an "iron jaw" act, a medicine-show barker, a silent-film actor, a nightclub straight man and a vaudeville drummer, he was perhaps uniquely qualified to grasp television's essential appeal. Lane was in Hollywood making "Boston Blackie" movies for RKO-Paramount, when a twenty-nine-year-old German refugee, an artist and technician named Klaus Landsberg, arrived in town from the East and, in 1942, founded an experimental TV station on the Paramount lot. The station was then called W6XYZ. In no time, Dick Lane was at the door, inside Landsberg's office, helpfully telling the young German how he should run the place.

One thing that Lane drilled home to Landsberg was that he should put wrestling on the air. Lane had a passion for it. As one of his hobbies, he managed a Texas grappler named Dangerous Danny McShain. The way Lane looked at it, wrestling had been around since three thousand years before the birth of Christ. The sport had paid its dues; it was ready for the big time. Lane badgered Landsberg until Landsberg agreed to rig up a full-scale wrestling ring inside a sound stage at Paramount and turn a camera on Lane's grippers.

Two years later the bouts were so big in LA that Lane moved the matches out of the sound stage and into the 10,096-seat Olympic Auditorium, where *Wrestling from the Olympic* began a thirty-year syndicated television run. W6XYZ, meanwhile, became licensed commercially as KTLA, and the youthful Landsberg began to consolidate his reputation as the West Coast's ranking visionary of TV.

Lane himself worked the microphone for those early telecasts. The young Steve Allen frequently sat in for him, tripping off into madcap digressions and Groucho-like wordplay to cover his utter and irreparable ignorance of the sport. Between the two of them, Lane and Allen brought stardom to such heroes and villains and assorted Great Pretenders as Lord James Blears, the fiendish Mr. Moto, The Destroyer, the hulking Tolof Brothers, Chief Strongbow, the Black Panther—and a

Texas-born grappler named George Weber, a man of such slovenly dress habits (he wrestled in blue jeans) that his wife, Betty, demanded one day that he march out and buy himself a decent suit of clothes. Weber obeyed. He returned looking so uncharacteristically dapper that his stunned wife exclaimed that he was *"Gorgeous, George!"* In that blurted cry was born one of early television's four or five most memorable personas.

No TV child of that repressive, sexually euphemistic era is likely ever to forget the delicious welling up of hilarity, seasoned with a strong redolence of *the forbidden,* as this platinum-coiffed, Roman-nosed creature appeared on the black-and-white screen, shed his flowing silk cape and stepped daintily into the ring—preceded, always, by his faithful valet, who had sprayed the premises with clouds of an atomized substance rumored to be Chanel No. 5.

Lane's wrestling matches were a ratings success in part because of a little touch of vaudeville he brought to each telecast: a half-facetious, half-serious, always semihysterical rambling interview that he conducted with grapplers to set up viewer interest for upcoming bouts. In a TV age that revealed athletes mostly as distant, faceless specks on a tiny screen—and years before Roone Arledge made camera closeups a hallmark of ABC coverage—Lane was fascinating and half-terrorizing his viewers with prolonged closeup shots of ferocious, broken-faced warriors as they bawled and bellowed and raged about how they would abuse their scheduled opponents next time they caught them in the ring. (A wrestler named Freddie Blassie, for example, was singularly piquant—he would invariably seize the microphone from Lane's hand and revile his opponent as a "pencil-necked geek.") No one could be quite *sure* that these individuals were speaking entirely in jest—after all, television was quite new, and behavior like this simply had no precedent—so Lane's pregame interviews established a TV wrestling tradition that persists, with refinements, to this day.

Four years after he introduced wrestling to television, Dick Lane created another sport destined for a kind of low-rent immortality: Roller Derby.

Roller Derby *cannot* claim a five-thousand-year heritage, as can wrestling. Its origins reach only to the Depression, when roller skating grew popular as a spinoff, as it were, from Dance-A-Thons, Walk-A-Thons and other time-killing amusements of the down and out. In the course of one lost 1930s evening in Chicago Stadium, boy-and-girl skating couples began to challenge other couples: they would skate in sprints around the stadium's perimeter, in a test of endurance.

It wasn't long before this aimless diversion developed into a money sport. With a dollar or so as prize money, the more aggressive couples began to skate out ahead of the pack, and then attempt to lap their rivals. Their slower competitors learned defensive tactics—blocking with the elbows, occasionally tripping—in an effort to prevent the leaders from winning the "prem," the premium money that had been bet.

KTLA aired the first TV Roller Derby match in 1949. Two years later, Klaus Landsberg established a year-round season for Lane's brainstorm. Eight mostly makeshift teams, purportedly representing various cities of the United States, competed—again, from Olympic Auditorium. The telecasts aired on Tuesday and Saturday nights.

Fancifully named (the New York Bombers, the Brooklyn Red Devils, the Jersey Jolters, the Chicago Westerners, the Los Angeles T-Birds, the Texas Outlaws) and outfitted with go-to-hell pads and helmets and uniforms, the contestants whirled around and around, followed by three KTLA Orthicon cameras and Dick Lane—again improvising a play-by-play style to accommodate the slightly hoked-up action.

"I liked those people," Lane remembered. "I never belittled them in any way—never criticized them, unless they did something very stupid. You don't throw rocks at people you like. But violent? Oh, my God yes, they were violent. Especially the *fans.* They were like the wrestling fans. I'd look at them out there in the seats sometimes, screaming and yelling and throwing things, and I'd say to myself, 'My goodness—they must eat their young.'"

There was another lively and imaginative source of TV sports in those primordial years: the DuMont Network, an entity that might have altered the course of American television history had it not been crushed out of existence in 1955.

DuMont is the Atlantis of television. Many, if not most, of the 1980s' most desirable viewing population would be astonished to learn that a legitimate fourth network existed at the outset of the TV age; or that for a time it seemed that DuMont, and not ABC, would blossom into equal competition with the two established radio-age giants.

DuMont not only existed, it set standards in terms of versatility, range of programing and public service. DuMont broadcast the first full hour of commercially sponsored TV—*The Original Amateur Hour,* underwritten by the P. Lorillard tobacco company, on January 18, 1948. DuMont carried the legendary Army-McCarthy hearings, which helped bring about the downfall of the demagogic Senator Joseph McCarthy of Wisconsin in the Cold War years. DuMont sent Klaus Landsberg out to Hollywood in 1941 to organize W6XYZ, later KTLA.

DuMont provided early training for such video craftsmen as Harry Coyle, NBC's master of baseball telecasts, and, briefly, Roone Arledge. DuMont carried television's first prime-time professional football telecasts in 1953 and 1954.

And it was DuMont that sank virtually without a trace in 1955, the victim not of its incompetence, but of stringent—some historians have said draconian, even punitive—FCC interpretations of its competitive status and corporate intertwinings.

Ironically, American television would not have been a mass-market medium without a technical breakthrough supplied by the doomed network's founder, a polio-stricken inventor named Allen B. DuMont. In 1932, working in a basement garage in Upper Montclair, New Jersey, with ten thousand dollars in capital and three assistants, DuMont produced a cathode-ray scanning tube (the TV set's picture screen) that could be sold at low cost and that lasted for thousands of hours, instead of the hundred-hour tubes in development then.

For several years after that breakthrough, DuMont seemed destined to dominate the new television industry. The founder incorporated his company as early as 1935. By 1939 he had an experimental station going in Passaic—W2XVW—and was demonstrating the first all-electronic, commercially available receiver at the 1939 World's Fair. DuMont was showing a profit by 1941. The company's profits, sparked by sales of radar-related equipment to the United States government during the war, enabled DuMont to finance commercial stations in New York, Washington and Pittsburgh within months after the war's end.

The DuMont Television Network was only one of five divisions within Allen B. DuMont Laboratories, which showed fixed assets of $4.5 million in 1948: the company also manufactured cathode-ray tubes, transmitters, oscillographs and TV sets. The network consisted of sixteen stations on the Atlantic seaboard and in the Midwest. By contrast, NBC had two owned stations on the air; CBS had one, and ABC had construction permits for five owned stations. DuMont had transferred its headquarters from New Jersey to New York's Wanamaker's Department Store at Ninth and Broadway, which it converted to a five-thousand-cubic-foot television facility, the world's largest.

Unlike the cautious lords of CBS and NBC, Allen B. DuMont had grasped the desirability of sports programing at the outset. Through the late forties and early fifties, DuMont presented a full range of prime-time boxing, wrestling, football and sport-related feature programs. But DuMont's earliest leap forward contained the seeds of the network's eventual downfall. One of the ways in which Allen B. DuMont obtained some of his operating capital in 1938 was to sign a contract with Paramount Pictures, under which Paramount was allowed to buy stock in the company at premium prices in return for a thirty-six-thousand-dollar loan. Because Paramount already owned TV stations in Los Angeles and Chicago, the FCC decided—arbitrarily, many experts later felt—that DuMont was not entitled to increase its own three-station ownership to the legal limit of five. In other words, DuMont and Paramount were one and the same entity in the FCC's eyes. This inability to gain a full complement of owned stations dealt DuMont the first in a series of fatal blows.

On September 30, 1948, came the crusher. The FCC called a historic freeze, a halt in its processing of pending license applications, while it considered several technical questions regarding color transmission and UHF reception. The freeze was to last four years. During that time, most of the existing 108 "pre-freeze" stations, owned by interests who had radio affiliations with NBC or CBS, cast their lot with one of those two giants. This left ABC and DuMont as minor networks. On February 9, 1953, ABC forged a merger with United Paramount Theatres. This move—which the FCC approved without a murmur—pumped $30 million in new capital into ABC. The network, rescued from a marginal fate, used the money for program acquisition. Overnight, ABC was the third major network, and DuMont was headed for oblivion. The end came in May 1955—less than a year after DuMont, in a final and tragic burst of false optimism, had opened a $5-million "Tele-Center" on East Sixty-seventh Street in New York. DuMont's remaining equipment and assets formed the genesis of Metromedia Broadcasting, Inc.

With DuMont's passing, a bright flowering of promise in American television faded. As if in some weird sort of sympathetic response, the first vivid cycle in TV sports programing came abruptly to an end.

V

"HOW'RE YA FIXED . . . ?"

The Eisenhower-era neighborhood saloon crowds who gathered to drink Carling's Black Label beer and watch the Friday fights or the Monday wrestling or the Saturday-afternoon *Game of the Week* probably never even sensed it, but 1948 heralded the beginning of a Dark Age for television sports. The darkness would be considerably more apparent by the mid-1950s, as DuMont failed and westerns and situation comedy shows began to crowd out the live games and matches that had flourished on the prime-time network schedules.

With one shining exception, the *Gillette Cavalcade of Sports,* the Dark Age would last for more than a decade—until an extraordinary collection of maverick professionals began to assemble at ABC and forge an empire, using the castoff elements of sports programing as their foundation.

Otherwise, 1948 was television's boom year. TV set production exploded by five hundred percent over 1947 totals. Within two years, 4 million sets would be in use in America. Audience figures jumped four *thousand* percent. Network relay facilities—microwaves and coaxial cables—were spreading like veins throughout the East Coast and the Midwest, enabling vast new audiences to view programs from central sources. Seven more were nearing operational status; 81 construction permits had been granted; 116 were pending.

Sports were among the very few programing victims of this boom. There were several reasons. For one thing, sports were seen as a males-only attraction, and market research had already begun to suggest that women, not men, controlled the family viewing choices in prime time. Then there was the matter of time. TV executives liked their programs to begin and end exactly at a predetermined instant; it made the listings so much more manageable. And finally there was the element of snobbery. Why dignify the grunting exertions of a couple of semicivilized Neanderthals in a ring, or two dozen colliding behemoths with mud on their pants, when one could offer America the sophisticated sounds of Sammy Kaye, *Four Star Revue*, or *Kay Kyser's Kollege of Musical Knowledge*?

It was no accident that the first two sports that CBS television did deign to become involved with were horseracing and golf. Horseracing and golf were hardly what a fair person could describe as proletarian pursuits. Working-class people tended to bowl, rather than play golf. As for the track, their involvement stopped with betting on horses. They seldom owned any. Horseracing and golf were among the chief amusements of the monied, Eastern managerial class in American society—a class that closely corresponded with CBS's own governing elite, beginning with the conspicuously aristocratic William S. Paley, the company's founder and chairman.

As for the less savory forms of competition, such as baseball, the CBS brahmins' hauteur sometimes approached the status of an art form. William C. MacPhail, the first full-fledged president of CBS Sports, painfully remembers a sales meeting in the mid-1950s, at which the name of Dizzy Dean, the legendary rustic play-by-play man, came up. One of Paley's highest-ranking lieutenants recoiled at the mention of Dean's name. Slapping his palm on the table, the executive declared that no personality as uncouth, as ill-spoken, as vulgar as Dizzy Dean (this was a few years before *The Beverly Hillbillies*) would ever get on the CBS Network. "We wouldn't *have* him on this network," the chieftain scoffed. There followed an excruciating silence. Finally an agency man representing the Falstaff Brewing Corporation cleared his throat, glanced helplessly around the room, and advised the network chieftain: "He's *on* your network. Every Saturday. Doing the Falstaff *Game of the Week.*"

In those beginning years, CBS and NBC did not even bother to form distinct sports divisions. Their sports "departments" functioned as vague, informal appendages of the news divisions. The news divisions, especially at CBS in the thrall of Edward R. Murrow, did their best to ignore that fact. Camera crews covered news and sporting events interchangeably—with the result that ball games on TV had the same distant, formalistic look and feel as a presidential ceremony. "Documenting the event" was the sober philosophy in either case.

No spectator present at the 1954 U.S. Open Golf Tournament at Baltusrol was likely to forget NBC's elephantine conception of a "portable" camera to record closeup action—if the spectacle of a wealthy

WASP hunched over a putter may be called action. The camera protruded through a hole that had been cut in the roof of a black Cadillac limousine. NBC News had converted the vehicle to provide mobile pans of such events as inaugurations and parades. But Baltusrol was not exactly Pennsylvania Avenue. Lurching and bumping around sand traps, its bobbing cameraman like a gunner at his turret, the mutilated limousine suggested nothing so much as some demented invasion of the golf course by an underworld hit squad, or a wayward hearse cut off from the funeral.

NBC was *the* first network for sports programing. CBS, preoccupied with its news division and with prime-time prestige, never really developed a taste for the subject until the 1970s; ABC was still a decade away from being taken seriously for anything. But even NBC Sports, in those formative years, would have been nothing without A. Craig Smith and the *Gillette Cavalcade of Sports*. It was Gillette, not NBC, that owned the rights to the World Series and All Star Game until as late as 1965. The network itself had not yet attained any real comprehension of sports' appeal.

A 1954 memo from NBC's Television Network Division to Perry Smith, then the network's "supervisor" of sports, advised in part: "Let's forget the Masters, any tennis at Forest Hills (the U.S. Open and the Davis Cup competitions), the Cotton Bowl . . . and let's take a hard look at baseball."

In this vacuum of comprehension at NBC, the redoubtable A. Craig Smith spotted and seized a historic opportunity. It would be stretching the truth to suggest that Smith ran NBC Sports from his office within the Gillette building in Boston. But there is no avoiding the evidence that this small, compulsive and ferociously alert marketing man—alternately plump and cadaverous, depending upon the cycle of his frequent crash diets—put his personal stamp upon the genesis era of TV sports. No network executive approached his penetrating grasp of this programing genre before Arledge (or, to be fair about it, before ABC Television President Tom Moore, who gave Arledge the operating leeway he needed). A. Craig Smith was TV sports' man of the fifties.

Smith was off and running, in fact, almost before World War II had drawn to a close. Television had not yet been released from its wartime licensing deep-freeze by September of 1944, but Smith couldn't wait. Global conflict for freedom and democracy or not, Gillette had to sell its Blue Blades. Radio had been a tremendous blessing, but now the company had to leap forward again; it had to increase its broadcast boundaries. In September of 1944, Willie Pep was scheduled to fight Chalky

White for the featherweight boxing championship. Smith decided to use that bout to extend the fabulously successful Gillette radio fights to television.

No matter that, of New York's three embryonic TV outlets, only WNBT had the capacity to telecast the bout—and no matter that the signal would be received by a mere handful of viewers; fewer than six thousand mostly gathered in neighborhood bars. If WNBT was the best outlet available, Craig Smith would take WNBT.

Thus began the implantation of the *Gillette Cavalcade of Sports* on television. WNBT later became WRCA and then WNBC, the NBC Network's flagship station. NBC and Gillette were to enjoy an exclusive mutual relationship that lasted until 1959, when Smith began to sense the coming sports revolution within ABC.

The *Gillette Cavalcade* was perhaps the greatest programing achievement of television's first two decades. At the time it finally left the air, in 1964, it was the longest-running series in TV history, having presented six hundred nights of boxing alone, not to mention dozens of America's most venerated sporting classics.

The *Cavalcade* was a masterful, and in many ways prophetic, demonstration of television's overwhelming suggestive force. A *Cavalcade* telecast did not merely cover a contest, it presented an *attitude* about the contest—and, by extension, an attitude about America, and about Gillette Blue Blades as a sort of steel-coated embodiment of American optimism. The *Cavalcade* accomplished this through Smith's shrewd and complex blend of programing components. The most obvious were the built-attractions of the contests themselves: Smith played every chip his company could afford on rights to such events as the Rose, Cotton and Orange bowls, the Series and the All Star Game, the Army-Navy game and the ranking fights of the period.

Not quite so obvious were Smith's meticulous choices of announcers (Mel Allen possessed a voice that somehow projected a Norman Rockwell-like note of sustained delight about the sunlit playing fields of All America), his early use of cartoon animation in commercials; his inspired selection of music and even his felicity in hitting on a title: "cavalcade" was just the word to suggest grand, triumphant continuity.

Craig Smith actually devised the *Cavalcade* several years before its television debut. In the afterglow of his 1939 World Series triumph, Smith immediately understood the need to consolidate it, to keep Gillette's name on the radio airwaves on a regular basis, regardless of the event being sponsored. Boxing was the least seasonal sport. There were bouts every week of the year. Boxing, then, would become the bedrock attraction for advancing Gillette's image. On June 18, 1941, Smith paid $14,820 to secure rights to a Mutual Radio broadcast of the first fight between Joe Louis and Billy Conn. This broadcast marked the inception of the *Gillette Cavalcade of Sports.*

That first Conn-Louis fight was notable for a couple of reasons besides inaugurating the *Cavalcade.* One reason was the intense drama of the fight itself. Conn, an audacious pretender out of Pittsburgh, came close to stealing the title from the legendary champion. Boxing with control and intelligence, Conn led Louis on points after twelve rounds. Then hubris intervened. Sensing his victory, Conn began to open the fight up; he started slugging toe-to-toe with his lethal opponent. In the thirteenth round, an exhausted Louis glimpsed a microscopic opening in Conn's defense. Louis plugged the opening with a vicious uppercut and Conn lay on the canvas, thinking faraway thoughts.

A rematch between the two men would not occur for four years—not until the close of World War II—but the anticipation, fueled by the stirring radio description, obsessed thousands of sports fans. "I recall that for the next four years my friends and I wanted to win the war and listen to the return bout, in that order," wrote Peter Andrews in *Signature* magazine a generation later.

The other reason had to do precisely with that stirring radio description. It marked the announcing debut of a thin, tenor-voiced twenty-eight-year-old with an apparent knack for never having to breathe in. Don Dunphy went on to become Gillette's signature blow-by-blow voice for the next twenty-three years, frequently teaming with Win Elliott as color man. But Dunphy might never have won the opportunity had he not been struck with a burst of inspiration, one of those instinctive hairbreadth choices that consistently seem to grace the fortunes of broadcast giants.

A. Craig Smith's first choice for the job was Ted Husing. But Husing was under a binding contract to CBS. So Smith, with his customary zeal for the absolute nuance, decided to hold auditions. Sixteen applicants responded, including Bob Elson of World Series radio fame (and a future Sportscaster Hall of Famer himself) and the popular movie actor Paul Douglas. The contenders were to take turns calling rounds of a light-heavyweight championship match in New York. Their voices would be recorded on 33⅓ rpm disks and shipped up to Boston, to be judged by the master's very own ear.

No one will ever know for sure whether that audition fight was selected purely at random, or whether Craig Smith was indulging some hitherto-concealed taste for sadism. Whatever the case, the boxing contestants bore the names of Gus Lesnevich and Anton Christoforidis. It would be hard to imagine a more Gorgonian test for a nervous, straining applicant for the country's most prestigious sportscasting affiliation than the prospect of babbling: "And there's a left by Christoforidis . . . another left by Christoforidis, a right by Christoforidis and now a quick counter by Lesnevich . . . Lesnevich again, and now Christoforidis . . ."

Don Dunphy called the third and fourth rounds, then came back to do the tenth and eleventh. As Craig Smith later sifted through the stacks of recordings at Gillette headquarters in Boston, one clear young tenor immediately distinguished himself from the pack. Alone among his fifteen tongue-tied competitors, this applicant, Smith noted, had the wit to refer to the ring combatants as "Gus" and "Tony." Here was an innovator after Smith's own heart. Dunphy got the job.

If fortune's favored sportscasters occasionally paused to marvel at their fate, such tremors never seemed to trouble the thoughts of A. Craig Smith. Smith was too busy *ordaining* fortune; his own and that of the people in his expanding orbit. Craig Smith understood his expanding power. He had long since grasped the fact that TV network executives remained innocent of sports' strategic role in programing. For Craig Smith, fate was not a matter of trembling wooden stepladders and ill-considered second cups of coffee; it had nothing to do with whether boxers survived a given round. For Craig Smith, "fate" meant being blessed with the capacity to fill a void that more conventional men—the early network presidents—could not even comprehend as a void.

"We used to say that Craig could see money in the Charles River," recalled a former employee, speaking as though he still half-believed the jest. "Craig used to swing around in that oversized swivel chair of his during our budget meetings, and gaze out his window—he had a wonderful view of the Charles—and mutter, 'I can see a hundred fifty thousand in that.'"

There was in fact little jesting in Smith's presence. Many people at Gillette had come to fear him by now. He shocked his staid associates by separating from his wife, Lillian (although he remained a solicitous father to their two daughters, Betsy and Jean). He took up an elegant bachelor's apartment in the Beacon Hill section of Boston, where he indulged his domestic requirements with an exotic assortment of Japanese valets. He had also taken up the habit of disappearing from Gillette headquarters for two and three weeks at a time. Intertwined with these sorties was a curious, almost self-punishing need for hard physical exercise: Smith would spend solitary hours prying himself furiously up and down the Charles River in a single-shell scull. No longer was Craig Smith the earnest, bright-eyed idealist who would push doorbells and peddle housewares in order to find out how the common people talked.

But even as he acted out these darker affectations of success, Smith showed an almost eerie sense of the future. Even in dissipation he was ahead of his time. A coming generation of network TV executives would refine and extend this sort of willful behavior, elevating it into a weird kind of industry etiquette.

No one dared admonish Smith when he returned to work—often bloated and steeling himself for one of his contrapuntal crash diets— because he always resumed his pursuit of Gillette's broadcast fortunes flawlessly, and because he was, after all, the company's savior in 1939.

"I had my own way at Gillette," an eighty-year-old Craig Smith affirmed in a telephone conversation from his retirement home in California. "I could get away with any undertaking at all."

As with most powerful executives, Smith's most casual remark was often interpreted as a literal command—inevitably, with extravagant consequences. A marketing vice-president at Gillette told Smith that he would be flying off to England on vacation one day in 1959, and asked politely whether there was anything he could bring Smith from that country. Smith snapped: "Yes. Bring me a scull." The marketing director showed up for work in a few weeks—several days later than his scheduled arrival. He had had to make the return trip by ocean liner, owing to the bulk of the custom-made, single-seat rowing shell that he had spent most of his vacation attending to.

If the people around him at Gillette lacked nerve, Smith himself had plenty to go around. Smith had enough nerve to supply the entire broadcasting industry. In 1946, Smith gazed into the Charles River and "saw" $14 million of Gillette's money there: $1.4 million a year for ten years in return for exclusive radio rights to the World Series and the All Star Game. Now Gillette could afford such extravagances: in 1946 its profits were $10.5 million.

"People thought Craig Smith was even crazier than when he swung that '39 package," recalled a colleague of the times. "But in fact, it was a helluva deal."

Not in Smith's scheme of things, it wasn't. By now, radio was an afterthought to the Gillette advertising director. Television was the coming medium in sports broadcasting. Smith saw that, even if the networks didn't—even if the sports establishment itself didn't see it.

In the 1940s, major-league baseball was still clattering along under a ruling cadre that might have performed splendidly at the helm of a landlocked eighteenth-century central European principality. Albert B. "Happy" Chandler, the former United States senator from Kentucky, had succeeded the late Kenesaw Mountain Landis as commissioner. To his everlasting credit, Chandler would support Jackie Robinson in Robinson's painful passage through baseball's color barrier in 1947. But in most other ways, Chandler, along with the team owners who elected him, was a traditionalist. He saw baseball as The American Game, an expression of the Republic's most ancient myths and values, a ritual to be performed in a pastoral setting on sunlit summer afternoons. Chandler's duty was to protect The Game from the corrosive, transitory whims of commerce and what, in a later age, would be called "secular humanism." Already Chandler had struck down a very attractive sponsorship proposal for a World Series broadcast because the sponsor was a beer company—Liebman Breweries, Inc., of Brooklyn. "It would not be good public relations for baseball to have the Series sponsored by the producer of an alcoholic beverage,"* Chandler moralized—a sentiment that would ring impossibly quaint to a later generation virtually baptized in Lite Beer.

Chandler and his ring of owners had little more regard for broadcasting than they did for Demon Beer. There was still a strong suspicion that baseball broadcasts amounted to "giving away free" the same product that fans paid for at the turnstiles. As late as 1939, all three New York teams—the Yankees, the Giants and the Dodgers—barred radio broadcasts of any home games. Small wonder that television, with its greater arsenal of pilferage, only compounded that paranoia.

There was in fact some valid basis in the owners' distrust of television. While the medium never cut seriously into major-league attendance, it devastated the minors. In 1949, according to statistics compiled by William O. Johnson, 42 million Americans attended minor-league contests. Ten years later—at the end of baseball's first TV decade—that number had plunged to 13 million; in another decade it had diminished to 10 million. The number of minor-league teams dropped from 488 in 1949 to 155 in 1969. †

---

* Russel Adams. *King C. Gillette*. Boston: Little, Brown, 1978.

† William O. Johnson, Jr. *Super Spectator and the Electronic Lilliputians*. Boston: Little, Brown, 1971.

Craig Smith had to fight his way through the major-league establishment's resistance to the changing times.

The first part was easy. Gillette, in fact, benefited from baseball's prejudice against beermaker-sponsors. The second part—smashing the resistance to television as an alien intruder—involved a talent that Smith had long since made uniquely his own: the shrewd and nerveless spending of cash.

In 1947, the year before television's breakthrough as a bona fide mass medium, Smith risked thirty thousand dollars for the right to cosponsor the Yankees-Dodgers Series in conjunction with the Ford Motor Company. The partnership was a matter of economic need, not bosom corporate friendship—at least as far as Smith was concerned. To Smith, Ford was an opponent—the rival team in Smith's own private World Series.

Here again, A. Craig Smith was acting upon tendencies that would be considered typical of network warriors two generations in the future. For him, the real competition in TV sports lay not on the playing fields but among the programers, the money people, the advertising crowd. In Craig Smith's eyes, Ford was the odds-on favorite and Gillette was the underdog. Smith had beaten the wealthier rival once before, in 1939, making money where Ford had failed. (He must have smiled at an early, and typically Old-World pronouncement made by Edsel Ford on the eve of the 1934 Ford-sponsored Series: "The Series [belongs] to the entire American public, and will not be interrupted by unwarranted comment concerning the sponsor of the broadcast or its products.") Smith had gone on to unmask that attitude as hopelessly naive; yet here he was in 1947, forced to share the national TV airwaves with these same pious dandies—who were now billing themselves as "Television's Number One Sponsor of Sports Telecasts." Ford had a twelve-month deal going to underwrite boxing matches at Madison Square Garden; it cosponsored the home baseball games of four big-league clubs, and it shared in the sponsorship of Dick Lane's boxing and wrestling matches out in Los Angeles.

As if the mere presence of Ford as a cosponsor were not grating enough, Smith and his Gillette colleagues had to watch with helpless chagrin as the imperious motor company unveiled its commercials. What commercials they were: miniature movies, self-contained filmed pageants touting the virtues of Ford. Produced by the prestigious J. Walter Thompson advertising agency, these ads amounted to a prototype for television's luxury commercials of the ensuing decades. Gillette, by contrast—to Smith's everlasting humiliation—could offer only the most primitive form of pitchmaking: "mikeside plugs," in the withering description of a Ford *doyen.*

Jointly telecast by CBS, NBC and DuMont, to an audience of only about 3 million in the cities of New York, Philadelphia, Washington and Schenectady, the 1947 Series hardly amounted to a national mortification for Gillette—not that a vaster audience would have noticed the disparity in the commercials' quality anyway, or cared. Viewers were far more enthralled with the dramatic relief-pitching duels waged between the Yankees' Joe Page and the Dodgers' Hugh Casey, and with Cookie Lavagetto's pinch double that broke up a Bill Bevens no-hitter with one out left in the fourth game, and with Al Gionfriddo's unbelievable stab of a 415-foot line drive by Joe DiMaggio in the sixth game. But as far as Craig Smith was concerned, a gauntlet had been thrown down. The next year, Gillette sponsored the Series alone, even though it cost the company $175,000. The year after that, Smith's competitive pride cost Gillette even more dearly: $800,000. But by now the television universe had changed. Instead of beaming the Gillette message to sixteen thousand American TV sets, Smith could now reach 10 million.

As he began engineering his masterwork, Smith knew that he already had one ingredient upon which to build: a three-foot high, eighty-pound, lead-encased set of electric chimes that pealed out Gillette's identifying theme during radio commercials. Inside the company, this contraption was known as "The Bong," and it was treated with the approximate care that was accorded an American President's "Doomsday Box." The Bong even had its personal custodian. For a while, this job fell to a twenty-three-year-old apprentice adman with the Maxon agency, which had the Gillette account, a cherubic Princeton graduate in political science named Joel Nixon. "For three years of my life I lived, traveled and slept with that thing," Nixon recalled, somewhat fondly, in his office at National Hockey League headquarters, where he eventually became publicity director.

Inside The Bong's lead casing were affixed three slender, hollow tubes made of silver. Inside each silver tube was a rod. Each rod was connected, electronically, to a tiny hammer—which was in turn wired to a panel of three buttons, attached umbilical-style to the exterior lead casing. When Joel Nixon pushed one of the buttons, it would activate the electronic hammer. The hammer would strike a rod. The rod would cause one of the hollow silver tubes to reverberate according to a scientifically calibrated note on the musical scale. There were three notes, one represented by each rod: F-sharp, A-sharp and C-sharp. Struck in the proper sequence, near a live radio microphone, the notes would set the airwaves aquiver with the motif that connoted, to an almost Pavlovian degree, the *Gillette Cavalcade of Sports*.

"Look sharp," the play-by-play man would cry, and Joel Nixon would *"Bong!"* (F-sharp).

"Feel sharp," and *"Bong!"* (A-sharp).

"Be sharp!" and *"Bong!"* (C-sharp).

Joel Nixon was thus perhaps America's ultimate trivia figure: the man behind The Bong.

"I lugged that thing to a different fight town every Friday night," Nixon recollected. "I'd sit at ringside, in violation of all known union rules, holding onto the damn contraption."

Why couldn't Nixon have bonged on something smaller—a hand-sized xylophone, for instance? "Craig Smith liked the sound of that machine," was Nixon's unsurprising reply. "He was a perfectionist."

The Bong itself was not perfect. There were moments—many moments—when Win Elliott would cry, *"Look* sharp!" and Nixon would stroke the first "bong" button—and all the electronic coruscations, the interconnecting system of cybernetic palpitations and dilations, the whole process of onrushing energy, flooding toward its rendezvous with the organism's cupreous nerve ends, would culminate in a . . . click.

"We finally had to find a guy who knew how to fix the damn thing," mused Nixon. "His name was George something. Luckily, he loved boxing. We always took him with us; he always had a seat behind me at the fights. When the bonger would click, George would get up and come over and fiddle with the wires."

But even a perfectly chiming bong was no longer enough for Smith. Not that he wanted to discard it; it had the makings of a framework, of a theme. A melody, a musical argument. That was the ticket. A. Craig Smith did what he always did when faced with a signficant vacancy to fill: he held auditions.

The musical world responded. Tin Pan Alley songwriters, jingle specialists, band leaders, Broadway lyricists. Their mandate: to create a unified melodic idea around the "Look sharp, feel sharp, be sharp" notes.

The winning composition came from no less than Mahlon Merrick, the orchestra leader for the great radio comedian Jack Benny. Merrick labored through several reams of drafts before he settled on a bracing, buoyant ditty set in march tempo. The Gillette Blue Blades March became as identifiable, in time, to Americans as the music of John Philip Sousa. So deeply did it penetrate into the national consciousness that it served as a musical paraphrase for the very word "sports." High-school bands squeezed and thrashed it out on ten thousand dusty half-time fields; spangled studio orchestras tootled through its opening bars to usher famous athletes onto the talk-show couch. It far outlived its own era. In 1981, a computer-electronics manufacturer applied to Gillette for rights to the music for use as the sound effect for a boxing video game.

Mahlon Merrick, by the way, did not get rich on the jingle—surely his life's masterpiece. Smith paid him a flat fee; there were no royalties. Perhaps Merrick should have consulted with Red Barber before he offered up his services.

So Craig Smith had his jingle—the ultimate jingle. Now he wanted a little visual flourish to go with the music. Smith consulted with Ralph Hotchkiss, the creative director of Maxon. Hotchkiss was very glad that Smith asked him: Hotchkiss had been kicking around a concept involving an animated parrot. Parrots talk, Hotchkiss pointed out to Smith. We could have this animated parrot, and he could say witty things, like "Do you have any blades, sir?"

Smith liked Hotchkiss's concept, for the most part. The strategic impetus behind the parrot's question, of course, was to prod the shaver-viewer; remind him that he had to replenish his worn-out blades. This impetus accomplished the dual goal of boosting turnover and forestalling customers' irritation over dulled edges. For the actual creation of the parrot, Smith ventured once again into the world of show business. He commissioned Chuck Jones for the job. Jones was just then reaching an early peak of fame as the leading Warner Brothers cartoon animator; his other creations included Bugs Bunny, Porky Pig and, later, the Road Runner.

For A. Craig Smith, Jones came up with a strutting, baggy-eyed, somewhat Walter Mitty-ish bird of plumage who fluttered and whistled and shaved his way across American TV screens throughout the fifties and well into the sixties: Sharpie the Parrot. Not only was Sharpie one of the very first animated commercial characters; he was the first to interact with real human beings on the screen. Sharpie the Parrot became a recognizable symbol to countless millions of TV viewers—some of whom might have had trouble correctly identifying the American Eagle.

So now Craig Smith had a bong, a parrot and a jingle to populate his commercials during that drop-dead 1952 World Series telecast, his personal comeuppance for the Ford Motor Company. But something was still missing.

It was that phrase! "Do you have any blades, sir?" What a flaccid, white-bread sort of . . . Smith plunged into thought. He rowed his scull back and forth along the Charles. He forced his mind back to those more innocent times of his life, back to those door-to-door days in Detroit, back to when he would use any pretext to get next to the common people, to absorb their vernacular.

Do you have any blades, how are you on blades, how are you for blades, how are you fixed . . .

Thirty years after it hit him, A. Craig Smith could not recall exactly where he was when that incantatory slogan swam into coherence. *"How're you fixed for blades?"* One likes to imagine that he was in his office at Gillette, that, at the decisive instant, he swiveled around in his chair and gazed once again into his beloved Charles River.

If he had seen money there before, he must have seen liquid gold there now.

VI

OL' DIZ

The first modern TV sportscaster—the personality who launched television toward its rendezvous with billion-dollar league contracts and ultra-tech saturation coverage of media megagames—was Dizzy Dean.

The notion seems ludicrous. Modern? A generation of viewers has come of age that was born after Dean's farewell telecast in 1964. Ultra-tech? To older Americans Dean is a blurry image from black-and-white summer Saturdays of the Eisenhower years, a flickering ham face in a white stetson, a Falstaff bottle in one fist, a "Howdy, Pod-nuh" on his lips.

Dizzy Dean is never mentioned in the same breath with Mel Allen, Curt Gowdy, Lindsey Nelson or Ray Scott. Dizzy Dean never covered a pro football or basketball game. He probably never saw an Olympics. Students of baseball history are more likely to associate his name with the hell-for-leather St. Louis Cardinals of the 1930s, the fabled Gas House Gang for whom Dean fireballed his way into the Hall of Fame. Taking account of his athletic past, it is too easy to dismiss him as a primitive manifestation of a broadcasting subspecies: the ex-jock behind the mike.

But Dean's legacy on the airwaves demands more respect than that. The evolutionary chain that has spawned Howard Cosell and Don Meredith, among others, traces directly back to him. Strange as it is to contemplate, Jay Hanna (or Jerome Herman; at any rate, *Dizzy*) Dean stands as the primordial on-air mover in the evolution of ABC Sports, and thus of all the glittering supervideo that flowed therefrom.

Dean's brief tenure on ABC, in 1953 and 1954, amounted to the cornerstone upon which programers such as Roone Arledge and Fred Silverman would later assemble a television dynasty. And his ensuing ten years at CBS, while driving grade-school grammar teachers into fits of frothing apoplexy, created a new legitimacy for vernacular speech. Dean forever demolished the supremacy of the "golden-throated" professional narrator. If Dean made the broadcast booth safe for the "jockocracy," he also set an early standard for jockocracy excellence.

But Dizzy Dean did not make it to the TV airwaves on his own. Nor was he the happy discovery of some alert and innovative TV network sports chieftain. In fact, if it had been left to the people running the networks, Dizzy Dean almost certainly would never have broken through into television at all. Like so many other pivotal advances in TV sports, Dizzy Dean's reign as a television sportscaster was a gift to the networks by an outsider, an advertising professional. This unseen presence could not have been in more radical contrast to the homespun Arkansas farmboy-athlete: he was a twenty-eight-year-old Phi Beta Kappa from Harvard, an urban Jewish intellectual turned advertising man.

Just as A. Craig Smith had done from his offices at Gillette, this new benefactor was destined to preside for several years as a kind of ambassador without portfolio to TV sports. Like Smith's, his name and face would never become known to the general public. But fame was not his ambition; his ambition was power. And in the end, he would vastly outdistance Craig Smith's pioneering achievements in fashioning an esthetic for televised sports. In the end, he would mastermind an ad-hoc business enterprise of his own that would become ABC Sports. And he would personally handpick the men who formed ABC Sports' original coterie: a collection of young, fiery, rough-edged intellects who could never have abided CBS's or NBC's staid organizational restraints, but who formed ABC Sports' imaginative core for the next quarter century. Among this handpicked coterie was Roone Arledge. The young adman's name was Edgar J. Scherick.

One afternoon in 1953, Edgar Scherick and a friend sat hunched in a rowboat that bobbed gently in the swells of Reynolds Channel off Long Beach, New York. A couple of young Madison Avenue go-getters on their day off, just fishing and batting the breeze. But Ed Scherick, then a pale and intense twenty-eight-year-old, couldn't get the furies out of his mind.

His thoughts kept flashing off to the Polo Grounds. He was *inside* the Polo Grounds, amidst thousands of screaming fans. And yet not inside the ballpark, but somehow above it. He imagined himself a part of the charged air that hovered above a hundred stadiums; his thoughts were of the airwaves. Scherick was suffused for a moment with a vision of tremendous power, an intimation of beginnings. He turned suddenly to his startled fishing companion and announced: "There is a revolution coming—I'm going to be in the middle of it."

Ed Scherick was not prophesying the social and political revolution that would erupt across America within a decade of that afternoon. He was talking about a narrower, more mercantile revolution, a revolution of television forms, a revolution that Ed Scherick himself would ignite.

And yet the two revolutions cannot be isolated from one another. They shared common implications, they involved the same mass society in simultaneous and competing ways. The years 1960-1974, the most traumatic period the United States had endured since the Civil War, coincided with the greatest mass absorption in sports—particularly football—in the nation's history. Television provided the largest conduit toward that absorption. Particularly ABC.

ABC, in telecasting superbly produced college football games, also transmitted an equally masterful—and packaged—attitude toward those games, and, by extension, toward the colleges and universities that sponsored them: an attitude essentially of numbness. By carefully keeping its cameras trained on the helmeted, disciplined players and the wholesome cheerleaders and the snappy, euphemistic, Salute-to-Old-Glory marching bands at halftime, and not on the beseiged administration building, the smoldering ROTC headquarters just over the stadium's rim, ABC perpetuated—however passively or unintentionally—a myth of stability, of tranquil, disengaged campus life, for those who yearned for such a vision.

The other networks were not noticeably at odds with this packaged attitude. CBS, the dominant carrier of professional football in the 1960s, was a passive accomplice to another payload of values that refuted most of the social revolution's aims. As seen on TV in the sixties, the National Football League leaped quickly from the status of an arcane, fringe sport to a full-blown expression of America's corporate and military ethos. It is by now commonplace to compare the pros' "bomb-blitz-penetrate" vocabulary with the argot of war, or to recall the glorification of martinet coaches such as Vince Lonbardi and Don Shula, or to point out that the NFL's emphasis on specialist players, one-skill drones who carried out their atomized task to robot perfection, suited the megalomaniac dreams of both corporate functionaries and vicarious warriors—including the vicarious warrior-in-chief, President Nixon, brooding on offensive plays for the Washington Redskins while real bombs blitzed and penetrated Vietnam and Cambodia, and watching a televised pro game while demonstraters chanted outside the White House.

TV sports became a kind of psychic refuge for millions of Americans, a way of numbing themselves to the horrible convulsions that threatened to disintegrate society as they understood it. At the same time, TV sports provided Americans the pretext of engaging their hopes in something real, something vital, something collective and large . . . and emblematic of the status quo.

Edgar Scherick was the man who set all this in motion. Far more of an interventionist than even A. Craig Smith, and more doggedly willful in his opportunism, Scherick embodied the germ of yet another attitude that would set his era apart from Smith's. It was the tendency to disregard the past, to act as though tradition did not exist and television was thus free radically to assault all kinds of rules and conventions, to disrupt continuity of practice whenever convenient. Ed Scherick belonged to a small cadre of cold-eyed, unsentimental video bosses who began to grasp this hidden truth in the 1960s and rode it to great power. The best-known of this cadre was James Aubry of CBS. It was Aubry— the quiet-spoken "smiling cobra" of TV executives—who brazenly dismantled much of William Paley's lofty, Old-World prime-time programing fare on CBS and replaced it with *The Beverly Hillbillies, Petticoat Junction, Green Acres, Gomer Pyle* and other vidfood that lacked connection to CBS's corporate traditions, but naturally suited the new medium.

Aubry and Scherick were among the first programers to sense that this kind of breakthrough programing could be achieved, that television left no record. It dwelt in an eternal time-present. Whereas print was about record, and was therefore obliged to conform to its own history, television could revise itself at will. The "time-present" insight would propel Ed Scherick through several incandescent years in television sports. Passed on to his discovery and disciple, Roone Arledge, it would help transform the video expectations of American society for a generation.

At the time he sat bobbing in that rowboat off Long Island in 1953, Scherick was an obscure figure in the advertising world. He had never even planned to be an advertising man. His thesis at Harvard, delivered just four years previously, had dealt with the Federal Reserve, the interest rate and bond market. Scherick's interests lay in politics, in economics, in theater—just about everywhere except advertising and television.

Scherick had gravitated to the ad firm of Dancer Fitzgerald & Sample in the manner of so many other bright young men entering media in the 1950s: on a whim. Scherick had been intrigued by a newspaper ad that promised a salary of sixty dollars a week for a young time buyer. The ad stipulated that applicants "must know the Nielsens." "Who the hell," Scherick remembers wondering to himself, "are the Nielsens?" He got the job despite this rather central gap in his knowledge. He learned soon enough who the Nielsens were.

Scherick was hardly the prototype Man in the Gray Flannel Suit. A small and quick-tempered man, his green eyes flashing about under a scowl of furious intensity, Scherick was an individual in a world of conformers. His voice, accenting its vowels with a slight Long Island nasal overlay, was a voice for issuing abrupt commands. Fussy about detail, compulsively thorough and above all poised like a falcon for the main chance, Edgar Scherick tried to restrain his natural impatience and adjust to his new world.

It was a world quite alien to Harvard. Scherick's new boss was a rough-and-ready son of a retired railroad man, J. James Neale. Neale had risen through the ranks of NBC radio in Chicago, where one of his principal duties had been to dangle a microphone cord outside a window in the Merchandise Mart and pick up crowd noise to be mixed in to the *Amos 'N' Andy* show.

"Neale was an uneducated man, but he had the itch," recalled Scherick. "He had a sense of what would work and what wouldn't. One of our main accounts at Dancer Fitzgerald was a beer company named Falstaff. Falstaff was a regional—not a national—beer; it was strong through the Midwest; and sports sponsorship was vital to its identity in the marketplace. Falstaff figured in the beginning of an operation Neale and I conceived that culminated in the establishment of ABC Sports."

In 1953, there was no ABC Sports; at least, not as a formal division. There was scarcely an ABC Television Network. ABC had been spliced into existence in 1943—not as a hopeful business enterprise but as a surplus appendage, a government-created transplant out of NBC.

As a subsidiary of the giant RCA, NBC had grown so rapidly through the 1930s that the Federal Communications Commission began to fear a communications monopoly. (CBS had stations in all the major markets, but lacked the enormous resources of a parent corporation, which NBC enjoyed.) So in 1941, the FCC required RCA to get rid of one of its two highly profitable NBC radio networks—either the "red" network, which concentrated on popular music and comedy programing, or the "blue," which carried the dutiful discussion shows, public-affairs and other high-prestige, low-audience programs. Naturally, NBC chose to lop off the "blue." The purchaser was Edward J. Noble, the creator of Lifesaver mints. The price was $8 million.

When the television era dawned, ABC became the network with the hole. It lagged far behind NBC and CBS in affiliate stations around the country, and its TV losses in 1950 were almost $2 million. The merger with United Paramount Theaters in 1953 probably saved ABC from going out of business, as it provided an infusion of $30 million in capital. But even with that windfall, ABC in the 1950s was a scavenger enterprise—marginal identity in the national marketplace, no coherent programing philosophy, no real money with which to experiment on attention-getting program forms.

"The situation at ABC was both a grave problem and a fantastic opportunity, as far as we were concerned," said Scherick. "ABC had no capital; it couldn't invest in any kind of programing—so whatever packages we at Dancer Fitzgerald offered them, we had to own ourselves, and hope to recoup our investment from the sponsors we'd lined up. At the same time, this meant that we had a chance to sell stuff to ABC that we could never hope to sell on the bigger networks. We started thinking about concepts."

With Falstaff as a client, the one obvious concept involved sports. The one mass-appeal sport that had quickly proved itself compatible with beer-drinking male viewers was baseball. Boxing, then near the end of its first great TV vogue, was regarded as narrowly Eastern-urban in its attraction.

But aside from A. Craig Smith's World Series and All Star telecasts on NBC, baseball had always been a local-station enterprise, never a network commodity. Which game, out of the several available on a given day, would a network choose to telecast—and why? What would Pittsburgh fans, for instance, care about Cleveland at Chicago?

Ed Scherick considered such objections, and dismissed them. Scherick reached for a hypothesis that no network chieftain, and not even the redoubtable Craig Smith of Gillette, had thought to consider: that insofar as television was concerned, it was not so much the game in question as the *packaging* of the game that counted. Pittsburgh fans didn't care about Cleveland at Chicago? Well, then, maybe they would care about something called the ABC *Game of the Week*—especially if the main attraction was not the Indians or the White Sox or any other team, but some surpassing personality who would provide the real continuity; who would in essence be the show. That role would fall to Dizzy Dean.

In a strict sense, Ed Scherick did not invent the Game-of-the-Week concept. Nor did he discover the broadcast phenomenon that was Dizzy Dean. Both entities were established on the radio well before 1953. What Scherick and his boss at Dancer, Jimmy Neale, did manage to accomplish was the successful transplantation of Diz and The Game to television—a significant achievement, given the great differences between TV and radio audiences in those days.

Dean had been a popular play-by-play man for both the Cardinals and the American League Browns in St. Louis through the 1940s, after an arm injury shortened his superb pitching career. In that era before conglomerate pressures killed off most competition, colorful beer labels flourished throughout America. Most big cities west of the Mississippi boasted one or two or three breweries, and the breweries liked to keep their identities high by sponsoring sports broadcasts. Many of these companies competed for the same audience in a major-league town. Dean, the most popular of several voices calling the St. Louis games on the radio, was owned by Falstaff.

The man who spotted Dean in St. Louis and elevated him to the national radio airwaves was an outrageous Texas genius—the Ted Turner of his era—named Gordon MacLendon. MacLendon, known as "The Old Scotsman," had rigged up a Texas-based empire called the Liberty Network. MacLendon's laissez-faire attitude occasionally prompted Northern broadcasters to grumble that their signals were being pirated down South. Whatever his technical transgressions, MacLendon was a superb judge of unorthodox talent. In tapping Dizzy Dean for his radio baseball broadcasts, MacLendon gave rural American listeners a homespun hero straight out of Fenimore Cooper by way of Uncle Remus. But Dizzy Dean was more than a living reference to folklore; he was a portent of broadcasting's future as well. The countrified Dean may not at once suggest many parallels with ABC's later creation, the heavily urbane Howard Cosell. But the connecting threads are there. Dean, like Cosell, was a brash, unterrified individualist with his own way of talking and a shrewd sense of his own show-business appeal. Like Cosell, Dean was an anti-authoritarian figure (he once shredded his St. Louis Cardinal uniform for press photographers in the heat of a salary dispute) who at the same time managed to suggest a first-name familiarity with the rich, powerful and famous.

By the time Mutual Radio purchased *Game of the Day* from MacLendon, Dizzy Dean was a subcultural superstar, for reasons quite apart from his pitching heroics.

"In those days, the Game of the Day meant the Game of the *Day*," recalled Robert (Buddy) Blattner, a longtime partner of Dean's on radio and TV. "We'd be in a different big-league town six days of the week. And on the seventh, on Mondays when the big leagues weren't scheduled, we'd do a *minor*-league game. We'd do Oklahoma City versus somebody. Mutual figured that this was a good-will gesture to baseball; the fans could follow the better minor-league players as they went up the ladder. But for *us*—well, I mean, getting Diz to work on an everyday basis was impossible. He liked the racetrack, he liked the golf course, and I think the biggest factors pushing him into broadcasting in the first place were his wife and his own wonderful love of being recognized. Now, the greatest way for Diz *not* to work would be to put conditions, sometimes stringent, on the network, so as to get himself excused. Diz, in his quest to do very little, would say things like, 'Al Helfer [another on-air partner] and I don't get along.' Well, the result was that Falstaff would acquiesce—sort of. They'd say, all right, Diz. Then, instead of excusing Diz, they'd send *me* in for Helfer. So I ended up working with Diz on those days when he was—more or less—assigned."

Blattner recalled another peculiar trait that linked the "primitive" Dean and the "sophisticated" Cosell, a trait that the two sportscasters applied in diametrically opposite ways. It has to do with an instinctive appreciation for the power of the self-created on-air persona. "Don't be fooled by all those stories about how Diz would say, 'He slud into third.' Diz was dumb like a fox. Not an intellectual, maybe, but very, very sly. He knew what made Dizzy Dean popular. Diz did a ball game the way he knew you wanted him to do it. I will never forget one time when we were in Detroit, and Diz did the first two innings—he liked to handle the first shift so he could get the hell out of the ballpark and go visit the racetrack. In that first inning, Diz turned out a play-by-play that was as professional as you could ever want it. Just very basic, meat-and-potatoes stuff. His call was very, very sound. Then, during the commercial break, Diz turned to me and put on that big old possum-eatin' grin of his. He said, 'That's enough o' *that* poop. Now I'm gonna get down to makin' some money.' And the rest of the way, it was all 'slud into third' and 'The Wabash Cannonball.' The Dizzy Dean he knew his fans wanted to hear.

"That famous expression he used—'Pod-nuh'—he used it to the greatest advantage of any man I ever knew. At Falstaff distributorship parties, he'd come ambling up in that white stetson of his, and grab some salesman's hand, and he'd holler, 'Why, *hello, Pod*-nuh —' and the man would stand there goggle-eyed watching Dean walk away, and he'd say, 'My god—*he remembered my name!*'"

Dizzy Dean was not simply a great natural personality. He was a great natural resource. The only trick was to transplant this resource from radio to network television. It is easy to forget how relatively formal American television tended to be in the 1950s; how scrupulously the early announcers observed correctness in grammar and decorum, for instance. Moreover, TV-set owners of the early fifties tended to be considerably fewer, more affluent and more specifically urban than were radio devotees. This upscale distribution of audience bolstered the innate snobbery of the network presidents—most of whom would have regarded Dizzy Dean, to paraphrase Ring Lardner, as if he were a side dish they had not ordered.

Finally, TV owners of the fifties were less likely to be bowled over by the mere *fact* of a major-league ball game on the air than radio listeners; the video-watchers would presumably respond only to games involving teams they rooted for as fans.

Ed Scherick and his boss at Dancer Fitzgerald, Jimmy Neale, were convinced that none of these myths held water. After all, did Americans—even sophisticated Americans—love Eisenhower for his politics, Gracie Allen for her sensitive nuance? Dean was his *own* subject matter. Once the ABC television audience got a jolt of this prodigious bubbling kettle of Americana, the Dancer people felt, they would keep tuning him in even if he did the play-by-play for ballroom dancing at Arthur Murray.

So early in 1953 Edgar J. Scherick folded an accordian string of railroad tickets into his suit pocket and set off on a tour of the major-league baseball cities—on behalf of a Midwestern working-class brew and a washed-up Arkansas pitcher. Scherick had every reason to believe that it would be a triumphal tour. His mission was to buy up network broadcast rights from as many teams as wanted to sell. And why wouldn't the teams want to sell? This was the big time—a national showcase every time *Game of the Week* came to their town! Scherick returned to New York several weeks later in a wrinkled suit and a state of tightly controlled panic. Of all the cities he had visited, of all the owners of all the teams he had negotiated with, only three were willing to sell TV broadcast rights to Dancer Fitzgerald and Falstaff: the Philadelphia Athletics, the Chicago White Sox and the Cleveland Indians.

But telecast rights in just three cities was not even the worst news Ed Scherick brought back to tell his superiors at Dancer Fitzgerald Sample. The worst news was that the ABC Network could not air any of its *Games of the Week* in any major-league city. The owners had slapped ABC—all network television—with an unconditional blackout. It did not matter if ABC wanted to beam, say, Detroit at Philadelphia into

Washington on a day when the Senators were out of town. No dice. No big-league telecast in any big-league town. Period.

These were draconian conditions. It would not have been surprising if the Falstaff Brewing Company had taken note of them, thanked Ed Scherick and Dancer for their trouble, and withdrawn its commitment to sponsor *Game of the Week*. Dancer would then have been left without a prepaid product to offer ABC. Dizzy Dean would have continued in hearty obscurity, another amiable minor character in American radio's vast gallery.

No one remembers just who it was at Falstaff that decided to take the unpromising risk and stick with *Game of the Week* anyway. The company went out of business in 1980 after years of declining profits; its internal records have scattered with its personnel. Perhaps the company's executives were astute enough to look at the mammoth population areas outside the Northeastern cluster of big-league cities: the whole continent west of St. Louis, and Dean's natural constituency, the South. These areas were filling up quickly with new viewers: between 1950 and 1954, American households with TV increased from nine percent of the total pool to fifty-four percent.

Whatever the company reasoning, the Falstaff *Game of the Week* made its ABC Network debut on June 6, 1953. For the first half of that first season, the results were indeed discouraging: the audience scarcely made a measurable blip. But Dizzy Dan's broadcast style defied indifference for very long. By the end of the 1953 season, *Game of the Week* commanded an impressive 11.4 national rating—and an even more astonishing fifty-one-percent share of sets in use on Saturday afternoons. Since all of these sets were owned by viewers outside major-league cities (owing to the blackout) it seems apparent that yet another historic indictment against television fails to stand up under evidence.

It was not solely television that killed the minor leagues. It was also the big-league owners, who decided to prohibit telecasts in major-league towns, which resulted in a concentrated dumping of these telecasts into minor-league strongholds.

"Howdy, *Pod*-nuhs, this' Dizzy Dean f'um Cleveland's Municipal Stadium, and lemme give you the dimensions of the playing field. It's two and a half wagon-greasings down the right-field line . . ." So spake Dean, and the big-city producers in the ABC truck outside the park fell on the floor in helpless glee. So did rural America. Television had not witnessed Dean's like before. Nearly all the new TV personalities up until his time, not only in sports but in prime time and news, had been either Eastern-urban, or, like Mel Allen, scrubbed and urbanized.

Dean was an absolutely unexpected blast from the heartland, the real
goods. The stetson, the string tie, the impulsive warbled snatches from
"Wabash Cannonball," the artfully cornponed usage—"Fawstaff—hit's
Amurica's P'emium Quality Beer!"—struck the Republic as authentic,
even somehow deliciously truant, a thumbed nose to straitlaced authority.

In 1954 the Brooklyn Dodgers and the New York Giants both saw the
benefits of Dean's mythologizing presence; both teams allowed ABC
inside their ballparks. Other clubs soon followed suit. After two happy-
go-lucky seasons on ABC, the *Game* moved over to CBS, although, as
Bill MacPhail discovered to his embarrassment, certain CBS Network
brass remained ignorant of the fact. In 1959, the great Dodger shortstop
Harold "Pee Wee" Reese replaced Buddy Blattner as Dean's sidekick.
Reese's honeyed Kentucky accents gave the telecasts a second Southern
voice, with Reese as the "serious" alter-ego to Dean's eternal Bad Boy.

As Dean's hair silvered and his girth expanded (his on-air patter
tended more and more to fond descriptions of legendary barbecues) so
did his fame. He became the apotheosis of his sponsor's product: a
Falstaffian figure selling Falstaff, ruddy and corpulent, his sly slanted
eyes mere slits now in the great meaty face. He was more than the ABC
ancestor to Howard Cosell in sports. He was precursor to a line of
magnificent television hillbillies from Tennessee Ernie Ford through
Colonel Sanders down through the cast of *Hee Haw*. Dizzy Dean was
the country daddy of 'em all. *Game of the Week* finally left the airwaves
in 1964. But Dizzy Dean went on making spot visits to broadcast booths
around the country until his death in Reno a decade later.

Dean probably never comprehended that ABC television, gathering
momentum for its massive surge toward number one in the national
ratings during his final days, received its first impetus from himself in
that forgotten summer of 1953.

Ed Scherick never forgot. More than twenty years after he had left
ABC Sports for Hollywood, Scherick recalled those times with Dean in
affectionate detail. On a lovely morning in Central Park in May of 1982,
strolling amidst a television-movie cast that included Bette Davis and
Christopher Plummer, as well as the extras, the production crew, the
horses, the giant lights, reflecting screens, cameras and directional microphones that were his to command—he was supervising the location
scenes for the television movie *Little Gloria—Happy at Last*—Scherick
talked *Game of the Week,* and his high, nervous voice grew almost
wistful.

"They were the best days I ever had in sports. When they were doing a game from the Polo Grounds, I'd meet Diz when he came into town on a Friday from his home in Texas. We'd go to Joe and Rose's on Third Avenue for dinner, and Diz would 'Howdy, *Pod*-nuh' everybody in sight. Then I'd go with him to his room at the Roosevelt Hotel where he'd get into his uniform—his pajamas and stetson—and he'd talk baseball and I'd listen. I still have a vivid picture of Diz, sitting on a trunk in the Phillies' locker room one afternoon, talking to Robin Roberts. You know, Roberts was a great pitcher, a Hall-of-Famer like Diz, but he would never ever throw a ball near a batter; would never brush anybody back. Diz couldn't understand that. I remember him looking at Roberts through those squinty eyes of his and saying, 'Hell, Robbie, you don't want to hurt anybody—but they's nothin' wrong with a few *eyeballs* lyin' around the plate.'"

It was a sentiment that Ed Scherick would adapt, in time, to his own uses as a competitor.

VII

SCHERICK AT CBS

The success of *Game of the Week* gave Ed Scherick his method. Now he looked for other ways to implant it.

At this stage, Scherick was still advancing along the trail blazed by his fellow advertising professional, A. Craig Smith. Like Smith, Scherick was exploiting the networks' vacuum of comprehension about the pluralistic appeal of the new "window on the world." The ruling circles at CBS and NBC were xenophobically locked into a narrow notion of television as *talking radio,* and were loading up the video airwaves with dozens of transplanted radio crooners, comedians and newscasters—which made for a lot of TV pictures depicting a large, smiling head in front of a spangled curtain.

Smith, Scherick and their advertising colleagues, of course, were burdened with none of the network chieftains' emotional commitment to the great, obsolete radio stars. Further, their sharply honed, disinterested analysis of the marketplace, bolstered by research, told them what the isolated TV barons could never grasp firsthand: namely, that people wanted to watch sports on TV. Neither Smith nor Scherick cared much personally for sports; it was not a matter of either man blindly seeking to justify his own taste. That error was the exclusive province of the Paleys and the Sarnoffs. What interested the outsiders, the admen, was the painless, prepaid, prepackaged implantation of a highly salable commodity—sports—in the leftover corners of the broadcast day. They would recoup their costs on commercial revenues, and wait for their chance to strike directly into the mainstream.

But Ed Scherick carried Smith's concept more deeply into ABC's territorial waters than even Smith was able to at NBC. He had to. Craig Smith enjoyed the luxury of dealing with an established and wealthy broadcast empire. Once Smith agreed to commit Gillette money to a

sporting event, there were layers of competent NBC technicians ready
to grapple with all the technological minutiae: securing AT&T transmission lines, arranging station clearances, coordinating the clerical
work.

But Scherick was obliged to master all these unglamorous considerations himself. The one man at ABC who showed much interest in
Scherick at all was a sly, drawling, deceptively elfin Mississippian
named Tom Moore, who was then in sales. As for the rest of ABC, its
attention was turned elsewhere—toward Hollywood, where the beacon
of survival shone weakly.

Leonard Goldenson had recently gained control of ABC television.
Goldenson had been president of United Paramount Theaters, and
he replaced Ed Noble at the top after the UPT-ABC merger. Goldenson's assistant at UPT, Simon B. Siegel, came on as ABC's treasurer.
In reality, he was Goldenson's second-in-command; these two show-
business operators would guide ABC's corporate destiny over the
ensuing generation. As soon as he was ensconced at ABC, Goldenson
began a series of bold new explorations for program sources—the
success of which would directly enhance Edgar Scherick's ability to
create his own power center inside ABC.

Goldenson appreciated at once the essential creative bankruptcy of
loading up a visual medium with audio programs. Reinventing radio was
not his goal. A lifelong denizen of the motion picture business, Goldenson believed the future of TV was in action, filmed entertainment—in
westerns and detective shows, like the movies.

The trick was to tell that to the movies. Hollywood, in the mid-fifties,
was paralyzed by fear and revulsion of television. Television was eating
into the industry; people weren't going to movies anymore, they were
staying home and watching Milton Berle and Jack Benny.

It was Leonard Goldenson's great genius to convert television from
Hollywood's destroyer to its most vital financial lifeline. It took years; it
took repeated visits to the big West Coast studios and long, searching,
prodding conversations with every movie baron he knew or knew of. But
finally Leonard Goldenson penetrated the movie colony's phobic defenses and persuaded studios to begin manufacturing product for the
small screen.

First came the financially moribund Walt Disney Studios, with
Disneyland. In return for Disney's commitment, Goldenson agreed to
purchase thirty-five percent of the stock—five hundred thousand dollars' worth—for Walt Disney's dream project, an amusement park in
Anaheim, California, also to be called Disneyland. The investment was

a good one; six years later ABC sold its stock for a profit of $7.5 million. Then came Warner Brothers, with *Maverick* and *77 Sunset Strip*. Then 20th Century-Fox and Paramount. ABC leaped into the forefront of television's great action-adventure era, and carved an early reputation as "The Network of the Young."

Its success with its movie-style programs did not make ABC instantly rich, nor did it close the gap in network size between itself and the two giants. But it did stave off the fate that DuMont had suffered. It bought some time.

But in 1955, all that concerned Ed Scherick was finding another coup with which to follow up *Game of the Week*. That coup involved a sport that, at the time, was lumped into the athletic grab-bag along with such other beloved mass-audience favorites as bronco-busting, Acapulco cliff-diving and longshoremen's brawls. The sport was called professional football.

The pro game in the early fifties had its small circle of devoted followers. But they were not, by and large, the same sort of genteel folk who went "Boola-Boola" at the Harvard-Yale classic. As early as 1948, the Chicago Bears had experimented with telecasts of six home games. The results would not pay Joe Namath's present-day cologne bills; the gross profits came to something under five thousand dollars. In that same year, the Baltimore Colts raked in upwards of fifty dollars for a telecast that went into the Washington market, and then presumably disappeared. In 1951, a couple of years before Scherick nosedived onto the scene, the Bears had assembled their own regional network of eleven cities—but had to pay two of those stations to transmit the games. The sportswriter Paul Zimmerman noted that those telecasts put the Bears into the red by $1,750. * Clearly, pro football was a television phenomenon on about the same massive scale as *Telephone Time,* or *Teenage Book Club*.

During that 1982 interlude in Central Park, Scherick recalled exactly how he came upon the National Football League and identified it as a hidden resource. "Even after *Game of the Week* got going at ABC, my basic job at Dancer remained that of time buyer. In that capacity I would routinely get on the mailing lists of TV stations all over the country. I was looking, sort of absently, at one of these circulars that came across my desk one morning. It was from some station out in Nebraska, KMTV. I was just turning the thing over in my hands,

---

* Paul Zimmerman, *A Thinking Man's Guide to Pro Football*. New York: Warner Books, 1970.

getting ready to flip it into the wastebasket. But I couldn't quite stop being intrigued with this little message, this *slogan,* printed on it."

The message that bemused Scherick was not exactly on the poetic order of "Give me liberty or give me death," or even, "I brake for small animals." In its entirety, it read: BUY CHICAGO BEARS–CHICAGO CAR-DINALS FOOTBALL.

"I got to *thinking,*" Scherick recalled. "If a station out in Nebraska, of all places, was telecasting pro football from Chicago, there must be others. I started checking around to see who they were, and how many." What Scherick stumbled upon was that obscure, eleven-station, ad-hoc network that the Bears and Cardinals had assembled to televise their home games. Scherick studied the geographical pattern of those stations a little more closely. And then he was on his feet, dashing through the corridors of Dancer Fitzgerald Sample. "I ran into Jimmy Neale's office, and I shouted to him: 'Do you realize this network covers just about the exact same territory as Falstaff's distribution area?'"

It was true. The St. Louis–based brewery marketed its product mainly in the northern Midwest—the same part of the country that received the Chicago team's feed. More fascinating still, the flagship, or originating station, for these telecasts was none other than Chicago's ABC-owned station, WBKB (whose call letters were later changed to WLS).

"We then went to Bob Kintner, who was president of ABC television. Kintner, to our astonishment, knew nothing about this! He didn't know that one of his major stations was originating pro football telecasts! So we got in touch with the Cardinals and the Bears. We told them: 'Dancer Fitzgerald, on behalf of Falstaff, will buy half the advertising time on your home telecasts, on a regional network basis, *and pay you the "B" rate card.'* The key thing here was the 'B' rate card. It was a helluva lot cheaper than the prime-time, or 'A,' rate card. They agreed! You know what it cost us to put on those games? Around two thousand dollars a week. *It was the greatest media buy in the history of television!*"

Great for Falstaff because it provided a cheap, centrally organized means of targeting its commercials to its buying public. Great for the Bears and the Cardinals because the Falstaff affiliation gave their names a new aura of major-media legitimacy that until then they had been lacking.

And great for Ed Scherick. The deal catapulted him forever out of the workaday "time buyer" echelon of agency work. It brought him within a whisker of a network sports presidency. "The Bears-Cardinals affilia-tion, coming on top of *Game of the Week,* really whetted Falstaff's appetite for sports," Scherick remarked. "When it became evident that ABC could not contemplate a really serious involvement in pro football telecasts—they just didn't have the good station hookups in enough cities—we took Falstaff over to CBS. *We got CBS into pro football.* They used the expertise that we had developed with the eleven-station regional network, and they brought the National Football League into the big time."

They certainly did. Actually, NBC and CBS transformed professional football from a fringe curiosity to a mainstream television event: CBS owned regular-season rights, and NBC telecast what was then called simply "the championship game."

Television's transforming magic had never worked more dramatically. In 1951, the entire NFL had realized only fifty thousand dollars in TV profits. From 1951 through 1955, the DuMont network paid the league a total of four hundred fifty thousand dollars for rights to carry championship games. But starting in 1956, the first year of CBS's historic, Falstaff-sponsored involvement with the sport, the NFL turned a decisive corner. It began to arouse the desultory attention of Eisenhower's America—a nation that until then had been almost umbilically attached to baseball. And yet, contrary to popular myth, the credit or blame for this new video sensation did *not* belong to network television. CBS, on its own, did not discover and colonize pro football. It took the imagination and the salesmanship of an outsider, Ed Scherick, and his advertising agency to shake TV out of its mulish indifference toward the game.

But it also took one transcendent pro football event to fix America's newfound interest in the sport and to consolidate all of Scherick's efforts. On December 28, 1958, that event burst forth in the frigid twilight of Yankee Stadium. The game that made the National Football League and married it to television, a brutal poem of football, unfolded. In that bleak urban dusk, with NBC's red-eyed Orthocon cameras peering spectrally into the dimness, Chris Schenkel and Chuck Thompson at the microphones and fifty million Americans watching on their black-and-white sets, the Baltimore Colts defeated the New York Giants, 23-17, at eight minutes fifteen seconds of a sudden-death overtime period.

Tex Maule, writing in *Sports Illustrated,* called it the best football game ever played. And in fact, a generation of Super Bowls and "immaculate receptions" notwithstanding, Maule's judgment may still hold up. Those long-ago viewers, their TV expectations already growing numb under the prepackaged neutralities of Perry Como and George Gobel and *Your Hit Parade,* sat there and watched as a new kind of live video

drama—an epic pageant of violence and grace, with real fortunes hanging in the balance—burned itself into their imaginations. They saw a
new national hero take form virtually out of the ether: Johnny Unitas.
The skinny, crewcut stranger with his high-topped shoes and his proletarian matter-of-factness under great pressure turned the small screen
into his personal crucible. In the closing seven seconds of regulation
time, Unitas brought his Colts seventy-three yards into field-goal range.
His movements, even in that twilight's blurry register, seemed eerily
elegant, even ritualistic. Scrambling back into the pocket on delicate
criss-crossing steps, gripping the football with both hands at his chin,
seeming almost to meditate as his line held and held and *held,* Unitas
whistled three consecutive completions to his gifted number-one receiver, Raymond Berry. These passes covered a total of sixty-three
yards. Then Steve Myhra kicked a field goal on a snap called without a
huddle. And regulation time ended with the score 17-17.

What the Colts then achieved in the overtime period has been enshrined in professional football lore as "The Thirteen Steps to Glory."
The Giants won the overtime toss, but the Colt defense stopped them
without a first down. Unitas shrugged off his dark Colts Cape, loped
onto the frozen field, and—in the opinion of many who witnessed it—
proceeded to create a new secular religion.

Starting at his team's twenty-yard line, the white-jerseyed number 19
called a sequence of thirteen plays that culminated in a savage one-yard
burst by Unitas's fullback, Alan (The Horse) Ameche, for the winning
score.

But it was the twelfth play of his masterful sequence that burns in
history. It could almost have been Unitas's homage to this marriage feast
of pro football and network television.

Raymond Berry had just caught a slant pass that moved the ball from
the Giants' twenty-yard line down to the eight. At this point, the logical
call would have been for a field-goal attempt from placekicker Myhra.
His success would have been almost automatic: recall that in those
years, the goalpost's crossbar loomed at the front of the end zone, rather
than at the rear.

But Unitas disdained this prepackaged, fail-safe route to victory. No
Perry Como certitudes in this new TV star's repertoire. Instead of a
cautious field goal, the young quarterback electrified the video millions
by risking a defiant, flat pass that found Jim Mutscheller on the one-
yard line. Ameche's plunge followed—and American television found
itself with a new hit programing form. It is emblematic of the TV–pro
football "marriage" that two decades later, three stars of that game were

TV announcing stars in their own right: Pat Summerall and Frank Gifford of the Giants, and, briefly, Unitas himself.

Unitas's salutary TV-era pass almost did not reach the TV airwaves. Only moments before Unitas threw it, the television sets tuned to the game across America had gone blank. PLEASE STAND BY graphics—a familiar sight of the era—flashed up moments later. A cable inside Yankee Stadium had been jarred loose from its power supply, and the greatest finish in pro football championship history came within seconds of oblivion as a TV event.

"Thank God there was a time out," declared Chris Schenkel. As the regular-season voice of the Giants, Schenkel called play-by-play for the telecast, along with Chuck Thompson, the Colts' regular announcer. "I mean a *real* time-out. It would have been *unthought*-of then for television to request a break in the action."

As a matter of fact, the first version of the notorious "TV time-out" had made its debut earlier that same year. But NBC directors were far too upright to dream of intervening in the action in such a nakedly self-serving way. Just four years later, network TV would manage to shed a great deal of this bashfulness—directors, trailing their head-set phone wires, barging onto the fields of the TV-created American Football League, treated premature kickoffs like some inexcusable flub-up in the control room.

The accident illustrated television's second-class status in that era. Schenkel, Thompson and NBC were working under conditions standard for the time, but quaint, if not downright belittling, in hindsight. The announcers were jammed into one of the NBC camera cages that had been suspended from the right-field upper deck in Yankee Stadium—in the very teeth of the raw December wind. Beneath them, threading through the crowd, lay the lines and cables connecting NBC's cameras to the remote truck. As the crowd began to surge toward the playing field in its overtime-induced frenzy—Schenkel recalls that the very grandstands had commenced to rock from the convulsive movement—someone kicked a cable at its connecting point, jarring the ends loose.

"The weird thing," Schenkel remembered, "was that we didn't miss any of the key action. Right after Berry's catch, the *Colts* called a time-out. That's about when the power went out. And in that brief span of time, one of our engineers—I wish somebody had recorded his name—actually climbed out of our cage and ran down on the field, into that mob, and *found* that disconnected cable and fitted it back together again."

Until that landmark football game, the NFL had been content to accept $200,000 a year from NBC in return for granting it the championship broadcast rights. But this time, when the contract came due for renegotiating, NBC's winning bid had leaped to more than three times that amount—$615,002. By 1962, the price tag approached $1 million.

The National Football League lost no time in grasping the significance of its rapid rise in value. As early as 1958, the league began to reshape its rules for a video environment.

Bert Bell, the NFL's first commissioner, announced a new rule in October of 1958: the league's referees could now call time-outs in the first and third quarters of a game without the request of a team— provided that nine minutes had elapsed without a normal break in the action. Sportswriters immediately pounced upon this provision as "the commercial time-out"—which, of course, it was.

Quite possibly, Bert Bell's decision was speeded along by the advice of Edgar J. Scherick. As soon as Scherick had forged the working link between Falstaff and CBS regarding pro football in 1956, he resigned from Dancer Fitzgerald and hopped aboard CBS. To people acquainted with Scherick's ambitions, there appeared little doubt that he was now on a very fast track. At age thirty, he was in position to advance quickly up CBS's ladder—perhaps to the unfilled position of director, CBS Sports.

It was not long before Ed Scherick himself knew better. "I *wanted* that job," Scherick affirmed on that afternoon in Central Park. "CBS Sports at the time had no clear focus, no leadership. They were a kind of subdivision of CBS News. What expertise they had was 'in the truck'— it was technical, not conceptual or strategic."

Scherick found his hopes bolstered even before he left Dancer. No one less than the stately Sig Mickelson, the head of CBS's TV news operations and thus the superior of Murrow himself, had approached the young adman to find out whether Scherick might be interested in the title of CBS's sports director—once the position itself got created. Scherick replied that indeed he would be. But Scherick was never to have the chance. Without the slightest warning, CBS offered the job instead to a forty-nine-year-old public-relations man for the Kansas City Athletics, a man named William C. MacPhail.

Scherick said nothing. But he was wounded. He had in effect been teased with, and then inexplicably denied, an executive position in network TV sports that he felt he had earned on merit—and the benefactor was a complete outsider to television, a man who affably admitted that CBS's offer had "come out of left field," and who just as casually would concede later than he "didn't know a camera from a boom mike."

MacPhail's hiring never elicited so much as a grimace from Scherick in public. Scherick even consented to a lesser job, a position in CBS sales. From that vantage point he provided the main conceptual thrust in establishing a master plan for CBS's city-by-city telecast breakdown, a plan that remains essentially intact today.

Scherick recalled that NFL experience with the same affection that colored his memories of the Falstaff *Game of the Week*. "I helped Bell and CBS decide how the various NFL teams would be plotted out into coverage regions. In those days, each region of the United States had its specific advertisers—regional beers, gasolines, and so forth. We'd work it out with the individual team owners. I was dealing with the Rooneys in Pittsburgh, the Bidwells and Halases in Chicago, the Maras in New York. It was great fun. Bert Bell himself ran the whole goddamn league out of his kitchen in Ballisn, Pennsylvania. He'd call me up every morning, just as I was soaping myself up in the shower, and we'd work out our arrangements by telephone."

Even to himself, Scherick tried to rationalize the shattering CBS snub. He told himself that CBS was an organization that valued *contacts,* and that the genial MacPhail had plenty of friends throughout the world of sports. Still, Ed Scherick could never quite shake the notion that he was passed over by CBS because he had a name like *Scherick*—while Bill MacPhail had a name like *MacPhail*—a solid, reptied, tweed-jacket, country-club, WASP name like MacPhail.

On the other hand, CBS's choice of Bill MacPhail was not without its own fortuitous logic. MacPhail proved to be a steady and competent, if unspectacular, executive, a classic of the CBS mold. And the man did have contacts. In those comparatively genteel, old-world days of network management, important business often got transacted within a closed community of kindred, privileged spirits.

William O. Johnson, the *Sports Illustrated* writer and editor, captured MacPhail and his milieu quite nicely. "MacPhail," wrote Johnson, "has pallid blue eyes, gray hair, and an unprepossessing, mild, nearly bland manner that seems better suited for the head usher at—well, at an Episcopal Church. Of course, appearances can be deceptive, for Bill MacPhail, like most of his CBS sports aides, is a team member in good standing at the upstairs bar of Toots Shor. In the gloaming of many a day, the scotch will flow in amber rivers and that brown-lighted barroom will slowly fill with the great and near-great of sports and the broadcast biz. . . . Soon the bar will be crowded, the stools filled, the drinkers perhaps three deep about the round rim, and MacPhail may start a game of Password, loser buys the drinks."*

One of the regulars in MacPhail's urbane circle was a fellow public-relations man with the Los Angeles Rams. As the years went on, this hail fellow took on a new job: he succeeded Bert Bell as commissioner of the National Football League. Pete Rozelle was a good friend of Mac-Phail and he was from the first a shrewd and penetrating appreciator of network television's importance to the sport.

In the early 1960s, this tranquil and profitable relationship was suddenly challenged. An independent sports consortium owned by Howard Hughes launched a series of moves designed, ultimately, to steal the NFL from CBS.

With the formidable Howard Hughes treasure at its disposal, the Hughes Sports Network presented a very real peril. If Hughes could gain the rights to any portion of the booming NFL telecasts, the company could conceivably parlay that plunder into the foundation of a fourth major network. Hughes's first maneuver came in 1962. The NFL rights for both regular-season and championship telecasts were up for renewal. CBS bid—as expected. NBC bid—as expected. The unexpected bid came from Hughes. The "outsider" consortium limited its target to postseason rights. In this arena, Hughes produced the highest bid.

It appeared for a nightmarish few hours as if network sports' most lucrative commodity was being snatched away from them, and that they were powerless to stop the heist. And then Bill MacPhail's good friend, Commissioner Pete Rozelle, an official putatively aloof from any sectarian TV interests, pulled a maneuver of his own: He called for rebidding. Instead of gratefully pocketing Hughes's millions, Rozelle decreed another round. Now CBS and NBC were back in the game. Given this reprieve, CBS unleashed some of its own financial might, and won the postseason rights. NBC, which turned up a secondary loser in all this maneuvering, was not overjoyed by the turn of events. But even NBC had to admit that at least it was still all in the family.

Bill MacPhail would dine out on that act of reprieve by Rozelle for the rest of his days in television. He believed—and his superiors at CBS saw no reason to doubt it—that Pete Rozelle had acted to block Hughes at

---

*William O. Johnson, Jr., *Super Spectator and the Electric Lilliputians*. Boston: Little, Brown, 1971.

least partly because he was MacPhail's good friend. Questioned about the episode in later years, MacPhail would smile and allow as how he and Rozelle had indeed hit it off well from their very first encounter. "We had an immediate chemistry," MacPhail would admit.

If that "chemistry" indeed contributed to Rozelle's decision to finesse the Hughes combine, then Bill MacPhail fulfilled his value to CBS on the basis of contacts, to say the least. Had professional football slipped through network TV's fingers, there is every reason to suppose that TV sports would continue as a loss-leader today—and even that the cable-TV challenge of the early 1980s would have made far more inroads against the networks than it in fact did. MacPhail was credited with an accomplishment that Ed Scherick, with all his aggressive shrewdness and brilliance, could never have brought off. It was perhaps the last victory for television sports' Old-World system of doing business.

Whether Pete Rozelle was actually moved by any Tom-and-Huck, blood-oath loyalty to an old chum from the social neighborhood is, at the very least, an open question, as Rozelle's later behavior toward CBS and MacPhail would make clear. But at least the perception of such gallantry remained.

VIII

THE SUNDAY-AFTERNOON GHETTO

emember the Sunday-afternoon ghetto?" Reuven Frank, president of NBC News, allowed a mist to cloud his otherwise steely eyes. He clasped his hands behind his head, his cufflinks glinting in the Rockefeller Center windowlight, and placed a wingtipped shoe heel tenderly upon his morning correspondence. "God, I used to love the Sunday afternoon ghetto," Frank murmured. "Now you can't get in there. They've wiped that out. Sports destroyed that." The mist evaporated from Reuven Frank's eyes. "Sports," he enunciated, making the observation sound almost like a proclamation of corporate policy, "is just a pain in the ass."

Reuven Frank is a gifted television journalist. Arguably, he is the finest who ever did battle against the armor-plated might of CBS News. Frank's attitude toward sports programing is not an intolerance for small annoyances. For news executives of Frank's generation—he arrived at NBC in 1950—the sports department was a natural enemy, an impediment to journalistic performance. Grafted onto the news divisions in those days, the network sports departments drained resources in budget, equipment and manpower. They did not return profits on the events they covered. And most unforgivably of all, they invaded and choked out the one sanctuary for enlightened experimentation in quality television—the one programing preserve in which guilt-ridden producers and directors could atone for the horrible concoctions they dumped into the rest of the airwaves like industrial waste: the Sunday-afternoon ghetto.

This languorous stretch of weekend hours was the period in which America barbecued, went to the beach, hula-hooped—did just about anything except watch television. So worthless was Sunday afternoon to advertisers that the networks did not bother to compete seriously for viewers. Instead, they opted for that chimerical quality, prestige. They encouraged "serious," intellectual programing, fare for men and women of taste, cultivation. Sunday afternoons in the 1950s displayed some of the best television that was never watched by the American public. "Stuff that pushed the frontiers," as Reuven Frank described it.

Perhaps the definitive Sunday-afternoon ghetto program was *Omnibus*, a Ford Foundation project that toured all three networks from 1952 through 1959. With Alistair Cooke as its host, *Omnibus* opened windows to dramatic themes, music and ideas that had never before reached a mass (or a *potentially* mass) audience; plays by James Agee, Maxwell Anderson, Chekhov; Eugene Ormandy conducting the Metropolitan Opera festival in *Die Fledermaus;* Orson Welles as King Lear; highlights from current Broadway musicals; showcase appearances by the likes of George C. Scott, Cyril Ritchard, Peter Ustinov and Leonard Bernstein.

The beginning of the end for *Omnibus* came as early as 1956, the year in which CBS acquired rights to the National Football League. It was also the year that *Omnibus* was dropped by CBS and picked up by ABC. That classic Colts-Giants championship telecast in 1958 (by Reuven Frank's own NBC crew, as irony would have it) was like an enemy flag implanted in the turf: from then on, sports would claim Sundays as its own.

"Techniques," sighed Reuven Frank. "Not *purposes,* but *methods.* That's what the Sunday-afternoon ghetto was. Sports destroyed that. Sports was purpose: to get an audience."

This managerial antagonism toward sports programing found expression at all the networks. CBS executives affected innocence that Dizzy Dean worked for them. Frank, at NBC, was a shade more forthcoming. "Curt Gowdy worked for me," he acknowledged, and then drew his lips back from his teeth. *"And I never met him."*

Back at CBS, Bill MacPhail quickly found that he would pay a certain price for the privilege of eclipsing Ed Scherick as head of the sports department. The price was almost continual frustration, a sense of walking along corridors and not casting a shadow, not hearing one's own footsteps resound.

"CBS had no *reason* to fool with sports," MacPhail pointed out. "CBS was *so* number one, overall, that its prime time was inviolate. There was no way I could get programing in there. I was the fifth wheel, the necessary evil. CBS would spend hundreds of thousands of dollars to develop prime-time pilots it would never use—and then ask, 'Why do we have to do the goddamn *Gator Bowl*?' Whenever I'd recommend coverage of something, the reaction was similar to, 'Oh, my God, we have to throw *MacPhail* another crumb. I remember when Sig Mickelson and I went up to see Lou Cowan—he was the network president then—about our coverage plans for the Squaw Valley Olympics. This was as late as 1960. We had to go up ourselves, make a special appointment with Cowan that was separate from his regular planning-board meeting, because Squaw Valley didn't come up in the planning board. Cowan heard us out, and then he said, 'But that's that *ski*, that *skating* thing. Unless we have an Arthur Godfrey or an Art Linkletter to host it, people won't watch.' That's how TV people *thought* about the Olympics before Arledge came along."

CBS did not do anything as outlandish as send Art Linkletter or Arthur Godfrey to Squaw Valley, of course. Instead, CBS sent Walter Cronkite. Cronkite joined such lesser on-air personages as Jack Drees, Gil Stratton and Bud Palmer. It was Palmer, however, who found himself with the most stirring assignment of those Olympics. In an eerie and utterly forgotten foreshadowing of what would happen sixteen years later at Lake Placid, New York, the United States hockey team staged a come-from-behind rally to upset the heavily favored Soviets. And Bud Palmer handled the play-by-play to a nation of largely deaf ears.

"People who saw and heard that game *cried*," declared MacPhail. "But, dammit, not many people saw it. CBS didn't bother to promote the Olympics to any degree, and the ratings were so bad that our sponsors felt they'd lost money on the whole thing." This despite the fact that CBS paid a mere fifty thousand dollars for rights to that Olympics— compared to the $225 million that ABC bid for the 1984 Games in Los Angeles. "And they had the audacity to keep reminding me," says Mac-Phail with acid humor, "'Just remember, Bill, for yourself and for all your people: when you go out into the world, you've got three big letters on your back: C-B-S.'"

It was this kind of attitude that obliged network regulars like Bill MacPhail to remain little more than caretakers of their departments. And obliged such true insurrectionaries as Ed Scherick to prowl the fringes restlessly, biding their time, waiting for some unguarded area of programing, some dead spot in the schedule, some technical or legalistic breakthrough—some as yet unforeseen chance to strike.

As early as 1955, that chance seemed as remote as a news president's goodwill. The first great postwar flowering of weeknight sports programs was virtually at an end. The boxing scandals involving James Norris's monopolies and underworld associations were breaking.

DuMont, the network most receptive toward sports, was skidding toward bankruptcy. And the surviving networks were looking not to the fight rings or the ballparks but to Hollywood for their content. The movie colony had long since retooled its "dream factories" to gratify this new demand. The home screens were filled with such prefabricated fare as *Loretta Young, You'll Never Get Rich, Name That Tune, Gunsmoke, People Are Funny, Our Miss Brooks*. True, there was the occasional oasis of live drama—*Studio One*, the *U.S. Steel Hour, Playhouse 90*. But the truth, contrary to affectionate memory, was that the network chieftains hated and distrusted live television. They would replace it with videotape—on the live shows that survived at all—as soon as that piece of technology became available. TV's ruling elite found live TV too random; there were too many chances for the unexpected, the uncensored, the ideologically unsound, to break through. An advertiser-financed medium wanted an audience as quiescent, as tranquilly receptive to the commercial's blandishments as programing could ensure. In the mid-fifties, television began to move away from its own inherent source of fascination, live programing, and toward a mode that closely emulated a previous mass-entertainment form, the movies. Sports was not a part of the grand design.

Given the network executives' passion for the controlled, the prearranged, the predictable, it may very well be true that their chronic aversion to sports programing went beyond mere apathy, class snobbery or thick-headed neglect. These cautious men may have sensed that sporting conflict rubbed some very primitive nerve ends in the human psyche; that it stirred untidy appetites that might strain the delicate sensibility required to yearn for New White Rain Shampoo or Speedy Alka Seltzer.

And of course they were right. The very next generation of TV executives would sense the same rubbed nerve ends, the same untidy appetites—and take direct aim at them, with college and professional football, the Olympics, boxing and auto racing. The difference was that television's eventual saturation of sports on the airwaves did not so much unleash those untidy appetites as convert them to a form of self-anesthesia.

But if the network rulers did not envision a future for TV sports, others did. Outsiders. Young advertising agency go-getters, nothing-to-lose guys, unfettered by the networks' stultifying caution.

While Ed Scherick was still tinkering with Dizzy Dean and the Falstaff *Game of the Week* at Dancer Fitzgerald, forces beyond his awareness were beginning to coalesce—forces that Scherick would shortly harness to create fortunes for himself, for ABC television and for countless sports figures over the ensuing quarter century.

The catalyst was named Tom Villante. In 1955 Villante found himself in the advertising business, as unexpectedly as had Scherick a few years before. Compactly built, dark-haired and handsome in a close-trimmed, starch-collared sort of way, Villante was the opposite of Scherick in several respects: no Harvard man was he, but a former New York Yankees batboy and aspiring professional second-baseman. He never made the majors. But like Scherick, Villante was smart, shrewd and aggressive. He ghost-wrote Joe DiMaggio's World Series column in 1950. After that, he drifted into the communications world, into advertising. At Batten, Barton, Durstine & Osborn, the young ex-infielder became a producer of Brooklyn Dodgers telecasts for one of BBD&O's star clients, Lucky Strike cigarettes.

"You'd better believe I had a challenge on my hands," Villante recalled. "In New York, during those years, a non-network station—WPIX—was carrying the home games of both the Yankees and the Giants. One of those two teams was *always* playing at home. So WPIX was doing telecasts just about every day of the summer. My team, the Dodgers, was on another independent station, WOR. They had a young guy, one of Red Barber's assistants, named Vin Scully, on the mike. In a way, these teams were lucky to be on local television at all. Most cities outside New York didn't have the luxury of non-network stations. And there was no way a network station was going to give up prime-time stuff to carry ball games in the summer. There was an audience out there for baseball, a big audience, but the big-time guys didn't know that. But my problem, in producing the Dodgers home telecasts for WOR, was this: I was on the air only *half* the summer. WPIX had games on the whole time. The only way I was going to compete, build an identity, was to do Dodgers road games as well. But that was an even bigger problem. *No* local station was doing road-game telecasts back then. Why? *Too expensive.* What killed everybody was the renting of telephone lines for transmission. It was something like a dollar-fifteen per hour, per mile. That was if you could even get them in the first place—if you didn't reserve 'em by the month, it was first-come, first-served. You had to be a CBS or NBC to afford those costs.

"Now, I started to sense a tremendous opportunity, if I could just figure it out. Something new had come into the television world a couple of years before, in 1952, that had the potential of blowing everything wide open. Changing all the rules around. I'm talking about UHF.

Ultra-high-frequency channels. The FCC allowed UHF in that year, 1952, and it suddenly—overnight—opened up about seventy new frequencies on the spectrum. But the new UHF stations in the big cities were poor. They were desperate for product. They wanted to get into local-team sports. Get an identity in the marketplace. WSGK in Boston was one of the first. They went on the air and couldn't get an *asterisk* in the ratings. Then they started telecasting the Red Sox games, and suddenly they were major. Same thing with WPHL in Philadelphia, and some other stations. There was a big baseball audience out there. The big guys just never knew it. But *nobody* was covering their team's road games. No one station could afford those telephone line rates.

"I started to do some investigating into the AT&T long-lines setup. I knew I had to find a way to do Dodgers road telecasts. It wasn't long before I stumbled on something incredible. I discovered that ABC had reserved lines into all the major markets. But *ABC didn't have any afternoon programing!* There they were, the lines, going unused. Teams still played some afternoon games on weekdays back then, plus all the weekend games were in the daytime.

"The first thing I tried to do, naturally, was sublease the lines from ABC. But the phone company said no. They said you couldn't barter on a common-carrier setup. So I was shot down. But in the *process,* I had gotten friendly with the guy at ABC who coordinated the network feeds through the long lines. His name was Dick Bailey. He showed me some ways to save money."

To say the least, that is what Dick Bailey showed Tom Villante. If Tom Villante had been a knight on some fabulous quest, and Dick Bailey had been a magical dwarf by the side of the road, it would have hardly been possible for him to show Villante the secret route to more riches. The twist in this particular fairytale is that Bailey got to keep most of the riches himself.

The secret route was the central nervous system of television: its transmitting telephone wires. AT&T had been a lifeline of the broadcast business since 1922, predating the existence even of NBC. Under the terms of an antimonopolistic arbitration of that era, the company agreed to stay out of active broadcasting, and to lease its lines, which in time interconnected all United States cities, to companies in the broadcast business. From then on, AT&T lines carried all radio and TV signals into markets from originating points that lay beyond the curvature of the earth. But while the lines were by law available to any broadcaster, economics of scale restricted their actual use to networks. Individual stations, as Villante pointed out, simply could not regularly afford the massive rates. Of course, individual stations had very little occasion to require long lines—since most of their programs originated in-studio—until the need to transmit sporting events over long distances became apparent.

When young Tom Villante of BBD&O approached the middle-aged Dick Bailey of ABC, his aims were modest enough: figure out a way to lower the cost of telecasting Brooklyn Dodgers road games. He had no idea that his question would trigger a combustion of ideas that would leave Bailey a millionaire several times over, summon Edgar Scherick from his Elba at CBS sales and back into the thick of the revolution that Scherick had anticipated back in his rowboat, and hasten the Big Sports era of television.

Dick Bailey was an unlikely candidate for extravagant fortune. The son of a Georgia ballplayer, Lemuel (King) Bailey, who pitched and won exactly one game in the major leagues, for the Cincinnati Reds, in 1895, Dick Bailey had served quietly and humbly at his job since 1938, five years before ABC split off from NBC.

"I kept meaning to get rid of that job and go off into business on my own," Bailey recalled from his horse farm in Connecticut. "But every time I was about ready to go, I'd get a thirty- or forty-dollar raise. That was a lot of money in those days."

Bailey listened with stolid, bureaucratic patience to the young advertising man's dilemma on that day in his ABC office in the fall of 1955. At the end of it, Bailey shrugged and told Villante that there really wasn't very much he could do to reduce the long-lines costs—as long as he was dealing on an occasional-service basis with just one TV station, and just one team. What you need, he explained, is to get several clubs together in a sort of pool arrangement—have them make one central deal with AT&T to rent the lines on a monthly basis, the cheapest rates available. Then, as each of the pool clubs came into a visiting city, each club could use the long lines in its turn.

As he outlined this commonsense procedure to his young visitor, the scales began to fall from Dick Bailey's eyes. A marvelous light began to glow, and it illuminated a long and shimmering corridor of his imagination.

"The major-league winter baseball meetings were scheduled for December in Chicago that year," said Bailey. "All the team owners, all the club representatives would be together in the same town. I told Villante and his colleagues at BBD&O to rent a hotel suite and arrange a meeting with as many of the club management people as they could, also to invite the advertising reps of all these clubs. I told them to keep the meeting top secret. I wanted the *utmost* secrecy from the outside. I had an important job at ABC, and theoretically, I suppose, what I had to propose to these people could be construed as not exactly in my company's best interest—though it certainly wouldn't hurt ABC in any way. Anyway, if my plan fell through, I wanted to be able to go back to my old job."

Bailey recalled that the meeting, held at the Warwick Hotel on Chicago's Michigan Avenue, was a setting for pandemonium. "It was standing room only," Bailey said. "All the agency reps for the various teams were afraid they were going to lose their jobs if my plan went through—be replaced by one central selling source. They wouldn't, of course. Then, hell, we couldn't make up our minds which *beer* to serve. Most of these teams were sponsored by breweries. You had Budweiser there, you had Carling, you had Hudepohl from Cincinnati, you had National Bohemian from Cleveland, you had Schlitz, you had Stag, you had Black Label . . ." They ended up serving some of each. But the real controversy, of course, centered on whether the owners and the agency people had any reason to trust Bailey. This new, unknown figure from New York, this person who promised to save the individual ball clubs thousands of dollars on their road-game telecasts—if they would accept him as the middleman between themselves and AT&T; if they would give him the money. "I'd already been to the telephone company," Bailey explained, "and they told me that such a pool arrangement was in fact possible—but they wanted two hundred thousand dollars posted in advance of the first telecast that following summer. That meant I had to talk these baseball people into coming up with that amount, and also into forwarding weekly checks to me so that I could meet AT&T's weekly rental payment.

"A lot of these guys, I found out later, ran security checks on me. A guy from Cleveland told me, 'I tried my damnedest to get something on you, but I couldn't.' Anyway, by the end of that meeting, we had an agreement. I went back to New York—hell, I'd used up a week of my vacation time in going out to Chicago—and handed ABC my three weeks' notice. And then I finally went into business for myself."

The business that Dick Bailey formed, in 1956, he called Sports Network. His basic service involved precisely what Bailey had promised the major-league owners on that uproarious clandestine night in the Warwick Hotel: he would secure AT&T long lines at the most economical rates for any consortium of stations or ad-agency representatives who wished to import distant athletic events into home markets. "I figured that we saved the big-league ball clubs a total of between eight

hundred thousand dollars and a million dollars in that first year alone,"
said Bailey.

Two years later, the son of a one-game, nineteenth-century National
League pitcher saved major-league baseball a fortune—and began to
harvest one himself. In 1958 the Brooklyn Dodgers moved to Los Angeles and the New York Giants moved to San Francisco, adding about
fifteen hundred miles each to their road-game line requirements. Dick
Bailey was suddenly one of the most sought-after figures in American
television sports. And just as suddenly, that "fringe" breakthrough, that
hidden route around the big networks' resistance to sports programing
that had seemed so hopelessly out of reach in 1955, had been achieved.
And the waiting insurrectionaries, prowling restlessly, lost no time in
pouncing on their main chance.

Almost before Dick Bailey knew what was happening, Edgar Scherick
was perched at his elbow. They were going to be partners, Scherick
explained. Scherick had prepared himself to resign his job at CBS sales
as soon as Sports Network began to surface as an entity within the
industry.

The first move Scherick had made was to pick up a telephone and call
Bill Reed. Reed was the commissioner of the best-known collegiate
athletic conference in the United States, the Big Ten. Scherick calmly
informed Reed that his conference's basketball games were about to be
canceled by CBS. "The CBS telecasts just weren't working," Scherick
later insisted, with an impatient shrug. "Nobody had ever mastered the
first quarter of the year in sports at CBS."

Then, having informed Reed of his doom, Scherick hit the stunned
commissioner with a plan for salvation. "I told him, 'You're gonna lose
your network exposure,'" Scherick said. "I told him, 'If you give me
your telecast rights, I'll guarantee you exposure where it counts the
most for you—right in the Big Ten area.'" Reed—no doubt a bit overwhelmed—agreed. The following morning, at 8:15 A.M., the advertising manager of Standard Oil in Chicago, Wes Nunn, received a long-
distance telephone call from a man who said his name was Scherick. "I
can deliver for Standard Oil," said the brisk, slightly irritable voice,
"twelve to fifteen Big Ten championship basketball games in the heart
of Standard's distribution area."

By 4:30 that afternoon, Ed Scherick had secured an order for the
games through Standard's ad agency. "I was in business," he declared.
His next move was to resign from CBS sales. And it was in that state of
armament that Scherick presented himself to the man who could get
him the necessary long lines, Dick Bailey.

"Ed was a great salesman, I'll say that for him," admitted Bailey. "I agreed to his suggestion that we split the whole thing. I put together the networking and Ed handled the sales. Jack Drees was our main on-air guy—Jack Buck later did it, and Bill Fleming. That was the beginning of an eighteen-year relationship with the Big Ten." It was also the beginning of yet another new TV sports-oriented business. The business was called Sports Programing, Inc. Its president was Edgar J. Scherick. In fact, the entire company consisted of Scherick and one assistant, a young man named Chet Simmons.

Years later, Dick Bailey still relished the farcical good luck that flowed from these events. "It was a funny thing," Bailey recalled, "Ed and I were never *formally* business partners—we each headed up a distinct and separate company—but because we worked together so closely, people were forever getting the names of our companies mixed up. Even industry people. They'd come to me with some kind of deal that was meant for Sports Programing, Inc., or else they'd go to Ed asking about Sports Network."

Bailey claimed to believe that it was just such a misunderstanding that elevated his onetime partner into the pantheon of the gods. "I was vacationing down in Florida one day in 1961," said Bailey, "and I got a long-distance telephone call from a friend at ABC. He said, 'We finally got you, you sonuvagun.' I said, 'What do you mean, you finally got me?' He said, 'We've been after you for years, and we finally got you. We just bought Sports Programing.'

"I said, '*I'm* not Sports Programing! I'm Sports *Network!* You guys didn't get me! You got *Scherick!*' They'd made the same damn mistake! They got our companies mixed up!"

This story may be a touch apocryphal. Tom Moore, the ABC programing chief who persuaded his network to buy SPI, did so only after working closely with Scherick as an informal partner for some eighteen months: presumably he knew the difference by then. Those eighteen months, moreover, were among the most decisive in ABC's history. By the time they had ended, Moore and Scherick had stunned the industry by snatching rights to some of the most popular events in American sports; Scherick had plucked Roone Arledge from the obscurity of a children's puppet show and launched him on his seminal career, and built around Arledge a staff of young geniuses whose careers would continue to flourish into the 1980s.

And all of this was before there was a formal division called ABC Sports.

Dick Bailey did not exactly fall destitute after Scherick ascended into ABC. Bailey continued to operate his Sports Network quite profitably until 1968. Then he sold it to Howard Hughes for $18 million.

In fact, the only player in this breakthrough drama who did not eventually realize a fortune was the ex-ballplayer Tom Villante, who remained with BBD&O until 1978. Then he assumed a job that was both prestigious and nicely symmetrical. Villante became the chief public-relations spokesman for major-league baseball.

IX

A TIME FOR BARBARIANS

Time," said the historian Arnold Toynbee, "is on the side of the barbarians." Oddly, he was not referring to television.

Actually, it is stretching the bounds of charity to call the people at ABC in the late 1950s "barbarians"—they wore suits, spoke a civilized tongue and seldom if ever sacked villages—but amidst the network-kingdoms of the day, ABC was indisputably the hirsute tribe: poor, small, ravaged, regarded generally with amused contempt, if regarded at all.

But now time began to shift toward the barbarians' side. To be sure, no one noticed the process as it began to develop, grain by grain. Not even Edgar Scherick himself, who set so many grains in motion, could grasp the enormity of the eventual onslaught. Scherick left ABC Sports for Hollywood nearly sixteen years before his ABC "tribe" threw off the last of its rags and stood alone at the pinnacle, in 1976. More tellingly still, the techniques and idioms nurtured in Scherick's tiny sports company fueled that influential victory, and revised the fundamental agenda of American television—and thus of much of America's popular style.

Call it a logic of the underdog. It had never before surfaced in broadcasting. It has never surfaced since, at least not on the scale that buoyed the ABC epoch. The logic is paradoxical: ABC was able to surpass its bigger, wealthier competitors precisely *because* it started out late, small and poor. Its very desperation compelled the network to take risks in hiring a collection of aggressive, brilliant mavericks who would not have been tolerated at the more orthodox CBS or NBC: not only Scherick himself, but also the men he handpicked—Roone Arledge, Jim Spence, Chuck Howard and Chet Simmons; and also such later arrivals as Chet Forte, Don Ohlmeyer and Cosell.

Scherick's protétéges, once ensconced at ABC, gleefully started running risks themselves. They invested sports with a hodgepodge of improvisations, brainstorms, impulses, notions expanded from notes scribbled on napkins and envelopes, technological scraps and fragments overlooked by other networks' news divisions—a video equivalent of found art—that somehow coalesced into the most intense infusion of ideas that had yet taken form in television's tepid pool of creativity.

A grain or two shifted up in Boston. Perched in his swivel chair above the Charles River at Gillette headquarters, an aging A. Craig Smith continued to direct a significant measure of NBC's sports schedule via his treasured brainchild, the *Cavalcade of Sports*. But Smith's reign as an absentee monarch was behind him. His days of influence at NBC were numbered, the times were silently but quickly overtaking this first great mastermind of broadcast sports. Within a few years, Craig Smith would be in premature retirement, his decline hastened by the consequences of a painful fall down some stairs in his Boston home. The fall damaged nerves in his right arm and left it nearly useless for long stretches of time.

Already it was no longer possible for Gillette to own outright many of the blue-chip events that had lent NBC its early identity as The Sports Network. The razor company managed to retain exclusive rights to baseball's World Series and All Star Game through 1965, and it still owned the Friday night fights on NBC. But beyond those properties, Gillette was selling off inventory fast. The result was that it could no longer claim equal partnership with NBC in sports programing; now, Gillette was receding to the status of just another sponsor. Skyrocketing rights fees for events that Gillette had elevated to national media prominence—the Rose, Orange, Sugar and Cotton bowls and the Kentucky Derby—obliged Smith and his lieutenants to relinquish absolute control, and share the commercial spotlight with other companies.

This new, diminished status could not have pleased the proud Smith, but he endured it. The fact that NBC allowed Gillette in at discount advertising rates—a courtesy tendered in honor of the company's baseball holdings—did not salve Smith's pride one bit. He drove himself as he always had, binge-eating and crash-dieting, savoring his liquor and then hitting the wagon, rowing his scull furiously up and down the Charles, negotiating and improvising. But somehow it didn't seem to matter as much as it used to. A. Craig Smith's "Look sharp, feel sharp, *be* sharp" days were behind him.

There were other assaults on Smith's sovereignty. Other shifting grains. One emerging annoyance was named Thomas Patrick Gallery. After several years of muddled indifference, NBC had finally gotten around to naming its own director of sports, Gallery, a hulking, florid ex-actor and promoter of boxing and football on the West Coast. And although Gallery enjoyed what might at best be called limited power at NBC (he reported for a time to Reuven Frank, for whom sports was "just a pain in the ass"), Gallery was nonetheless an NBC employee. As the 1950s wore on, Gallery proceeded, gently and discreetly, to ease the reins of authority from Craig Smith's hands and grip them himself.

In many ways, Tom Gallery was a perfect expression of NBC's genteel attitude toward sports programing. Like his counterpart Bill Mac-Phail at CBS, and despite his intimidating size—he stood six feet four inches, with a stevedore's shoulders and neck—Gallery was an intelligent, decent and sweet-natured man. Well over fifty when he joined NBC, Tom Gallery was known as a sociable fellow, a product of a time and place that valued loyalty and put personal honor above personal gain. In other words, he was the ideal prey for the legions of aggression gathering at ABC.

In fact, it was Tom Gallery's fate to be remembered best as the dupe in a chillingly effective mousetrap strategy in 1960—a hoax by which ABC snatched college football telecast rights away from NBC at rock-bottom rates. ABC would go on to use college football as the foundation of its 1960s image as the new leader in TV sports. The perpetrator of the hoax was Edgar J. Scherick.

Smith's most distressing problem centered around his most indispensable creation, the bulwark of his company's sales image. The *Gillette Cavalcade of Sports* itself was in trouble.

In February 1955, Gillette's jolly parrots and merry marches abruptly gave way to darker symbols: strangling octopuses. Gangsters.

Nikolai Bulganin had succeeded Georgi Malenkov as premier of Russia; the Soviets announced an H-bomb lead over America; United States political leaders debated the strategic importance of Quemoy and Matsu; racial integration began to take hold in public schools; and Hollywood unveiled a new cinematic toy called Cinerama, a frantic high-tech bauble designed to lure patrons away from their television sets. But for sports fans, the really sensational news of early 1955 sprang from boxing, the Supreme Court and the mob.

On the last day of January, front-page newspaper stories announced that the Supreme Court had reversed a lower-court ruling and held that professional boxing (along with legitimate theater) was subject to anti-trust laws. This decision opened the way for a series of Justice Department suits that would eventually shatter the vast James Norris monopoly over pro boxing, shed light on the shocking penetration into the fight world by racketeers and hoodlums, and tarnish the sport so badly that it all but vanished from network television.

Ironically, it was network television's saturation coverage of boxing that had spurred the antitrust ruling in the first place. James D. Norris, Jr., was a tycoon out of an F. Scott Fitzgerald novel, an almost Gatsbylike figure who brooded over the boxing world from 1949 until his empire was finally banished a decade later. As president of the International Boxing Club, and as owner or controlling partner of giant arenas in Chicago, New York, St. Louis, Detroit and Indianapolis, Norris was able to dictate the matchmaking and promotion of just about every fight of consequence in America. Editorial cartoonists routinely portrayed his empire in the form of an octopus. Indeed it was. At the time of the Supreme Court ruling, the IBC enjoyed exclusive boxing rights in Madison Square Garden, the St. Nicholas Arena, Yankee Stadium and the Polo Grounds. And that was just in New York. Norris also controlled fights in Detroit's Olympia Arena and in Chicago's Stadium. Fight managers who agreed to make matches without Norris's imprimatur, or who dared consent to import bouts outside his mammoth jurisdiction, faced permanent blacklisting from any ring more noble than a fleabag gym—or worse.

Jim Norris came from a wealthy Canadian family that settled in Chicago. His father had built his fortune as a grain broker; he put his capital to work buying up sports stadiums on the verge of bankruptcy at ten percent of their original worth. In this manner, the elder Norris acquired the string of stadiums that his son would turn into boxing duchies.

"The old man was one hundred percent clean, and Jim himself was basically clean," insisted Harry Markson, a former newspaperman who had known the Norrises as director of Madison Square Garden's boxing operations in the fifties. "The old man hated FDR and Leo Durocher, but I guess that don't make him a bad guy. He owned the Chicago Black Hawks, and his son Jim was mainly interested in pro hockey. That and horseracing. But he got to be a boxing czar almost in spite of himself. And that's what finally got him into trouble."

Before Jim Norris backed into the fight world in 1949, the most prominent matchmaking organization in the country was Mike Jacobs's Twentieth Century Sporting Club. Jacobs supplied fights to such sponsors as Gillette (Fridays on NBC) and Pabst Blue Ribbon (Wednesdays on CBS). Among the fighters under contract to Jacobs was the world heavyweight champion, Joe Louis.

In 1946, the scrupulous Jacobs suffered a stroke. He was never again

to assert full control over Twentieth Century. Three years later Joe
Louis decided to retire from the ring. Louis's press agent, a man named
Harry Mendel, conceived the idea of a four-man heavyweight tourna-
ment to determine Louis's successor. The contestants would include
Ezzard Charles, Jersey Joe Walcott, Lee Savold and the polysyllabic Gus
Lesnevich—the same "Gus" who had earlier figured in Don Dunphy's
successful blow-by-blow audition for A. Craig Smith.

With Jacobs in bad health and virtually helpless as a promoter, press
agent Mendel turned his sights west—to an up-and-coming sports impresario out of Chicago named Jim Norris. After consulting his business
partner, the real-estate magnate Arthur Wirtz, Norris agreed to run the
tournament.

Lesnevich and Savold eventually dropped out of the arrangement. But
on June 22, 1949, Charles and Walcott boxed in Chicago Stadium for
the Heavyweight Championship of the World. Charles won a unan-
imous fifteen-round decision.

Something else happened in the Stadium that night. Jim Norris, the
educated, cultivated scion of a Canadian grain baron, found himself
utterly bedazzled with boxing—with its diamond flash and mink-stole
glamour, to be sure, but also with other aspects: with its forbidden
intimations of pagan violence, its blood savagery, and perhaps most
compellingly of all, with its siren lure of the underworld. On that night,
Jim Norris's good judgment, moral sensibilities and restraints upon
narcissistic grandeur all were anesthetized. On that night, Jim Norris
became the prototype of the modern television sports fan.

"Jim Norris had a face like a handsome bulldog," recalled Markson,
"and he was a gentle, amiable, compassionate, generous and thoughtful
man. But he had many faults. One of them was his fascination with
unsavory characters. Jim was not himself a mob guy. But if ever there
was anybody who could be condemned for guilt by association, it was
Jim Norris."

Norris and his partner Wirtz bought the Twentieth Century Sporting
Club from Jacobs for one hundred thousand dollars—an impressive sum
in those days—and renamed it the International Boxing Club. Now it
was Norris who acted as the main organizing agent in the chaotic,
decentralized world of boxing. Now it was Norris who arbitrated the
fights that got sold to Gillette and Pabst. And it was not long before the
whispers started—whispers that would build to a Justice Department
roar in 1955.

Organized criminals had never been very far from the fight world—
all those Depression films about clean kid fighters defying the fat man

with the cigar and the derby hat were not exactly *Fantasia*—but it fell to the starry-eyed Norris to let the mob inside boxing's front door. Frankie Carbo, the most dreaded hoodlum among the many dozens working the fight game, hung out in Norris's Madison Square Garden office. Carbo was an extortion specialist who, in the words of one MSG matchmaker, "had his fingers on the throat of boxing and could squeeze the air out of it any time he wanted to make a move." * Carbo owned fighters, and he owned managers. He often dictated his wishes for a matchup to Norris's regular, salaried lieutenants, and the salaried lieutenants would always listen with great respect.

But Norris had a reason beyond mere boyish fascination to "walk and talk" with racketeers. That reason derived directly from the imperatives of television. When Norris and Wirtz took control of Jacobs's boxing federation, they inherited contracts that required them to produce fifty good fights a year for Gillette and another fifty for Pabst. "Much of the situation that Jim got himself in," says Harry Markson, "involved the fact that the so-called tough guys owned many of the leading fights of the time. So in order to ensure that he could keep furnishing talent for these televised shows, Norris found it convenient to tolerate—to work hand-in-hand with—the Frankie Carbos of the world. That and his natural preoccupation with the dark side of life got Jim ensnared with the underworld."

Although television contributed heavily to the pressures that propelled Norris toward the "tough guys," there is no evidence to suggest that either Pabst or Gillette, or the networks, for that matter, knowingly accommodated any illegal payments or pressure tactics. On the other hand, television did exactly nothing to *investigate* the persistent rumors of monopoly and corruption in the boxing world. The same held true for the country's newspapers. In the mid-fifties, as in Babe Ruth's time or Warren Harding's, the daily press did not go in for that sort of thing. Writers tended to identify with the great and beloved figures they traveled with and quoted each day, rather than something as abstract as "the public interest."

It was instead a disaffected insider who triggered the slow process that led to Norris's banishment. Jack Hurley, a brilliant manager of a mediocre heavyweight named Harry Matthews, finally got tired of being snubbed in his efforts to line up a profitable bout for his fighter. (Hurley

---

* Teddy Brenner as told to Barney Nagler. *Only the Ring Was Square.* Englewood Cliffs, N.J.: Prentice Hall, 1981.

was not a man to settle for the small picture: one of the opponents he accused of unfairly "ducking" his man was Rocky Marciano.) Hurley finally persuaded a couple of United States senators to take up his cause, and they in turn aroused a sluggish Justice Department to begin probing into boxing's internal operations. But before Justice could launch any such inquiry, it needed an explicit ruling that boxing was in fact an interstate commerce activity, and therefore subject to antitrust enforcement.

The need for such a ruling might appear ludicrous on its face to a reader of the 1980s. After all, boxers did quite manifestly travel from state to state to practice their trade—"carrying their shorts and fancy dressing robes in a ditty bag," as one justice witheringly characterized it. But in fact the case presented an embarrassing dilemma to the Court. In 1922 the Court decided, perhaps a shade sentimentally, that the dominant sport of the time, major-league baseball, was not an "interstate commerce," and therefore could not be prevented from enforcing the "reserve system" that restrained players from seeking deals with other clubs—that prevented, in other words, the free agent. But if baseball were held blameless from accountability for its business practices, why should boxing not enjoy the same protection?

Television inadvertently came to the High Court's rescue. The medium that had enriched the sport for a decade was now seized upon by the abashed justices as a device for proving that fights were indeed interstate. Since more than twenty-five percent of the International Boxing Club's total revenues were derived from rights sold to the TV networks, "which were admittedly interstate," the Court's majority declared that boxing was therefore itself fair game for antitrust action.

How that magical figure of twenty-five percent materialized is one of those mysteries that remain hidden in the judicial folds of history. No matter. The 1955 ruling triggered its desired effect. Within months, a chain reaction of "fix" charges, slander suits and confessions in several states began to convulse the fight world. The antimonopoly suit against Norris and the IBC dominated these upheavals. Justice charged that Norris and his associates had illegally monopolized championship prizefights in several cities; that in fact, since 1949, all but two of twenty-one title bouts in the United States had been promoted by the defendants.

In 1957, a district court ordered Norris and Wirtz to end their ties with Madison Square Garden and to dissolve the IBC. Two years later the United States Supreme Court upheld that ruling, and professional boxing in America lay in deep disarray.

Television suffered its share of the public blame. As early as February 2, 1955—just days after the Supreme Court's initial antitrust decision—*New York Times* columnist Arthur Daley wrote, with just the slightest hint of scattershot thinking:

> Everything in fisticuffing is geared to bigness until boxing has become a garish, monstrous facade without soundness or foundations. . . . Television is mainly responsible for boxing's steady disintegration, even though television paradoxically creates more fans and swallows up more boxers at the same time.
>
> Millions watch [Norris's] shows for free on their magic lanterns every Wednesday and Friday. How can a little neighborhood club buck such free competition? And never were those neighborhood clubs more desperately needed, because TV swallows up fighters faster than it does comics. Paying customers have virtually disappeared, and television has become the tail that wags the mutt. Unless a fighter can get a slice of the video dough, he's wasting his time. So the conniving that goes on to muscle into a few prized shots has opened up a whole Pandora's Box of evils.

In fixing the blame on television—rather than on the sports czars who willfully threw aside their better moral judgments and even their respect for the law to exploit television (to say nothing of the fans who continued to watch, despite the growing public awareness of underworld meddling)—Daley was committing a fallacy that would be repeated again and again over the next quarter century. He assumed that television was the *active* force, and not a *repository* for human greed, morbidity and narcissistic fantasizing.

But television heard the message. Or at least some of television heard it. In the fall of 1955, the ten o'clock Wednesday time slot on CBS was suddenly a bulwark of lofty thought and high prestige. The *20th Century–Fox Hour* alternated weeks with the *U.S. Steel Hour,* giving CBS an hour of high-quality, live dramatic anthology that featured such stars as Lillian Roth, Phyllis Kirk, Keenan Wynn, Paul Newman, Gene Hackman, Duke Ellington and Anne Francis.

Pabst Blue Ribbon bouts? What Pabst Blue Ribbon bouts? It was as though they had never existed. CBS was out of the fight game but good. DuMont was out of business completely. ABC quietly picked up the Wednesday fights, under different sponsors. And NBC, holding its nose but unwilling to rupture its good relationship with Gillette, allowed the Friday bouts to remain on its airwaves.

NBC was never at ease with boxing after the scandals broke. The public besmirching of the sport deeply mortified the network's conservative leaders. These cautious, bureaucratic animals began to live in terror that NBC's overall image of "See-the-U.S.A.-in-Your-Chevrolet" wholesomeness would be undercut by any lingering association with the ring or its denizens.

Craig Smith, sensing this corporate chill, heaped what coals he could muster upon it. Smith mobilized his company's own in-house research department to execute a marketing study of some four thousand United States homes to find out whether American adult males shared the general public revulsion toward boxing. Gillette aides who were involved in the project point out that the size of this sample was nearly four times the saturation of existing Nielsen surveys. The word came back that enough men still sought out TV boxing to justify a continued high return on Gillette's advertising dollar. This survey saved Smith's career for a while; it kept the Friday *Cavalcade* propped up on NBC for a few extra years.

But inevitably, the ratings began to slide. From twenties at mid-decade they had soon edged down to eighteens. Then sixteens . . . word began to float out that NBC was looking for a way to jettison the *Gillette Cavalcade of Sports*—at least its boxing arm. A. Craig Smith sat helplessly up in Boston and watched it all start to come apart. His power base at the network, seemingly impregnable just a few years before, was eroding before his eyes.

Late in 1959, A. Craig Smith reached for the telephone on his desk in his office above the Charles River at Gillette, and did what he had to do. He called—not ABC, not directly; he could not quite bring himself to go that far. Smith rang up a middleman, Lou Maxon, the head of the ad agency that had handled Gillette's account for years. It was Maxon who made the decisive call to the ridiculed, inelegant little network.

"We want to talk sports," Lou Maxon told the man at the other end, Tom Moore.

Moore. The second Southerner to plop like a benign Cheshire Cat upon Ed Scherick's trail, but this one, shrewder even than the Ole Pod-nuh, Dizzy Dean. It was Moore—sloe-eyed, deceptively gallant-mannered, filled with a private mirth—who had virtually annexed Scherick's Sports Programing to ABC.

Moore had given Scherick the informal title of negotiator and producer of sports for ABC. And it was Moore who would form a brief, but outrageous, personal partnership with Scherick in which the two men, so dissimilar in temperament and background, would swagger about like buccaneers, throwing together deals that by all odds could never have been made.

When Tom Moore heard Lou Maxon's voice on the telephone, his own voice went all honeyed with unctuous charm. Why, ABC would be purely *honored* to meet with the gentleman from Gillette, just name the time and place and we'll be there.

Maxon suggested his own apartment, a suite in the elegant Park Lane Hotel. Perhaps Maxon had meant to make some kind of symbolic statement about relative power: not only were ABC's main offices in a rather seedy part of town—the building on West Sixty-sixth Street had once been a riding academy, and it was no secret that the prevailing odor closely matched the description that frequently accrued to ABC prime-time programs—but it also was well known that Ed Scherick, the unofficial chief of ABC Sports, operated out of an even seedier two-room office on West Forty-second Street. "It looked like a bookie joint," Roone Arledge remembered.

"There, in this incredibly lovely apartment," recalled Moore, "were A. Craig Smith, Lou Maxon and two other gentlemen from Gillette. Ed and I came over representing ABC. I had the feeling that this was going to be quite an evening."

Moore didn't anticipate the half of it. Among the subdramas being played out in Maxon's living room was one that no one present could possibly have appreciated at the time: the first face-to-face meeting between the man who invented the mode for modern sports telecasting and the man who would project that mode toward its ultimate realization.

One of the Gillette officials in the room that night later observed that the introduction between Smith and Scherick lacked warmth. If Craig Smith sensed the implications of a torch being passed, he did not show it. He remained aloof, icily correct in a dark tailored suit, and seemed to take a bleak measure of the small, nervous operative, whose own couture was absent-mindedly adequate. As the Gillette sides later reconstructed the encounter, Smith's first instinct was to draw back from Scherick; he distrusted the young man. The old Gillette chieftain, perhaps forgetting his own headstrong recklessness of twenty years before, sensed something too eager, too shrewdly calculating about the young man at Tom Moore's side. Scherick generated an aura of raw matter, poised to rush into the nearest vacuum.

Nevertheless, realities were realities. A. Craig Smith cleared his throat and offered the first gambit. "He told us that Gillette regarded its

Friday night fights as the backbone of its advertising program," said Tom Moore. "They'd taken note of the fact that we now had a Wednesday-night boxing schedule, sponsored by Alka Seltzer and Kool cigarettes. Smith told us that Gillette would come in as an advertiser—if we would get rid of the other sponsors and move the bouts to Friday nights."

Warily, Tom Moore parried. He replied that while ABC would welcome Gillette as a sponsor, ABC could not think of breaking into its Friday night entertainment schedule (which then included 77 *Sunset Strip,* followed at ten by something called *Robert Taylor: The Detectives*).

"Get rid of the sponsors," replied Smith in an even voice, "move the bouts to Friday nights—and Gillette will come in with an advertising budget of $8.5 million."

Tom Moore, as he later recalled it, felt breathless. Even Ed Scherick sat staring, his customary aplomb flattened. *Eight and a half million dollars*—it was a fortune, it was a gold rush. Moore had not dreamed that Gillette would quote a figure remotely like $8.5 million, nor that Smith would submit the sum so early in the negotiation, with so little hint of resistance on ABC's part. *They must be desperate,* Moore thought. Whatever mood Lou Maxon had sought to establish by inviting ABC to his sumptuous apartment now lay shattered. Smith had overcommitted himself virtually before the hard bargaining began.

Sensing this weakness, Moore now began to exploit his upper hand. Friday night was out, he calmly informed Smith. Saturday night—that was a different matter. On Saturday nights, an ABC songfest called *Jubilee U.S.A.* was failing against *Gunsmoke* on CBS. Moore could offer Smith a Saturday night boxing showcase. But there was one other stipulation: because of promises ABC had made to its existing sponsors, Gillette could not have exclusive rights to those bouts, at least not in the first year. That is, it couldn't be called the *Gillette Cavalcade;* at least not right away. But after a season, Moore assured Smith smoothly, there was every chance. . . .

There is no way to accurately gauge what A. Craig Smith must have felt at that moment. Not even for $8.5 million dollars could he get his way with the *Cavalcade,* transplant it intact and without interference from other advertisers, even to the lowliest television network on the spectrum. A. Craig Smith looked at Tom Moore and at Ed Scherick, and he told them that he would take the deal.

"We didn't walk out of that room, we *flew,*" Tom Moore remembered. "All of a sudden we had more money to spend than we'd ever imagined. It was Christmas! Gillette couldn't *possibly* spend all of that $8.5 million on the fights. They'd given us what amounted to an uncommitted bank-roll to spend on what we pleased."

Moore and Scherick were hardly down to the Park Lane lobby in the elevator before they had hit upon the main item in their new shopping list. They wanted NCAA college football. The telecast rights to that sport would instantly catapult ABC out of its pauper's status and into something like parity with CBS and NBC in sports.

Tom Moore phoned up Ollie Treyz, the ABC television president, and demanded to see him that very night. He knew that bidding on NCAA football would activate some old traumas within the ABC hierarchy. Five years before, in 1954, ABC had bid $2.5 million on the NCAA and won. The resulting fiasco nearly bankrupted the company. But now there was some new talent running the network's sports operations—men who knew what they were doing. Moore knew that if ABC got college football rights this time around, he and Scherick could make the other networks look shabby in comparison. Treyz agreed to Moore's plea for the right to bid—but he set a condition. Don't overcommit, he warned. Don't get us in trouble again.

Now Moore and Scherick went back to Gillette with a further demand: Free enough of the $8.5 million to back us one hundred percent in an NCAA bid, they said. In return, we will try to sell up to fifty percent of the backing to other advertisers and reduce your liability by that amount. Smith agreed.

There was a certain cold-bloodedness in this request. Moore and Scherick were asking Craig Smith in effect to turn utterly against his great historic benefactor, NBC. NBC and Tom Gallery then owned the telecast rights to college football games. That contract would be up for renewal in 1960; NBC had every reason to expect that its renewal would be automatic. Even though NBC had to go through the formality of sealed bids, there was no reason to expect a serious challenge from CBS; certainly not from ABC. CBS had pro football. ABC had trouble paying its bills. Thus there existed a comfortable, self-perpetuating status quo, an Old-World arrangement of mutual courtesies that satisfied everyone.

But not for much longer.

If Tom Moore and Edgar Scherick felt any remorse for their manipulation of A. Craig Smith, they did not discuss it at the time, nor have they since. Besides, it was nothing compared to what they planned to do to Tom Gallery.

Tom Gallery never knew what hit him. Perhaps he never let himself know. Late in his life, decades after the event, Gallery would insist, with the most guileless sincerity, that he'd never been aware of the plot, that he had no memory of it unfolding—that it couldn't have happened that way, or he would have taken note and exacted a terrible revenge.

But it did happen. The story is a classic in the folklore of TV network intrigue. The perpetrators, twenty-two years later, could certainly recount its details with loving relish. Perhaps it was best that Gallery did not remember.

Treyz's warning to Moore meant that he could not unleash an unlimited amount of money in the NCAA bidding competition. Moore and Scherick would have to bid frugally. But there still existed a slim chance that even a modest bid would bring home the rights. That chance lay in a peculiar money-conscious strategy that Gallery himself practiced at bidding ceremonies.

Moore and Scherick knew that Gallery like to show up for these occasions carrying not one sealed envelope, but two. Each envelope contained a separate monetary figure. The figures were several million dollars apart. It was Gallery's practice to make a careful study of each face in the room, mentally cataloguing every person who had business there. Gallery knew the faces of all the people from the various leagues and conferences and athletic committees, and of all his rivals at CBS and ABC. If Tom Gallery spotted someone in the room from another network, he would assume that NBC had a serious competitor for whatever property was up for acquisition. Depending on how badly NBC itself wanted the property, Gallery would then drop the envelope with the higher figure onto the table. If Gallery did not spot a representative from the other networks, or if he sighted a rival who was likely to make only a token bid, the NBC Sports chief would produce the second envelope, the one containing the parsimoniously lowered figure, and place it into contention.

It was Moore's and Scherick's plan to mousetrap Tom Gallery: to lull him into committing that lower-priced envelope before he suspected that ABC was even in the room. But how? Gallery knew Moore's face. They could not risk assuming he didn't know Scherick's face. There were damned few faces at ABC to begin with, and Tom Gallery was in the face-knowing business. Before he came to NBC in 1953, Gallery had built a colorful career on the West Coast as a cowboy movie actor and later as a promoter of boxing and football. As a young veteran of World War I, having served at the Argonne front in the tank corps, Gallery drifted out to Hollywood where he starred in some fifty-six early movies—he was the hero in the first Rin-Tin-Tin series. "The damn dog went for my ear the first day we met," he recalled many years later.

"We never got along too well." But Gallery had a knack for getting along with human beings. He met and married the movie actress ZaSu Pitts, with King Vidor and his wife standing up for the couple at their wedding.

But sports were Gallery's main love, and he left the movies to begin promoting prizefights at the Hollywood Legion Stadium. "It's a bowling alley now," he said not long ago, "but in the old days it held four thousand people and was sold out fifty-two weeks a year. I sold front-row seats to guys like Al Jolson. Bing Crosby was calling the fights on the radio." From boxing, Gallery branched into wider endeavors. He was an active force in establishing the Rose Bowl as a national event. He helped organize professional football's Pro Bowl game. Returning East during the years of World War II, Gallery took over the operations of the old Brooklyn Dodgers professional football team as a favor to his friend Daniel Topping, the team's owner, who was then a Marine Corps officer. In this capacity, Gallery pioneered nighttime telecasts of the Dodgers's games on the DuMont network—anticipating ABC's *Monday Night Football* by nearly a quarter century. He then moved over to DuMont for a few years, dickering at one point with A. Craig Smith for rights to the World Series on that small network. He came finally to the attention of David Sarnoff at NBC by proposing a method of wiring Yankee Stadium for static-free public-address announcements using RCA equipment.

An example of Thomas Gallery's adherence to the old-fashioned codes of loyalty and obligation occurred a couple of years after he had been named director of sports for NBC. "I met Bill Paley (the founder of CBS) at a dinner party one night," Gallery recalled, "and we fell to talking, and one thing led to another and finally Mr. Paley made me a deal to leave NBC and come over to CBS. I was awfully tempted by the offer—he was the biggest name in broadcasting, after all—but I had to say, 'I don't jump contracts, Mr. Paley.' When I said that, Bill Paley threw his arms around me and hugged me. He told me how much he respected that, and he said, 'If you ever need a job, call me.'"

This was the nature of the man whom Moore and Scherick fixed in their crosshairs.

The NCAA telecast bidding ceremony was scheduled for a Monday, March 14, 1960, at New York's Royal Manhattan Hotel. Scherick and Moore did not plan even to go near the neighborhood. They had to figure out a way to "be" in the Royal Manhattan without being there. It didn't take Ed Scherick very long.

"All I needed to do was find a face that Gallery would not recognize," he explained that afternoon in Central Park. "I didn't even bother with the guys at the corporate level. I ran my mind. I went into one of the control rooms. I spied this lower-echelon guy; tall, thin, sort of Lincolnesque. Unobtrusive. Frankle, I think was his name. Yes. Stanton Frankle. He was *perfect*. Just the sort of fellow you never notice in a room; the kind of guy who blends into the wallpaper. Stanton Frankle became our main hope."

The next problem was utterly to seal off ABC's intention from the outside world. "If NBC got the slightest inkling that we were in the game, they'd come in with their high bid," said Scherick. "We were pretty sure we could top their low bid. Their high bid would be way beyond us."

To prevent a fatal security leak, Scherick himself typed out the bid letter—and left blank the space for the dollar amount until moments before Frankle was to depart for his mission. Then he wrote it in with ink. Moore and Scherick estimated that Gallery's *low* bid for the rights would be about $5,500,000—a routine ten percent increase over the last contract. To be safe, they hit upon the figure of $6,251,114. The odd dollars represented Scherick's notion of a little bidding humor. No one could say that the ABC commandos were not a fun bunch of guys.

There were still other precautions. It was conceivable, for instance, that no one would believe that ABC had the money to back such a bid. ABC's lawyers drew up a document, waxed and stamped to create the fullest mystique of legal rectitude, that attested to the network's solvency.

Then, on the day of the bidding, Scherick threw on one final layer of precaution: against the remote possibility that Stanton Frankle should meet with disaster en route to the Royal Manhattan, Scherick assigned a *second* faceless ABC emissary to trail Frankle by a few blocks. "I explained to this man," said Scherick, "that if he should see Stanton Frankle fall injured in the streets, he should let Frankle lie where he fell and proceed on to the consummation of his mission."

In an unusual gesture of self-restraint, Scherick decided against dressing Frankle in a tuxedo and inserting him into the bidding suite disguised as a waiter. "It didn't matter," insisted Scherick. "By that time, Stan Frankle had practically become a *mystic* over his mission. He would have walked over burning coals for me. I took him aside and I put my hands on his shoulders and I gave him his final instructions. I told him: 'Stan, if anyone asks you who you are, I want you to tell them the truth. Don't lie. Otherwise, be utterly silent. You are to speak to no one. There will be one man in that suite whom I want you to pick out right away, because that man is your enemy. He will be rather corpulent, bald, quite tall, a hail-fellow-well-met. Pick this guy out and *watch him.* When the NCAA officials announce that the bidding is to begin, *do not move.* Wait. Wait for Tom Gallery to make *his* move. When, and only when, he removes his fingers from his envelope, you are to come forward and say, "I represent ABC," and place your envelope on the table. Now go, and Godspeed.'"

Perhaps one of the deep regrets of Edgar Scherick's life is that he could not be present to witness Stanton Frankle's performance at the Royal Manhattan Hotel that day. The historical consensus is that it was a masterpiece. Frankle made it to the hotel without tragic incident, proceeded to the bidding suite, strode expressionlessly among knots of men he had never seen before. Many heads turned toward him, but no one so much as offered a handshake in greeting.

Frankle found a shadowed spot near some draperies and molded himself against the wall. With his head motionless, he swept the room with his eyes until he spotted a tall, balding man straddling a chair that was turned back to front. Stanton Frankle narrowed his eyes and waited.

Finally, the television director for the NCAA, a man named Asa Bushnell, called the gathering to order. Bushnell announced that the bidding was to commence.

Near the curtains, Stanton Frankle assumed the attitude of a statue. As for Tom Gallery across the room, he, too, froze into the aspect of a man attending a seance. Not a muscle of his huge body so much as twitched. For several tomblike moments, it must have seemed to the NCAA officials that no one would carry their college football games that fall.

Then Tom Gallery shuddered to life. Taking a final, penetrating glance about the room, he stepped forward and placed one of his two envelopes on the table before Asa Bushnell.

The atmosphere in the suite relaxed. Men turned to one another and began to chat; some drifted toward the cash bar.

Now came the moment of Stanton Frankle. With the dramatic flourish of a stovepipe-hat villain emerging from the draperies in a riverboat melodrama, the ABC secret agent strode toward Bushnell. As heads swung toward him, Frankle—following Scherick's orders to the finest detail—announced himself, thrust forward the ABC envelope and slapped it down. Gallery was trumped.

"The NCAA committee just about went into shock, the way I heard it," said Scherick. "The last people on earth they expected to be doing business with was ABC. They took the envelopes into a back room, and I understand that they were back there a long time. But they couldn't remain back there forever. The by-laws were the by-laws. They had no choice but to come back out, finally, and declare that ABC had won the bid. And that," added Scherick, as a chilly edge crept back into his voice, an edge undiminished over twenty-two years, "was the end of Tom Gallery."

It was also the beginning of ABC Sports.

X

BUILDING THE ABC EMPIRE

BC's commando raid on the NCAA football contract produced a kind of nervous hilarity in bars favored by network professionals. There was something comic about Scherick's elaborate cloak-and-dagger theatrics, but there was something feral beneath the comedy. How far would these new people at ABC go to get what they wanted? And *why*—now that the professionals were on the subject, dabbing at their lemon twists with just the tips of their manicured nails—would ABC want the college games in the first place? College football telecasts had almost bankrupted the ABC network six years ago. The causes of that failure were no secret. And those causes, in 1960, had not gone away.

The main cause was starkly simple: ABC didn't have as many affiliated TV stations around the country as did CBS or NBC. The network fell short of parity by about twenty percent. That gap may not have seemed very large by any conventional measurement, but by advertisers' standards it was the Grand Canyon. It meant that ABC could probably never win a national ratings race and thus demand top dollar for its commercial time.

A related curse hanging over the network was UHF. A good many of the ABC affiliates that did exist around the country were new stations operating on the recently introduced, and generally unfamiliar, ultra-high-frequency band. Most TV sets in those days could not even receive UHF without a special adapter. And who was going to go out and buy an adapter? The sheer fact of television was still enough to fascinate viewers in the 1950s. People didn't watch programs, they watched TV. What were they going to get on UHF, with those cumbersome adapters, that was better than *The Buick Circus Hour* on NBC, or *Biff Baker, U.S.A.* on CBS? Soft-core pornography was still a quarter century away.

It was Tom Moore's task as ABC programing chief to come up with something better than *Biff Baker*—some kind of programing the viewers felt they could not be without. Moore thought the something was sports, never mind the 1954 NCAA disaster. Back in 1954, nobody at ABC knew how to put on a sports telecast. Now Moore had some professionals. He had Ed Scherick. And he had someone else. A human secret weapon, a discovery that Moore had made within the network. A natural resource: a towering intellect packaged inside the face and squat body of a character from *Guys and Dolls*. A Phi Beta Kappa in mathematical statistics at Columbia University who wrote his master's thesis on the possibilities of rolling dice.

Julius Barnathan. A great character in the ABC maverick mold; perhaps, when it was all counted up, the definitive ABC character. Barnathan, the child of Spanish-Jewish immigrants, growing up poor in Brooklyn, with his deep-set sad eyes in a large, square skull and his side-to-side barrel-chester gait, heavy Flatbush neighborhood accents and profane, back-slapping barroom joviality, all concealing a great, humane heart and a piercing, sophisticated grasp of the emerging science of market research. Barnathan, who could and perhaps should have risen to the ABC Network presidency, but was deflected in favor of leaner, smoother, more punctilious men ("Julie is a masterful individual," Sy Siegel once assured his rival Tom Moore, "but he'll never be head of this network. He just isn't the *type*"), was banished to the Siberia of engineering. Refusing to think of engineering as Siberia, he would learn engineering, of which he knew zero, and turn that dreary department into an Oz of technical resources that would elevate ABC's visual and aural effects into the forefront of the industry.

Julie Barnathan—"Bar-nuthin'," as he was respectfully known among some of his colleagues. Barnathan shared Tom Moore's belief in salvation through sports. But with Barnathan, it was not just a hunch. Barnathan had joined ABC in 1954, as supervisor of ratings. He did not exactly "get in on the ground floor"; at the time, the network's offices were above an A&P grocery store on Upper Broadway. "With a pair of binoculars you could look right into the red-light district," Barnathan remembered. While everybody else above the grocery store was trying to figure out how the hell to do television, Barnathan was figuring out television audiences.

ABC had always been the network most aggressively committed to market research as a tool for tailoring its programs to specific audiences. The credit for this is due Barnathan. He was exploring demographics, the science of subdividing audiences according to age, sex and income, while everyone else still thought that mere ratings—body counts—were the last word in Orwellian wizardry.

"I was there when ABC built its schedule around the Mickey Mouse Club," Barnathan liked to growl. "We were doin' market research before anybody else. We knew that a lot of the audience was loyal to either CBS or NBC. But we also found out that there was a big part of the audience that wasn't loyal. That was *young people*. Young people were fickle. Great! We decided to go after 'em. We decided to become the Network of the Young. And the way to do that, in the beginning at least, was through sports."

Julius Barnathan became Tom Moore's ally on the inside of ABC, an advocate of Moore's causes to Leonard Goldenson and Sy Siegel, just as Scherick was his ally on the outside. It was Barnathan—glowering, barging in, waving his survey sheets—who had backed up Moore's petition to bid again on the NCAA. And after that bid had been secured, it was Barnathan who helped Moore develop a scheme that would make the raid on NBC look like a small act of charity.

Now, with Julius Barnathan's urging, Moore and Scherick were going to go and steal themselves—all right, perhaps "borrow" would be a better word—some television stations. "We stopped thinking *affiliates*," Moore explained, "and started thinking *clearances*. If we could talk some CBS and NBC stations into carrying ABC football telecasts, it didn't matter whether they were our stations for keeps or not." Here again, the ABC barbarian was blasting holes in an Old-World system that had served the large networks nicely.

CBS and NBC had divided up the largest and strongest local-station affiliates before the orphaned ABC was ever on its feet. Many cities of significant size did not even have an ABC-connected station. But "affiliated" did not mean "owned"—not by a long shot. Each network owned five stations. The other hundred-fifty-odd in each grouping carried a given network's programs under the terms of working agreements. Because the FCC held that local stations should ultimately be accountable for programing, it prohibited any network from compelling any affiliate station to broadcast what that network sent down the line.

Of course, in practice, the local stations had generally opened up their transmitter-spigots and let the parent network supply a program flow until sign-off time. Only in rare instances—say, in a city that had just one TV outlet—would the local station accept programs from two or more networks. It was an arrangement that stabilized viewer expectations and made money for everyone. Everyone except a clawing underdog that didn't have many affiliate stations, ABC. Under Moore and

Scherick, ABC began to treat stations that had working relationships with CBS or NBC like so many stray cattle whose brands could be altered. They began to rustle.

As Moore put it years later: "My argument to the top brass was, 'You let us get into college sports, and we'll get the games cleared in markets where ABC has no affiliates. *Because the public doesn't give a good god damn* about a station's loyalty to NBC or CBS.'"

Brooklyn-bred Barnathan perceived that most of ABC's station pilferage would have to be accomplished in Dixie. "If you have the NCAA in the South, it's like God," he reminded them—as if Mississippian Moore had to be told. "If you go after stations down there, they'll come over. And as for cities that do have ABC stations on the UHF bands— why, there we'll stand our ground. We'll *make* the public go out and buy the goddamn special adapters. Because they won't see NCAA football if they don't."

As head of ABC programing, Tom Moore would have to stay mostly aloof from this crusade—although as a Mississippian he would have relished the adventure; he would have been like a politician stumping through the hollows and the backwoods towns. Instead, it was Julie Barnathan—by now the head of affiliate station relations, who took the point position: Barnathan working the phones, calling up stations in places like Columbus, Georgia; Raleigh, North Carolina; Lexington, Kentucky; Birmingham, Alabama; Cincinnati; Austin. Barnathan's gruff urban voice, falling heavy on the Southern ear, the hated voice of the New York City devil, fast-talking and twisting things around, this time was selling the local station manager something he wanted to buy; something he was willing to bend those traditional working agreements just a *shade,* now, to obtain—college football.

The Southern NBC affiliates, especially, fell into Barnathan's grasp without a whimper: they had been traumatized when they found out their parent network had been bamboozled out of the most popular programing they could offer their football-crazed viewers. For these willing turncoats, Barnathan was ready to give the winch a couple of extra yanks. "If we *do* decide to give you the NCAA," he'd bark into the telephone, *"how many hours of our prime-time programs are you prepared to take?* We got *Maverick,* we got 77 *Sunset Strip,* we got *Disneyland . . ."*

The scale of deflections and concessions was phenomenal; it was more than the New York schemers had dared hope. Baton Rouge may have been Barnathan's finest single achievement. In Baton Rouge, Barnathan persuaded the CBS affiliate, Channel 9, to drop *Gunsmoke*—Marshal Matt Dillon being a folk hero roughly on the scale of Huey Long—and air the Gillette Saturday fights, all for the right to those football games.

The convention of the National Association of Broadcasters was coming up in Chicago. Local-station executives from all over the country would converge on the Conrad Hilton Hotel for three days of self-congratulatory handshaking and backslapping and nametag-wearing and cocktail hours and . . . Tom Moore couldn't stand it. All those cattle in a single pen—decorum or not, he had to be in Chicago.

Moore, Scherick and Barnathan flew off to Chicago to attend the NAB convention. But, typically of those giddy, swashbuckling days, they didn't exactly melt into the crowd. They descended on the NAB with a giant NCAA banner, which they draped above the ABC exhibition booth. They hired models tricked out like college cheerleaders and set them high-kicking. "We put on a *helluva* show," Moore recalls. "Before we were through, those station managers had it drilled into them that college football was tied into everything that ABC did."

The NAB convention allowed Tom Moore to enter the affiliate-rustling campaign without being brazen about it. He could operate in the softly lighted, carpeted suites of the Conrad Hilton, where big, prosperous men in their best going-to-the-city suits stood belly to belly and swirled the ice in their scotches and tried to think of one more friendly commonplace to utter to the stranger in front of them. This was the old aristocracy of American television, the feudal lords, who despite their facile received wisdom about "markets" and "demos" and "dayparts" and "lead-ins," didn't have a clue as to the true power of what flowed through their transmitters, nor as to how greatly that power would soon be enhanced and manipulated by the three smiling, good-natured men filtering among them, who paused to drape an arm around their shoulders and talk a little football—the men with that bang-up NCAA booth and the cheerleaders, from the desperate little third network in New York, ABC.

By the end of that three-day convention in Chicago, Moore, Scherick and Barnathan had coolly completed their plunder. They had all the clearance commitments they needed to advance their revolution onto the airwaves.

In the span of a few weeks at the beginning of 1960, the outwardly moribund ABC Television Network had struck a series of competitive blows virtually unmatched, in the short history of television to that time, for sheer headlong nerve and remorselessness. Every one of those blows had been engineered by Tom Moore and Edgar J. Scherick.

Was ABC going to get away with all this? It was. The only question remaining was whether major sponsors would support this kind of plundered programing. As it turned out, Moore and Scherick did not even have to enforce the commitment they'd extracted from Craig Smith and Gillette—a promise to underwrite all the commercial minutes on the football telecasts, if necessary. "By the *night* of the day we began soliciting sponsors, we'd sold half the time," recalled Moore. "We could have gone on selling more, but Gillette said, 'Stay there. We'll take the other half.'"

So it had not been an altogether bad start for ABC in 1960. John Fitzgerald Kennedy had been inaugurated as the thirty-fifth President; his administration brought with it a sweeping mood of eagerness, optimism and vital elegance. All at once the country began to shrug off the darker morbidities of the Cold War and of McCarthyesque paranoia; it plunged into a dance to its own regeneration. The Kingston Trio composed a ringing folk hymn to "The New Frontier." The Word went forth and the Torch was passed, and now it was "Pepsi—for those who think young." The pop-cultural catchphrases were "vim and vig-ah" and "A-OK" (the first, a Kennedyism; the second, a scrap of NASA jargon); and on back roads and front lawns across America, imitators of the Kennedy clan's athletic style seemed to be plunging off on fifty-mile hikes or heaving footballs around.

Perhaps no company in America identified with this imagery of rebirth as profoundly as did ABC. After all, had not ABC personified the downtrodden, the outcast orphan? And was not ABC secretly pulling itself up from stagnation and despair by the same application of pluck, vigorous enterprise and youthful boldness that the new administration embodied?

Youth was suddenly in the very air that people breathed; it hung there, waiting to be incorporated onto the airwaves, and neither CBS nor NBC appeared inclined to notice. It fell to ABC, urged on by the clever Barnathan, to transform itself into the Network of the Young, and sports would be the catalyst of that transformation. (ABC's successful "youth" image would conceal a bit of a paradox as the sixties went on: while its sports and prime-time programing tapped into young and progressive audiences, the network itself was ideologically conservative at its highest levels. In 1965 it nearly merged with ITT, an international conglomerate famous for its defense contracts and counter-revolutionary activities in South America; and Howard K. Smith, ABC's prime commentator, was to be recognized as the one TV newsman palatable to the tastes of Richard Nixon and Spiro Agnew.)

At any rate, ABC's mandate became increasingly obvious to people like Moore and Scherick as the new decade began. Here at last was the revolution that Scherick had intuited seven years before, in that bobbing rowboat off Long Island. The fact that ABC still did not formally contain a sports division—Sports Programs, Inc., remained Scherick's personal company—only added to the giddy aura of long-shot adventurism. Anything was possible. Scherick and Moore had virtually willed a college football schedule out of thin air.

It seemed a good time to be thinking about a staff for the nonexistent sports division: a few hands who might have some ideas about how to put those filched games on the air. And so began the most enduring phase of Ed Scherick's legacy to ABC: his inspired assembling of Chet Simmons, Roone Arledge, Chuck Howard and Jim Spence as the original cast of the dynasty known as ABC Sports.

It is hard to imagine exactly what special gifts Scherick was able to discern in each man, at the time each was hired. They were all young, anonymous, unproved. None, save Arledge, was an established television professional—and Arledge was established only as the producer of an in-studio kiddie puppet show. Of the rest, one was a former adman, another was a Korea veteran who'd done a little radio sportscasting in college, and the third was fresh from an Ivy League campus, a scrapbook full of collegiate sports columns under his arm.

Perhaps Scherick sensed in each a shred of temperament similar to something in himself: in Howard a quick nervous intelligence tinged with obsession; in Spence a random aggressiveness and thirst for competition; in Simmons a dogged, clerical attention to detail; in Arledge, the sheer primal appetite that Scherick later summed up as "a will to power."

They were mavericks. Of the four, only Simmons could have controlled his impulses enough to pass for the blandly competent "organization man" that stately CBS and NBC were promoting through the ranks in those days. And only Simmons would have the chance to prove it. After four years of competing against Arledge to fill the power vacuum created by Scherick's abrupt departure, Simmons crossed over to NBC Sports—where it became his thankless fate to compete against Arledge for the next sixteen years.

But whatever qualities Scherick noticed in these men, they were not fleeting. Arledge, Spence and Howard flourished at ABC for the ensuing quarter century, and played fundamental roles in lifting ABC to the status of a major, frequently dominant, network. In 1983, even Simmons returned to the fold, in a way: as commissioner of the new United States Football League, whose existence was keyed to telecast contracts with ESPN, the cable network—for $18 million over two years—and with Arledge's ABC Sports.

Simmons was the first of the lot—if only because he came with Scherick as the other half of SPI. Scherick had known Simmons at Dancer Fitzgerald and admired the young man's stolid thoroughness, and also his ability to mix with others, to smooth over frictions with a glad hand and get ahead with business. Round-faced, earnest and fastidious, Simmons at the outset was Scherick's Scherick—carrying out an assortment of detail assignments, doing liaison work with collegiate officials, nailing down ABC's technical and engineering needs. This experience would invest Simmons with an administrative expertise that he would later put to good use at NBC.

Howard and Spence came aboard Scherick's bandwagon in August 1960. Spence was twenty-three, a handsome, dark-haired young graduate of Dartmouth College, where he had majored in Spanish and edited the school paper's sports page. "I planned to be either a foreign correspondent or a sportswriter," Spence said. Upon his discharge from military service in 1960, Spence had first sought employment from Bill MacPhail at CBS Sports. Sitting outside MacPhail's office, waiting for his interview, Spence fell into conversation with a young CBS production assistant, a former All-American baseball player named Chet Forte. "You don't want to be here," Spence recalled Forte warning him. "You want to be over at ABC, where it's all happening." Spence went ahead with his appointment in MacPhail's office, but afterward, he followed Forte's advice and sought an interview with Scherick. (Chet Forte later followed his own advice. He fled CBS for the hot new outfit in 1961, and stayed on to create the on-air look of *Monday Night Football*, which he produced from the very first telecast.)

At Sports Program's Forty-second Street offices, young Spence waited more than an hour for an audience with Scherick. This time there were no smart young assistants telling him to go somewhere else. In fact the place didn't seem like a television enterprise at all. Spence felt more like he was auditioning for a part in a Broadway musical. He sat in the small anteroom fidgeting, his scrapbook of Dartmouth sports clips on his lap, waiting for someone to usher him in. Finally, from the other side of an office door, Spence was startled by an impatient, high-pitched bellow: *"Spence! Get in here!"* Spence scrambled to his feet, dashed inside and nervously thrust his book of clippings at the sharp-featured small man before him.

Scherick took one look at the scrapbook and snarled: *"I don't wanna see those!"* Spence felt confused. It sounded as though he had been rejected before he could even utter a word. But now Scherick was looking down below the scrapbook. He was looking at Spence's feet. *"You know what I*

like about you?" Scherick demanded savagely. *"Your green socks!"* he
answered himself. Scherick had spotted Jim Spence's Dartmouth colors
down there above his shoes, and recognized a fellow Ivy-Leaguer. What
would later come to be known as the Preppy Code had worked for
Spence. Scherick hired him for sixty-five dollars a week. His assignment
was to help out on football telecasts as a production assistant. "I also
changed a lot of water in the copy machine," added Spence.

Beginning in 1977, when Roone Arledge assumed the dual presidencies of ABC News and Sports, it was Jim Spence who assumed the day-
to-day operations of the network sports division.

And then came Chuck Howard. Tall, sandy-haired, lean and ramrod-
straight in the manner of a military man—he had run an Army PX in
Korea—Howard came to ABC from, of all places, the Chase Manhattan
Bank. "I was working in some training program there when a friend
introduced me to Scherick," Howard said. "I'd broadcast some football
and basketball games at Duke University, and I was interested in getting into sports in any way I could." Like Spence, Howard came on as a
production assistant. Over the years, he pioneered and perfected the
ABC college football telecast "look"—working always in close tandem
with Arledge. Howard also played a key role in the creation of *Wide
World of Sports.*

Howard and Spence were the first products of what became an organizational philosophy at ABC Sports. ABC rarely hired talent away from
other sports divisions, even in the years when the raiding of news stars
became an Arledge hallmark. Instead, ABC scouted emerging young
collegians as meticulously as an NFL team, hiring the brightest and
most innovative as production assistants and blending the best of them
gradually into the system. "This nurturing philosophy paid off best for
us," noted Howard, "when we got into the Olympics. We needed an
army of trained, specialized production talent, and we'd developed that
army on our own."

But as the years and decades were to prove, it all came down, ultimately, to Arledge.

XI

THE COMING OF ARLEDGE

His very entree into the medium was consistent with his reputation as a sort of Messiah. It involved an inn, late travelers, no room, an act of grace.

He was laboring as an humble headwaiter at an inn on Cape Cod in the spring of 1954; it was called the Wayside Inn. Recently turned away from a community newspaper on Long Island, he had come to this menial station seeking only the barest sustenance while he awaited his induction into the Army.

Late one evening a family arrived at the Wayside Inn. Too late to be seated for a meal. "I am sorry," he said, "I cannot serve you dinner; the kitchen has closed." And as he looked at them the young headwaiter took pity on the family, and said, "Oh, come on in, and I will wait on you." And he gave them food to eat, saying, "Don't hurry, enjoy your dinner." And as the family was leaving the inn, the father asked for the young headwaiter's name.

Many days passed, and the young headwaiter went to New York, where he had lined up a job interview at DuMont television after his stint in the Army.

And as he passed into the office of the head of programing, the young headwaiter saw that a miracle had transpired; for the man who sat behind the desk of the head of programing was the same father who had appeared that late night at the Wayside Inn. And in the revelation of that moment, the young headwaiter saw that it was good, and that it was going to get better.

Arledge's timing was always uncanny; it was *digital*. His arrival in television coincided with the perfection of three technologies that would transform television's impact on the world, and he was among the medium's very first thinkers to understand their value and adapt them to his use. Those technologies were videotape, communications satellites, and commercial jet travel.

Timing and adaptation were near the center of Arledge's intuitive genius. He applied them to equal advantage in his use of machinery and of men. There is the case of Howard Cosell. Cosell was a fringe commodity when Arledge inherited ABC Sports, a personality virtually blackballed by his own network. That Arledge rehabilitated Cosell and adapted his unorthodox talent to enormous advantage is part of TV sports' folklore. Less well known is the fact that Cosell's greatest access to notoriety depended entirely on the quirk of scheduling that placed ABC's pro football telecasts in prime time, on a weeknight. If ABC had telecast pro games on Sunday afternoons, in parity with CBS and NBC, Arledge has said, he would not have chosen Cosell for his broadcast team. The same attributes that made Cosell exactly right for prime time made him exactly wrong for the rhythms of Sundays.

Arledge was never an inventor. But he held to a boy's fascination for what technology could do. It was the fascination of a boy who had gone and peered at the DuMont display inside the World of Tomorrow pavilion at the 1939 World's Fair. This fascination nurtured in him a compulsion for prodding his real technicians to produce the actual circuitry that would make tangible some piece of Arledge dream gadgetry. He could visualize the adaptive possibilities in existing equipment, or combinations of equipment, as well as in people and in situations, almost like a writer seizing upon an unlikely metaphor and converting it into something artistic.

He sat and listened one hot day in 1961, over a beer and a hamburger at a little bar near the Los Angeles Coliseum called Julie's, while one of his engineers, a professorial man named Bob Trachinger, droned on about something he'd seen on a recent trip to Japan—a concept that might make it possible for television to slow down images, approximating the slow-motion effect familiar in motion pictures. This was in the early days of videotape, a process invented by the Ampex Corporation in 1956, but not perfected for commercial use until 1959. Videotape was a cumbersome kind of equipment, requiring heavy machines and the most excruciating kind of editing. Most TV people tried to avoid using it. But Trachinger thought that the Japanese might have been on to something quite novel.

It required, Trachinger explained to Arledge, one TV camera that would take a picture of an image being picked up on another camera, and recording that image on videotape via a process that would allow it to be replayed at half speed. "Scan converter," Trachinger was calling it, and he began to sketch out his idea on the napkin under one of the beer mugs. He ended up using several napkins, which in turn required the drinking of several beers. The napkin kept getting wet with beer foam, and Trachinger's ballpoint pen kept tearing the fiber, but when he was finished drawing, Arledge knew that he had something that neither of the big networks had, a way of slowing down time.

A couple of weekends into ABC's fall 1961 NCAA telecast schedule, Jack Concannon of Boston College swiveled and cut and twisted for eighty yards and a touchdown against Syracuse. And at halftime, instead of the conventional and tiresome marching bands, ABC audiences saw Concannon's flickering image—slowed down to a graceful, dreamlike waltz, while Paul Christman's voice explained the atomized strategies of each cut, each twist. (In this as in other innovations, Arledge and his people were not only ahead of CBS and NBC, they were ahead of ABC. The pre-Barnathan heads of the engineering department sneered at Trachinger's concept. They refused to allocate a budget necessary to put it on line. So Trachinger did some adapting of his own. He adapted funds that were earmarked for other projects and diverted them into the machinery needed for the slow-motion replay.)

Trachinger's breakthrough brought ABC some early, deserved prestige. But as the years went on, the event betrayed one of Arledge's less statesmanlike tendencies—his tendency to ascribe all significant advances in television to his ABC, and, by extension, to himself—much in the vein of the comic-strip Soviet commissar who gave Mother Russia the credit for all the great inventions ("Can't you see the Russian name on the bottom—'Reg. U.S. Pat. Off'?"). As the years went on, Trachinger's slow-motion breakthrough became blurred, in Arledge's reminiscences, with the instant replay. "When we were finished," Arledge told *Playboy* magazine in 1976, [Trachinger and I] had the plans for the first instant-replay device."

But ABC did not invent the instant replay. Viewers did not see that Concannon slow-motion run until halftime, because the modified tape machines that recorded it were located back in the New York office, not in the ABC remote truck. It was not until two years later that a young CBS director named Tony Verna was able to solve the maddening technical problems necessary to rerun a videotape immediately after a play. "In those days," Verna recalled, "there were no such things as footage counters or electronic readouts. It wasn't like film. When we rewound the tape we didn't know where we were. I finally ordered one of my technicians to coordinate a 'beep' tone to the point at which the quarterback took the snap."

A former West Point cadet, Verna labored to have his jerry-built device completed in time for the Army–Navy game. He succeeded. His hope was to capture the tricky movements of Navy quarterback Roger Staubach, but as the game wore on, one attempt after another to hit the replay button at the precise moment failed. Finally, late in the contest, Verna managed to cue up some usable footage of Army quarterback Rollie Stichweh galloping for a touchdown. In the truck, Verna spoke into his headset phone, reminding Lindsey Nelson that he would have to explain the replay. Nelson, the old literalist, took the advice to heart. *"This is a videotape!"* Nelson kept screaming. *"They did not score again! They did not score again!"* "If you did that now," Verna remarked to an *Inside Sports* columnist in 1980, "they'd throw a net over you."

Similarly, Arledge never resisted taking credit for coining one of the most quoted mottoes in broadcast history—"The thrill of victory, the agony of defeat." This was the phrase that became the slogan for *Wide World of Sports,* and the legend that surrounds its creation has some of the aspects of Lincoln's drafting of the Gettysburg Address. According to myth, Arledge scribbled out the phrase on the back of his airline ticket while traveling back from Japan in 1961. The notion is appealing. But some old hands at ABC are wont occasionally to cough into their fists and murmur, discretely, that—*ahem*—one might want to check this version out with Jim McKay, who, in revisionist doctrine, at least, is the *real* author of the Thrill-Agony epigraph.

Confronted with just that inquiry by telephone one day, McKay paused for a long and agonizing moment before replying. One had the sense that McKay was watching his whole resume pass before his eyes. Finally McKay's voice managed to pronounce the following sentence: "It was a joint effort."

But if Arledge exaggerated certain of ABC's technical breakthroughs, in truth the exaggerations were few. ABC led the way in electronic innovations throughout the sixties and seventies. It led the way because Arledge, unlike his competitors, never failed to listen to the talented engineers under him. He listened when Trachinger or the prodigious Barnathan reported in with the latest visual or acoustic breakthrough— a miniature mike to put inside a golf cup, or a mike that would record the sound of the Olympic Games' Eternal Flame being lit (just as the mike itself was being immolated), or a mike to fasten onto a basketball rim (to record the swish), all of which came under the heading of ambience. Many of these devices were perfected by Trachinger only after furious improvising, prompted by some Arledge whim, an offhand question that began, "Why can't we. . . ?"

Just as Arledge was never an inventor, neither was he an exceptionally gifted administrator. At least, not in the conventional sense, in the ways that rigorous organization men like Tom Moore entirely understood. "We'd have a lot of trouble with Roone about his expense account,' Moore recalled. "Eight, nine thousand dollars at a crack, with no accounting for how the money was spent."

And a young woman whose television work brought her into contact with Arledge and his coterie in the early days remembered, not disapprovingly, that "they were charming, fun-loving, entertaining people whose lives were their jobs. They were like rock stars. In a sense, Roone and his core group were sports stars in their own right. The sport they were stars of was television. They were jumping through hoops of fire all the time, and they had to let off steam."

But others who knew Arledge then—members of the coterie—put a slightly different interpretation on these aspects of Arledge's leadership. Dick Ebersol, who spent several years in the 1960s as a youthful aide to Arledge before moving on to NBC (where he created *Saturday Night Live*), insisted that the expense-account vagueness did not reflect a wastrel style. "You have to understand," Ebersol said, "that the bigger networks, CBS and NBC, ran their own sports departments like traveling country clubs. There was a constant cocktail atmosphere; it was as if they didn't take themselves or their coverage all that seriously—it was a gentleman's club, everybody knew everybody else, nobody competed too seriously. Roone was never like that. His competitors were essentially businessmen; they thought about going through channels, about how to survive within their organization. Roone constantly thought about two things: show and audience. If he spent his department's money, it was to advance ABC Sports' interests. Example: he'd spend a lot of money flying program sponsors—sales guys, you know—down to ABC golf tournaments and horseraces and that stuff. The salesmen just *ate that stuff up*. They loved to be around famous athletes and big events. It made an incalculable difference in sponsor loyalty. It was one of a thousand little things Roone thought of to help his network win."

It would be hard to make a case for Arledge as a classic administrator. Like many creative men, he distrusted or ignored the rules of bureaucracies. Subordinates frequently found him remote, inaccessible. When, in 1977, ABC President Elton Rule awarded him the dual presidencies of ABC News and Sports (a move that would release the Arledge's idiom forever into the news division of all the networks), an elfish aide named Beano Cook cracked: "Now he won't be returning calls on *two* numbers."

The deposed Simmons was a better administrator. So, perhaps, was

Spence—level-headed, a good negotiator, a man of budgets and schedules and organizational flow; the man, in fact, who has administrated ABC Sports on a day-to-day basis since Arledge moved into the news.

What was it, then, that made Arledge so great? Edgar Scherick may have found the phrase for it: a will to power.

His associates have vivid memories of that will made manifest:

Of Arledge walking into the jury-rigged control tower of the 1968 Mexico Olympics to find his two chief associates, Jim Spence and Chuck Howard, at odds over some technical problem. Arledge excused both men, assumed the controls and single-handedly directed a marathon forty-four unrehearsed hours of broadcast—the largest TV sporting event of its time.

Of Arledge defying the powerful National Collegiate Athletic Association's television committee by mandating—in an almost unthinkable break with tradition—that ABC would not submit its college football play-by-play announcers to the committee's approval.

Of Arledge sticking with his choice of Howard Cosell as a *Monday Night Football* announcer in the face of pressure that included a letter from Henry Ford to the ABC board of directors demanding that Cosell be taken off the air. Among those leaning toward Ford was the board chairman, Leonard Goldenson.

One of the most competitive souls in all of competitive corporate America—more competitive, no doubt, than many of the athletes his ABC cameras glorified every weekend—Arledge at times unleashed his enormous manipulative instincts in ways that others thought ruthless, even immoral. His negotiations for Olympics rights involved promises that some rivals genuinely felt were indefensible on ethical grounds. And his eventual success at superimposing his TV sports style upon ABC's network newscasts and public-affairs programs (from where it quickly spread out to the other networks) struck critics across the country as an irreparable attack on journalistic tradition.

But tradition was just where people tended to misread Arledge most grievously. If there is one abiding hallmark of Roone Arledge's personality, one impulse that has animated him from that first futuristic telecast in Birmingham through his revision of network news' imperatives to his exotic video architecture for the 1984 Summer Olympics in Los Angeles, it is a refusal to take the past into account. Arledge is a kind of Luddite in reverse: instead of rejecting the future, he rejects history.

It may be suggested, without intending to justify any of Arledge's more roughshod revisions of convention at ABC, that he did not so much disrespect traditional behavior as simply ignore it, on the ground that it did not apply to television. As a medium, television (along with radio) uniquely retains no trace of a past. On its flat screen, the field of electromagnetic dots, shifting at the rate of once every fifteenth of a second, is constantly rearranging itself into a new time-present. Roone Arledge—whose own freckled face and penchant for polka-dotted shirts and ties imitate that field to an almost satirical degree—may well have grasped, at some point, that television in its own way stands outside time. Especially "linear" time and the accumulation of cultural values that have accrued to linear time. The media analyst Tony Schwartz, a commercial-maker and expert in the field of auditory perception, may have articulated Arledge's instincts in a 1974 book titled, *The Responsive Chord.*

"Truth," Schwartz announced in that book, "as a social value, is a product of print. . . . Electronic communication deals primarily with effects. Electronic media have been viewed merely as extensions of print, and therefore subject to the same grammar and values as print communication. [But] The patterned auditory and visual information on television or radio is not 'content.' Content is a print term . . . a whole new set of questions must be asked, and a new theory of communication must be formulated."*

Arledge habitually concealed any public evidence of being an introspective man. His circular face concealed emotion. It was the face of an overgrown boy; the Scottish skin fair, red beneath the freckles, the blue eyes saucerish and watchful as if from perpetual mild astonishment. The thin Celtic mouth seemed designed for silence, tucked back into his strong jawline and fixed by an indented welt, like a tailor's dart, at either end.

In fact Arledge relished good talk and good wit, but only when there was *time* for it. Telephone messages to him could go unanswered for days, weeks, months; but when he did return them, he was ready to bear down on the issue at hand, and let the caller beware. He cultivated an economical dry wit of his own, an Algonquin Round Table–like skill at deflating with the well-chosen *mot.* One Wednesday morning early in Howard Cosell's tenure at ABC, Cosell was pacing about Arledge's office during a staff meeting in full Cosellian cry. Perhaps partly to assure himself that he deserved his sudden great bounty of network stardom, Cosell was ranting at those present, "You are all *priv*-i-leged to be able to lis-ten to me. You should *all* pay two hun-dred mill-ion

---

*Tony Schwartz. *The Responsive Chord.* N.Y.: Anchor Press/Doubleday, 1974.

doll-ars for the right to lis-ten to me." And Arledge, without looking up from the new edition of *Variety* whose pages he was thumbing, murmured, "Howard, in one way or another, we all do."

But Arledge was always wary of conversations in which he was urged to explair himself, to peel back the layers of his personality and expose the core of the appetite that drove him. It was as though he did not want to stray too near the core himself, and peer into the whiteness. "Ed Scherick is the guy who taught me how to compete," he allowed once, after considerable prodding, lacing and unlacing his thick fingers in his lap as he sat stiffly on the edge of his office sofa. But it was not Ed Scherick who taught Arledge, for instance, to mount an ABC camera on the roof of Veterans Hospital in Pittsburgh, its lens aimed into nearby Pitt Stadium, for the second telecast of Arledge's career.

"That was before the Goodyear Blimp days," said Beano Cook, who remembers standing dumbfounded as Arledge's technicians lashed the Image Orthicon to the roof, "and of course Roone was just after a panorama shot. But in those days, nobody did panorama shots. We couldn't believe it."

Like many of Arledge's eccentric notions in the sixties, the camera-on-the-roof gambit does not age well. Its novel force deteriorates with the perspective of hindsight. But then, so does much of the visually surreal TV comedy of Ernie Kovacs, psychedelic lampshades and Andy Warhol's film *Kitchen*. It helps to remember that in the early sixties, American culture was just beginning to stir from a long repose inside an almost paralytic orthodoxy that imprisoned not only American politics and American educational systems but also American popular artistic forms, including visual forms.

Whatever unexamined compulsions propelled Arledge, they could not be explained by any conventional notion of rags-to-riches ambition. He was born to privilege. The year was 1931, the place Forest Hills, Long Island. His father, Roone Pinckney Arledge, Sr., was a North Carolina lawyer of Scottish stock who had moved northward, attracted by New York's barristerial opportunities and the tree-lined elegance of suburban Long Island. Roone Jr. lived a conventional, unremarkable childhood, at least on the surface. But surface circumstances are not always the most revealing measures of a childhood. Arledge later remembers what fond respect his family accorded the radio in the household. The senior Arledge listened gravely to the evening news broadcasts on CBS by Gabriel Heatter, especially during the World War II years ("Ah, yes, there's good news tonight . . ."), and the great, swirling currents of history relayed on the airwaves became topics of probing dinner-table discussion. Roone Jr. lived for the sporting events. He would lie sprawled on the living-room carpet and absorb, trancelike, the faraway voices of Red Barber and Graham McNamee and Bill Stern. Arledge recalled listening to Barber's 1939 World Series broadcasts. The nine-year-old boy was only passingly aware of the Gillette Blue Blades. What attracted young Roone's attention were the 1939 Cincinnati Reds. "The Reds were the first team I ever followed," he said once. "I was a big Bucky Walters fan."

That little Roone Arledge should choose the distant Bucky Walters, of all people, for his hero-worship, may have been nothing more than a childhood whim. But a glance at Walters's career record does yield up one surpassing event; an event that made Walters different from almost every other major-league player. Walters had come up to the big leagues as an infielder. But in 1936, he abruptly discarded his past: he became a pitcher. And as a pitcher, he eventually won 190 games. What Bucky Walters did in baseball in the 1930s, Roone Arledge was to do in television in the sixties, and beyond.

At school, Arledge competed. He played baseball and wrestled at Mepham High School in Merrick, Long Island, and edited the sports page of the school's paper. Sportswriting appealed to him, and he decided to get the best education in journalism that was available. No journalism school in the country had a better reputation than Columbia University.

In choosing Columbia, the youthful Arledge committed an inexplicable blunder. For most young men, it was the kind of blunder that would have brought a shamefaced withdrawal, a confused switching of plans; enrollment in another school. For Arledge, it was simply a small matter of adaptation—and the educational opportunity of his life. He showed up on the Columbia campus ignorant of the rather fundamental fact that the journalism school he intended to enroll in was a graduate journalism school. But instead of leaving, Arledge took a look around the campus, decided he liked what he saw, and enrolled in a liberal-arts curriculum.

It was 1948. Columbia proved an extraordinarily good place to be, especially for a smart but sheltered upper-middle-class kid from the shaded lawns of Forest Hills. The McCarthy era was just beginning in America; a regressive chill of political conformity, paranoia and super-nationalism would soon envelop universities and communities everywhere. Columbia, then a relatively small, prestigious intimate bastion of urban intellectualism, was among the few schools that escaped the prevalent chill.

Roone Arledge was still something of an innocent when he plunged into this environment. He continued to seek out the avocations that had interested him in high school: he wrestled, edited the undergraduate school's yearbook, ran successfully for his class presidency and also made president of his fraternity, Phi Gamma Delta. But along the way, the intensity of Columbia's pedagogical ferment began to burn its way into Arledge's consciousness.

First, there was the matter of college pals. Arledge found himself befriended by a trio of roommates, each of whom would go on to leave his mark on American communications. There was the tough-talking, worldly city kid, Larry Grossman, who in 1976 would become president of the Public Broadcast System. There was the pale, ironic young phrasemaker, Richard Wald, who would become a distinguished president at NBC News before Arledge himself coaxed Wald to ABC News as a senior vice-president. And there was the scholarly Max Frankel, who in 1973 would win a Pulitzer Prize for his stewardship of *The New York Times* editorial page.

"These guys helped form an atmosphere for me at Columbia that was incredibly stimulating," Arledge remembered. "They made me think in ways I'd never thought before. I remember Frankel, how he used to argue that you couldn't understand an idea unless you understood what the idea stood against. And they made me appreciate the value of curiosity. I guess my dad had that effect, too; at our dinner table the talk was always, 'I bet that Omar Bradley is thinking this right now; I bet President Roosevelt is planning to do that.' But, I mean, these guys— they never let an idea alone until they'd examined it to exhaustion. It changed me. After that kind of stimulation at Columbia, I could never understand a reporter, or a cameraman, or any kind of journalist, or *anyone* who wasn't curious."

But as stimulating as his new pals were, they did not account for the most significant means to enlightenment that Roone Arledge experienced at Columbia. His most intense introspections, apparently, were prompted by the superb faculty, and in courses that had nothing directly to do with sportswriting or journalism. "My God, Mark Van Doren was teaching in humanities then," said Arledge. "Lionel Trilling was teaching courses in literature. Van Doren was just a towering figure. I remember conversations from his classes as though they happened yesterday. One day we were discussing *Don Quixote,* and some kid in the class said he thought that Don Quixote represented God, and I thought that was a pretty wonderful, pretty intellectual remark. And then Van Doren replied, 'I wonder whether there has ever been a great story written in which God has *not* been one of the characters.'"

From Trilling, the master of the art of narrative, Arledge began to understand the elemental appeal of *story* to the human imagination. He listened as Trilling explained how the wisps and fragments of narrative drama lay beneath the surface of the most random behavior, and how it was the task of the artist to sift and isolate this drama, and heighten it, and render it in such a compressed and ordered way that the reader could respond, with his spirit as well as his intellect, to its ageless compelling themes. Arledge's standing orders to the announcers who do the play-by-play for ABC Sports events—to find the human drama inherent in each contest, a concept that became "story line" on *Monday Night Football*—is a direct homage to Trilling.

At its best, a sporting event expresses a dramatic vision that is greater than the sum of its statistics, injury list and betting line. All announcers have to talk about something. Better they seek a "story line" than drone on about the weather, the great crowd and the rugged determination written on the head coach's face.

Arledge enrolled in graduate studies at Columbia University's School of International Affairs after he received his bachelor's degree in 1952. He soon became restless with the confinements of campus life. Scholarly contemplation was not, over the long haul, his true style. He wanted to put his hands on something and set it in motion, to test his newly enlightened instincts in an arena. Within a year, Arledge dropped his graduate studies, left Columbia and began looking for work.

At about the same time that Ed Scherick was sitting in his rowboat, dreaming of a "revolution," Arledge was making his first job inquiries at DuMont—the network whose futuristic displays he had gazed upon as an eight-year-old at the New York World's Fair. "I wanted to be in something that had to do with sports," Arledge remembers. "All the guys I'd met at Columbia kept telling me, 'Don't get into sports because sports isn't creative.' I didn't believe that, but I sure remember feeling the pressure to do something that was noble and uplifting."

In that exalted spirit, Arledge began looking around for an outlet into which he could pour his expensive Columbia erudition. The nearest outlet seemed to be a small Long Island daily newspaper. Arledge applied. To his shock, the editor turned him down: "No experience."

"It was the best thing that ever happened to me," Arledge observed later, as if there might have been any doubt. A bit deflated, Arledge accepted the practical limitations of his marketability. The headwaiter's job at the Wayside Inn followed. And that job led to his chance gesture of kindness toward the late-arriving family, whose name was Caddigan. James Caddigan rewarded Arledge with a job at DuMont: an errand-boy's job, really; one that involved chasing after this and that for whichever floor director called his name, but still, a classic entry-level television job. Arledge lost no time seeking out his superiors, shaking hands, making his higher ambitions known.

But first he had to fulfill the demands of Selective Service. Arledge entered the Army in 1954, and defended his country in such exotic theaters as the Aberdeen Proving Ground in Maryland. When he was discharged a year later, he found that there had indeed been a casualty: not himself, but the DuMont Television Network. It had folded.

But Arledge's handshaking paid its dividend. His contacts at DuMont steered him to NBC, where a stage-manager's job awaited him at the New York flagship station, whose call letters then were WRCA. One of his assignments was to help produce a children's puppet show, then called *Shariland,* hosted by the ventriloquist Shari Lewis.

Arledge may have been on the inside of NBC on the wispiest of credentials—behind-the-scenes menial to a kiddie puppeteer at the local station. On the other hand, he was *on the inside.* And like Ed Scherick, Roone Arledge appreciated the opportunities that accrued to those on the inside. As he had at DuMont, Arledge began to explore the NBC organization. His explorations led him up and down the elevators at Rockefeller Center; to floors that housed command posts far superior to those of WRCA. He visited the executive offices of "General" Sarnoff himself, the chairman of the board of RCA. Like all top-level executives, General Sarnoff employed the services of a personal secretary, a beautiful and jolly young blonde woman named Joan Heise. Arledge presented himself to Miss Heise. He asked her for a date, courted her. They were married in December 1953. The couple took up residence in a seventy-five-dollar-a-month rent-controlled apartment in Brooklyn, where their neighbors included Arledge's great chum from Columbia, Larry Grossman, and Grossman's own bride. Grossman by then had taken a junior editor's position at *Look* magazine.

Arledge and Grossman had never lost touch since Columbia. Now they were reunited in Brooklyn, family men now, and scrimping for a living, *responsible;* but, reflected in one another's eyes, still the dashing young romantics from university days, and sworn to lavish their gifts upon the world. In the long tenement evenings, with both families' budgets too thin to allow much on-the-town entertaining, Grossman and Arledge rekindled their great collegiate passion for talking, for exploring ideas and conjuring the sublime.

"Neither of us had a dime to waste," Grossman recalls, "but, God, did we have big ideas. We both had this dream of breaking through; of doing something that mattered."

Over many long evenings, the dream sharpened. Arledge and Grossman began to toss back and forth their notions for a mythical television
program: the most earnest and yet scintillating program ever conceived,
a television program that would dramatize the loftiest achievements of
history's greatest artists and generals and statesmen. High-minded and
rigorous in content, yet written and photographed and paced according
to state-of-the-art slick production values, it would win over the most
hopelessly low-brow members of the mass audience. It would have story
line! The series had a working title: "Masterpiece."

In the throes of this fantasy, the two young idealists imagined that
they would render such immortal themes as Beethoven's early admira-
tion of Napoleon and how that hero-worship led him to compose the
Eroica symphony; the political battles between Michelangelo and Pope
Julius II that formed the psychological backdrop for the painter's great
murals in the Sistine Chapel; the currents of muscular American popul-
ism reflected in the poems of Walt Whitman's epic *Leaves of Grass*
("Would you hear of an old-time sea fight? Would you learn who won by
the light of the moon and stars?").

"We worked like slaves on that idea for nearly two years, off and on,"
recalls Grossman. "We haunted the New York Public Library. We did
incredible volumes of research. The death of Lincoln—I can't tell you
all the ideas we had for that program."

The mythical series presented its practical challenges, of course.
Once a proposal was on paper, who would look at it? Roone Arledge and
Larry Grossman had no credentials in the television industry. Away
from the fame-laden vapors of their Brooklyn rent-controlled apartments, they weren't so famous. They were nobodies. On the other
hand, Roone Arledge was, however tenuously, on the inside. He could
operate within NBC. Now, for the first important time in Arledge's
career, the cool and calculating pragmatist took over from the inflamed
idealist. Roone Arledge began to adapt—to employ the tools at hand to
his own unique uses.

The immediate problem was to get someone in authority to look at the
proposal once it had been written. Someone, say, like NBC President
Sylvester (Pat) Weaver. One way to ensure Weaver's attention would be
to present the document to him on stationery bearing the letterhead of
General Sarnoff, the chairman of NBC's parent corporation, RCA, and
the company's guiding spirit since 1919. Better still, the letterhead
stationery should contain the personally scripted initials of the General
himself.

But how? There was no chance that Sarnoff would read and initial the proposal, or even provide his personal stationery—unless the document was typed up beforehand and dropped on his desk, along with his daily stack of routine correspondence. By his personal secretary.

As it happened, Roone Arledge was married to the very woman who was General Sarnoff's personal secretary. Joan Arledge, always game for a lark, agreed to carry out the crucial task of typing and delivery; it was fairly certain that the busy chairman would scrawl his mark without reading the document closely. After all, that was what secretaries were for.

The plan worked perfectly. "Masterpiece," flawlessly typed on RCA corporate letterhead and duly initialed by the chairman of the board, arrived on the desk of Pat Weaver. Weaver was impressed. So impressed that he decided at once to meet the two young NBC geniuses who had caught the eye of the General.

"As soon as he came into Roone's office, and saw a basically empty room and these two young guys and a typewriter, he knew he'd been had," remembered Grossman.

"Masterpiece" was never again mentioned, either officially or unofficially, at NBC television. Perhaps taking Arledge's youthful zest into consideration, and no doubt with a measure of respect for his audacity, Weaver allowed Arledge to remain among the employed.

So Roone Arledge had arrived in television and presented his calling card. As if to atone for his bureaucratic fast shuffle with "Masterpiece," he plunged into the production of Shari Lewis's puppet show—retitled *Hi, Mom*—and even won, on its behalf, a New York Emmy in 1958.

And then Arledge began to pull his own strings.

XII

NOT FOR MEN ONLY

Winning Emmys for puppet shows was not Roone Arledge's idea of the noble or uplifting. After the collapse of "Masterpiece," an Emmy for a puppet show was almost tantamount to a cruel joke, fate's pie in the face. Arledge never quite got over a certain melancholy at the memory of this impossibly gallant, callow dream-program; it had for him some of the lingering purity of a first love, which, in the context of his developing obsession with video, it was. Years later, when he had otherwise hardened himself to the most ruthless varieties of combat on network television's bleak battlegrounds, when his ambition had expanded to the point where he could throw a bargaining figure down before the eyes of an Olympics committee chairman and then tell that gentleman in a passionless voice to think hard and fast about that figure, because within a few minutes its value would be sliced—even at that stage of his power, Arledge never quite put aside his fondness for the failed possibilities of "Masterpiece." "Masterpiece" was his Rosebud. Nearly twenty years after Pat Weaver had seen through the letterhead ruse and slapped the idea into oblivion, when Larry Grossman became president of the Public Broadcast Service in February of 1976, Grossman received a telegram from Innsbruck, Austria, where ABC Sports was deployed to cover the Winter Olympics. The telegram began: CONGRATULATIONS ON THE PBS JOB. HAVE A GREAT IDEA FOR A DRAMATIC SERIES BASED ON GREAT WORKS OF ART, MUSIC AND LITERATURE . . . Grossman cabled back: TERRIFIC IDEA. I HAVE THE PERFECT TITLE. LET'S CALL IT "MASTERPIECE THEATRE" . . .

Commuting from Brooklyn to Rockefeller Center each day, where he spent his days refining the production values of a puppet show, the twenty-seven-year-old Arledge began to feel a bit like a puppet himself. He started to tinker with program ideas again, this time by himself.

In the late 1950s, the last word in avant-garde urban male sophistication was a daring new magazine called *Playboy*. *Playboy* featured articles on jazz, clothing, wine, automobiles, sports—and photographs of women with actual naked breasts. *Playboy*'s founder was an eclectic-minded, pipe-smoking young magazine editor named Hugh Hefner. Hell. Arledge was young and eclectic-minded. Arledge liked jazz and sharp clothing. Arledge had some editing experience—didn't he supervise the suave Columbia yearbook? Arledge even smoked a pipe.

Arledge had his reasonable doubts as to the feasibility of showing women's actual naked breasts on the NBC airwaves. But in all other aspects, he perceived, *Playboy* amounted to a capital prototype for a male-oriented TV show, a "magazine" based on a magazine, as it were. Why read about good jazz when you could hear and see it? Why read about automobiles and sports . . . all right, it wasn't "Masterpiece." But on the other hand it wasn't Lamb Chop, Charlie Horse and Hush Puppy, either—no disrespect to Miss Lewis.

Hefner's influence even hung over Arledge's proposed title for the show: "For Men Only." In terms of the impending sexual revolution, this selection did not exactly enshrine Arledge as a social prophet; it was rather egregiously imbued with the prevailing dominant-male mythology of the late 1950s. On the other hand, one would be mistaken to suppose that Arledge's general comprehension of women could be summed up in that callow title. Whatever his personal successes and failures with women, Arledge's developing sensibilities as a programmer could not long contain such a reductive view.

His marriage to Joan Heise produced three daughters and a son, but it was not destined to survive the pressures of his constant travel. The breaking point would come in 1971, when Arledge abruptly jettisoned his plans to meet Joan in Honolulu for a brief vacation in favor of personally producing ABC's telecast of the Texas–Arkansas football game. Arledge explained to *Playboy* years later that his decision was based on the fact that President Nixon had decided to attend the game—which would decide the national championship—and Arledge wanted to be on hand in the event of an assassination attempt. Joan did not, apparently, find the explanation sufficiently mitigating. She filed for divorce.

Arledge's first marriage may indeed have been, as he suspected, a casualty of his impulsive preoccupation with running ABC Sports. But it does not follow that he dwelt solely in a "For-Men-Only" mythos. One of the most striking features of Arledge's TV-sports motif has been its attention to nuance, to subtle drama, to color and style, to all the various human relationships that unfold within the stadium—items of interest normally ascribed to a feminine sensibility. *Monday Night Football,* that male jock's Valhalla, overflows with such detail. Asked how he came to understand the power of this distinct perspective, Arledge recalled: "I had taken Joan to see the Army–Notre Dame football game with me once. Joan hated sports. But in the final thirty seconds of the game, she suddenly asked me if she could borrow my binoculars. I said, 'Hey, wonderful, she's getting interested.' It turned out that she wanted to take a close look at the plumes on the Notre Dame band. Right then, it occurred to me that if you can't get viewers interested in a sporting event as fans, there are other ways."

Shyness was always a hallmark of Arledge's dealings with women; but then, shyness frequently characterized his personal contacts. A female colleague, who liked and admired Arledge, described him as self-conscious in the presence of women. Dick Ebersol believed that the shyness was more general; that much of Arledge's overall isolation from his staff and from subordinates was due to his sense of pain at having constantly to explain, and perhaps justify, himself. The shyness was hardly incompatible with an appetite for power. In fact, Ebersol observed that as Arledge's public reputation grew, and he was less and less obliged to explain himself upon entering a roomful of strangers, his confidence seemed to expand.

Part of this growing assertiveness was reflected in his wardrobe. Arledge gradually shed his careful Ivy-League button-downs for a dress style that amounted to a catalogue of hypermasculine affectations: a veritable armor-plating of gold name bracelets, weighty watches, rings and chains; open-collared shirts in aggressive wide stripes or dots; Montecristo cigars, and slickly polished ankle boots. To this armament he added an appreciation for fine liquor, limousines and foods, and a relish for big-game hunting.

But there was always the airtight self-control. Few people ever knew him to lose his temper. Few people ever *knew* him. Dick Ebersol roomed with Arledge in New York for a few weeks after the divorce from Joan, and recalled that even in that most susceptible of periods, there was scarcely any pouring out of the soul. "I'd come back in from a night on the town and he'd be there with a book," said Ebersol. "Roone, in another life, would have been a writer or an artist. He's an incredible lover of art and nature—he can drive you nuts when he gets going—and he talks about *show*. I can't say I've ever heard Roone talk a lot about himself, in a deeply personal sense. But from talking to him in those days, I came away with insights into television that I fed directly into *Saturday Night Live."*

When Arledge remarried, it was to a beauty queen—Anne Fowler, a former Miss Alabama. Ebersol visited the couple once, at the height of Arledge's power at the top of ABC News and Sports, at their home in Sagaponack, Long Island. He recalled the climate of ease and affection between the two, but he was more struck by a single, oddly moving glimpse of Arledge that forever fixed the man in Ebersol's mind. "I had come out onto the patio to say hello to him," Ebersol said, "and he was sitting with his back to me, facing a strip of white beach that must be among the most beautiful in the world. His head was bowed. I thought he was reading. But when I got up to him I saw that he was looking down at a miniature TV screen on his lap. He'd torn the flaps off a cardboard box for a makeshift sun-shield. He was watching the first college football telecast of the season."

Arledge began to assemble the components for a pilot version of "For Men Only." He called up friends of his, people he had met or heard of in the television business, and talked them into coming over to NBC and helping him give his idea some form. Most of the participants donated their time. The rest Arledge paid out of his own pocket.

For the sports segment, he invited the up-and-coming sportscaster Marty Glickman to narrate a feature on track and field. Robert Rieger, whose powerful line drawings of athletes were then a staple of *Sports Illustrated,* showed up to display some sketches of a Carmen Basilio bout. There was a jazz feature. And for sex appeal, Arledge coaxed a young starlet named Donna Douglas to parade back and forth across the set in a bathing suit. Douglas was later to make her own mark in the medium; she starred for several seasons in *The Beverly Hillbillies,* Jim Aubry's contribution to the New Television at CBS.

As host of the pilot, Arledge might well have selected himself. After all, he personified the male that "For Men Only" would be aiming for. He wore the sharp, rakish clothes, he smoked the pipe, he affected the super-male's glib, confident impresario style, he even had the chin. But Roone Arledge never entertained a moment's wish to be before a television camera. From the very beginning, he understood that his place in video was at the controls. For the host's role he chose a young WRCA weatherman named Pat Hernon. And as things turned out, Arledge could not have made a more fortuitous choice.

This highly tatterdemalion crew, this bunch of players in video's version of a pickup game, assembled one night in 1959 in Studio 8G of

Rockefeller Center. Arledge had coaxed a camera crew, stagehands and technical staff from his superiors. On his own, he had supplied two final, essential components for a successful pilot production: two bottles of scotch, which he doled out to cast and crew. After a couple of rehearsals, and several toasts, the makeshift cast plunged into a half-hour "hot" take of the show for the TV cameras. In the control room of Studio 8G, a film camera recorded a "kinescope" of the production from a live monitor screen. (Videotape was still a few years from general use.)

It wasn't "Masterpiece." But the people who acted in it and the NBC people who later reviewed it recalled being affected by a certain brash energy that flowed out of the show, and also by a sense of novelty: nothing quite like this had been attempted before. It had pacing, it had humor, and it had a distinct, organizing point of view. Emmys had been awarded for less. As they looked at the finished film a few days later, Arledge and Hernon saw that all of this was true. Arledge was impatient to move. He scheduled an appointment with the general manager of WRCA and proudly reeled off the kinescope.

The general manager of WRCA was named George Heinemann. Heinemann was a sweet, plump gently whimsical man—and a factotum in the notorious NBC bureaucracy. In later years, Heinemann would rise through that bureaucracy to the position of vice president for children's programing. He would rise in the classic manner, by exercising tact, restraint and caution, and by not taking undue chances.

So here Heinemann sat, the future kiddie programing czar, looking at a show about jazz music, sports, and a half-naked girl strutting around. Well, George Heinemann *liked* it, but . . . but there was this problem of where to fit the darned thing into the tight WRCA schedule . . . Sorry, he said.

Arledge felt his energy drain out of him. For the second time, a legitimate and distinctive idea of his was sinking into the great bubbling morass of NBC indifference. (Twenty-two years later, asked what he remembered about "For Men Only" George Heinemann smiled and answered mildly, "It was a little ahead of the awareness line . . . I worried about public acceptance . . . it certainly became what everybody's now doing.")

For Arledge, it was beginning to feel as though Shari Lewis's puppet strings were weaving themselves into a net around his career, as though he had wasted two bottles of scotch. But Arledge had forgotten about Pat Hernon. The WRCA weatherman, who had played the host in Arledge's pilot, had become a believer in "For Men Only." If WRCA didn't want it, there were other people Hernon wanted to show it to.

One of them was a guy Hernon had met a few years before, when he was doing a newscast with another station. This guy had been with Dancer Fitzgerald & Sample; he'd had the Falstaff account. He was over doing something with ABC these days. His name was Edgar J. Scherick.

Hernon called up Ed Scherick and persuaded him to take a look at Roone Arledge's kinescope. Scherick agreed. When it was over, Scherick decided that he didn't want "For Men Only", either. But he wanted the man who made it. Scherick wanted Roone Arledge.

"I recognized the talent in Roone as soon as I saw that kinescope," Scherick declared. "I always had an eye for picking people. Maybe more than anything else in life, I'm proudest of my ability for picking men. Some people have a will to power, and others don't. I saw right away that Roone Arledge had a will to power."

If Scherick recognized Arledge's will and talent at once, Arledge recognized redemption when it beckoned. He instantly grasped that ABC was the arena he had been seeking. Most of his peers at NBC, hot young producers on the rise, would have sneered at the prospect of abandoning General Sarnoff's grandiose empire for a seedy little boot-strap outfit like ABC. Not Arledge. He saw that here was an organization without a rigid bureaucracy, without a calcified protocol that limited innovation—without a past, for all practical purposes.

Moreover, Arledge saw that ABC's very lack of an official sports department was a factor in his favor. That particular chain of command had yet to resolve itself. Anyone who got into the liquid system now had a chance to claim real power when things hardened.

Arledge signed on with Scherick as an assistant producer. But he began behaving almost immediately as though he were a part of the policy-making structure. He threw himself into another furious phase of concept-planning, unleashing the same intensity of vision that he had poured into "Masterpiece" and "For Men Only." This time his creation would not sink into some morass of apathy. In the late summer of 1960, a couple of months before ABC's first college football telecast, Roone Arledge placed in Ed Scherick's hands a remarkable memo. And although the memo has never been published before now, its chief arguments—often paraphrased by journalists—quickly became a matter of legend. And justly so. A feverish yet tightly reasoned burst of youthful idealism and exuberance, this document foretold with almost unnerving accuracy the technological and philosophical future of television sports. Most of its key concepts remain operative in the 1980s; in fact, most of its key concepts did not become standard with CBS and NBC until the mid-1970s. Only the advent of microcomputer technology, and the development of superimposed, compressed images within a corner of the videoscreen, have substantially revised Arledge's vision.

Much of Arledge's phrasing in the memo projects the surface image of a charming, earnest but rather callow young go-getter perhaps a trifle too anxious to please his superiors. There is his diverting (but shrewd) prefeminist stab at taking the fair sex's tastes into account ("Women come to football games to . . . see what everyone else is wearing"); there is the playful pun on "fixed cameras" that probably hints at the equipment's unreliability at the time; there is an almost childlike rhapsody as Arledge limns the appeal of romantic students sharing blankets and substitute halfbacks scoring seventy-yard touchdowns and the faces of the clean-cut players—"the pride of America, not hard-bitten old pros."

But underneath all that purplish rhetoric there is a completeness of vision that almost approaches a tableau in a John Dos Passos novel. And there is the ironclad conviction that television, using unheard-of techniques, can somehow capture the tableau. The memo is perhaps the best existing expression of what Ed Scherick perceived as Arledge's "will to power."

The memo's unifying theme, slightly misquoted in the familiar axiom "take the fan to the game, not the game to the fan," is stated in the opening sentence:

> Heretofore, television has done a remarkable job of bringing the game to the viewer—now we are going to take the viewer to the game!!
>
> We will utilize every production technique that has been learned in producing variety shows, in covering political conventions, in shooting travel and adventure series to heighten the viewer's feeling of actually sitting in the stands and participating personally in the excitement and color of walking through a college campus to the stadium to watch the big game. All of these delightful adornments to the actual contest have been missing from previously televised sports events. . . .
>
> To improve upon the audience . . . we must gain and hold the interest of women and others who are not fanatic followers of the sport we happen to be televising. Women come to football games, not so much to marvel at the adeptness of the quarterback in calling an end sweep or a lineman pulling out to lead a play, but to sit in a crowd, see what everyone else is wearing, watch the cheerleaders and experience the countless things that make up the feeling of the

game. Incidentally, very few men have ever switched channels when a nicely proportioned girl was leaping into the air or leading a band down field. . . .

We will utilize six cameras for our basic coverage of the game, but each man will have a complete schedule of additional assignments that will allow him to cover all the other interesting facets of the game when he is not actually engaged in covering a game situation. In addition to our fixed cameras (using the term advisedly) we will have cameras mounted in jeeps, on mike booms, in risers or helicopters, or anything necessary to get the complete story of the game. We will use a "creepy-peepy" camera to get the impact shots that we cannot get from a fixed camera—a coach's face as a man drops a pass in the clear—a pretty cheerleader just after her hero has scored a touchdown—a coed who brings her infant baby to the game in her arms—the referee as he calls a particularly difficult play—a student hawking programs in the stands—two romantic students sharing a blanket late in the game on a cold day—the beaming face of a substitute halfback as he comes off the field after running seventy yards for a touchdown on his first play for the varsity—all the excitement, wonder, jubilation and despair that make this America's Number One sports spectacle and a human drama to match bullfights and heavyweight championships in intensity.

In short—WE ARE GOING TO ADD SHOW BUSINESS TO SPORTS!

In addition to the natural suspense and excitement of the actual game, we have a supply of human drama that would make the producer of a dramatic show drool. All we have to do is find and insert it in our game coverage at the proper moment. And this we will do!

The moment we take to the air, we will start making the viewer feel he is at the game. Instead of the hackneyed slide to introduce the telecast, we will attempt to video tape a college cheering card section or a great college band spelling out NCAA FOOTBALL on a football field; and after our opening commercial billboards, instead of dissolving to the usual pan shots of the field, we will have pre-shot film of the campus and the stadium so we can orient the viewer. He must know he is in Columbus, Ohio, where the town is football mad; or that he is part of a small but wildly enthusiastic crowd at Corvallis, Oregon. He must know where in the country he is, what part of the town, what the surrounding country and the campus look like, how many other people are watching this game with him, how the people dress at football games in a particular part of the country and what the game means to the two schools involved. While the color man is setting the scene, after we get to the stadium, we will see people parking cars, possibly a group picnicking on the back of a station wagon before entering the field and still others getting their programs from the student ushers at the gates.

Then the viewer must meet the players—but he will meet them as he would if he were at the game. This will be accomplished by using a blowup of the cover of the actual game program and introducing the individual players by means of pictures of them in their normal street attire. These are enthusiastic college kids—the pride of America, not hard-bitten old pros—and we want everyone to know this.

The camera men who will be using long zoom lenses will have wide angle lenses attached for the pre-kickoff color and scene setting shots. They will have time to get back to their game lenses before kickoff. This will be an enjoyable show to work on, but it will not be the place for lazy cameramen, directors, stage managers or anyone trying to accomplish his job the easy way. The announcers will be as familiar with the college town, the players on the two teams, the relative merits of the teams involved, the traditions surrounding the game and the type of people involved in it as the most enthusiastic undergraduate actually present at the game.

We will use video tape recorders to enable us to replay the decisive plays of the first half during the half-time break. . . .

The audio man must know just when the referee is liable to speak so that he can open the pot from the remote mike we will try to have him wear. . . .

The personal satisfaction in such an undertaking will be great. We will be setting the standards that everyone will be talking about and that others in the industry will spend years trying to equal.

How true.

Beyond the practical purposes of the memo—it was distributed among prospective advertisers to whip up enthusiasm for sponsorship, and it also amounted to a successful job application for NCAA producer by Roone Arledge—it also aimed at drawing a distinction between the new ABC TV sports coverage and the flat, passive approach that had been standard up to that time. But given all the celebratory attention that its unifying theme has received over the years, surprisingly few people have noticed that Arledge really did have the thought backwards.

The effect of all his conceptual insights was, in a profound sense, to "take the game to the fan." An Arledge sports telecast saturated the small living-room screen with a rapid, eclectic and intimate barrage of images of a volume that no fan, however tireless, could ever hope to duplicate by actually going "to the game."

Arledge's reference to the "creepy-peepy" had an ironic touch, by the way. This cumbersome, hand-held camera (it actually required three people to hold it) had been developed by NBC News for the 1956 Republican National Convention. Its first telecast image was a dramatic shot of Thomas E. Dewey coldly eyeing his inter-party rival, Senator Everett Dirksen of Illinois, as Dirkson orated from the podium. Under Arledge, the "creepy-peepy" would become a standard component of a sports telecast, and would one day evolve into the mini-cam.

The original guiding genius behind the "creepy-peepy" was that implacable enemy of TV sports, Reuven Frank.

Ed Scherick was impressed—as who could fail to be—with Arledge's memo. Largely because of it, he awarded Arledge his first stripes: the young romanticizer of coeds with babies and beaming substitute halfbacks would produce NCAA football on ABC.

Arledge was twenty-nine years old on the afternoon of September 17, 1960, when he produced the first sporting event of his career—a telecast that forever separated ABC from the past. The site was the American Legion Stadium in Birmingham, Alabama, where Bear Bryant's Crimson Tide was to meet the Georgia Bulldogs.

Everyone in the ABC contingent had the jitters. "It was a group of people who'd never worked together under live broadcast conditions before," remembered Chuck Howard, who was a production assistant to Arledge. "Curt Gowdy, our announcer, had never done a game with Paul Christman, the color man. Bill Bennington, the director in the truck, had never worked at ABC Sports. We'd even tried to do a rehearsal game the Friday before, to take our cameras and equipment over to a high-school football game, but the game was rained out. So here were all these people, strangers, that Scherick had brought together, and the pressure was on us not to let down the network after it had staked all the money on the NCAA. And on top of that, here was Roone bringing a whole new concept of sports coverage to television in the very first assignment he ever had. Before us, NBC had just opened the lenses on its cameras and then closed them again after the game. And now here we came with stuff people had never seen: all kinds of crowd reaction shots. I remember the day before the game, I'd driven Gowdy over to record an interview with Bear Bryant. Bear talked for forty-five minutes about what a poor, sorry little team his Alabama boys were. Hell, Alabama went out and tore Georgia's ass. Bryant thought *he* had troubles."

Tom Moore had invited a whole delegation of in-laws from Meridian, Mississippi, up to Birmingham for the occasion: his two sisters and their husbands, and also his own wife. Moore had planned to sit in the stands with these good folks and enjoy the game and let his sports people take care of their duties without the added pressure of his official presence. But at the last minute, Tom Moore couldn't stand it any longer. He excused himself and squeezed his way back through the fans wending their way into American Legion Stadium and made for the ABC truck.

Perhaps Moore had psyched himself, as much as any of his subordinates, during an emotional speech to the ABC coverage crew in New York just before everyone disembarked for Alabama.

"I got 'em in my office and I said to them, '*Lissen*—we do not want to do a football game like NBC," Moore remembered. "'I want to see the good-looking gals! The chrysanthemums! The cheerleaders! The fans! The players sitting on the bench! I want to see the apprehension of the guy about to go into the game! I want to see the head coach pacing! I want you to capture the story of the moment!'"

Years later, Tom Moore swore that the speech had come directly from his own heart, that he had drawn on his own feelings as a sports fan and his newspaperman's instinct for color and detail—that his exhortation was, in short, the video equivalent of Knute Rockne's "Win-one-for-the-Gipper" harangue of the 1920s. In his excitement, it never dawned on Moore that he was in fact delivering a highly compressed précis of Roone Arledge's memo.

As for Ed Scherick—a fidgety man in the calmest of circumstances—his demeanor that day made Tom Moore look, by comparison, like Thomas Aquinas. "Scherick was all over everybody," Jim Spence remembered. "He was all over Gowdy and Christman, he was all over Roone. Roone finally turned to Ed and said—imagine the guts this took, from a twenty-nine-year-old kid, just hired—"*You gotta stay out of the booth!*' Ed just said, 'OK.'" Spence chuckled at the memory. "But it killed Ed to be away from the action. I remember two or three weeks later, when we're in Lawrence, Kansas, and Ed is *still* under banishment. So he walks over to this building near the stadium, a university office building, and he just walks in and starts combing the rooms until he finds one with a TV set. He turns the set to the game and sits down in the empty chair behind the desk. A few minutes later, somebody knocks on the door. Scherick yells, '*Quiet, quiet!*' The guy knocks again and Scherick yells, 'Goddammit, I'm trying to concentrate on the telecast!' So finally the guy bursts into the room and finds Scherick behind the desk and almost *throttles* him. It's the athletic director! Scherick is sitting in the goddamn athletic director's office!"

That was typical of the involvement that Ed Scherick brought to his tenure at ABC Sports. The revolution was most definitely here now; the guns were blazing, and Scherick was in the middle of it, smelling the powder and rallying the troops.

But on September 17, in Birmingham, Alabama, there was really only one controlling presence. People who witnessed Arledge's dominion over the ABC control truck that afternoon still speak of it with a kind of self-conscious humor in their voices, as though they remain unconvinced that they saw what they saw, and would rather not dwell on it, or take it too seriously.

Arledge ran that telecast as if he stood before a video control panel all his life—ordering up tightly framed camera shots of athletes in unguarded moments, shots that no one had ever seen on American television before, integrating the standard game-action shots with novel closeup glimpses of fans and cheerleaders and players on the sidelines, now panning back for the establishing ambience, now swooping close for the intimate glimpse.

It was as though Arledge stood at the controls of some private spaceship, and everyone else had wandered aboard—strangers at first, but integrated into a smoothly functioning unit by the game's end. It was an otherworldly performance: the twenty-nine-year-old kid simply had no established tradition to draw from as he worked. When it was over, every man in the ABC truck that day knew he had been looking at the future.

Just as Edgar Scherick had broken a mold by making Dizzy Dean the real star of the Falstaff *Game of the Week* seven years before, Roone Arledge now stood in the ABC mobile truck in Birmingham, Alabama, and calmly broke Scherick's mold. Now the real star of the show was ABC itself. Curt Gowdy and Paul Christman may have been calling the play-by-play, establishing the framework of their own great vogue through the sixties, but in the end, it was ABC that people would remember when they talked about TV football. Arledge was demolishing the implicit proscenium stage that had always separated the TV cameras from their subject matter. From now on, any ABC telecast of a sporting event stood to be a bigger event than the sport on the field.

Bear Bryant's "poor little" Alabama team won that ABC inaugural, defeating Georgia 21–6. The Georgia hero would one day work for Roone Arledge on the ABC airwaves: an unorthodox, scrambling young quarterback and team captain named Fran Tarkenton. Tarkenton would go on to illuminate many an ABC *Monday Night Football* telecast in the 1970s as the signal-caller for the Minnesota Vikings. And he would later ascend to a performer's role within ABC as an MNF announcer and as a host of the prime-time show *That's Incredible!* Just as that 1958 pro championship game on NBC had showcased three future TV-announcing personalities (Gifford, Summerall and Unitas), so this TV-landmark collegiate game discovered its own embryonic video star. The medium it seemed, was indeed the message, and the message was sports.

XIII

MADE-FOR-TV FOOTBALL

I n 1960 and 1961, riding the crest of their own long-shot adventurism, Ed Scherick and Tom Moore revised the universe of sports, television and audiences for all time by introducing two unprecedented program experiments on the ABC airwaves. These two experiments, and the great flow of programing forms that they unleashed, permanently reversed the dynamics that had connected athletic events to their audiences. They were telecasts of the new American Football League, which began in the fall of 1960, and *Wide World of Sports,* which premiered the following April.

Before *Wide World* and the AFL, television had selected the games and events and bouts it carried on the basis of pre-established public interest. TV sports had been a passive illumination of what people already cared about. Television did not invent the Rose Bowl or introduce Americans to the heavyweight boxing championship or generate the money necessary to form the National League. Television responded to an existing demand.

But now Scherick, Moore and ABC broke that passive pattern. With *Wide World* and the AFL, they made a seminal discovery: that instead of telecasting events because people were interested in them, they could make people interested in events *because they were on television.* In the years following this breakthrough, television would become an active, agenda-setting force in America's relationship with athletics—and with the styles, economics, political dynamics and moral values that devolved from that relationship as well.

Television's power to stimulate a mass following for a sport simply by airing it never became absolute, of course. Professional ice hockey and soccer are two prime examples of sports that could not penetrate the public's capacity to care (although in each of these sports, there was an important structural problem: the relative scarcity of breaks in the action made it difficult for sponsors to receive adequate time for their commercials). But if it wasn't absolute, that power was still enormous. *Wide World of Sports,* extravagantly successful in its own right, formed a kind of elite division-within-a-division: it became a training and experimental laboratory for the most promising of ABC's young cameramen, producers, directors, logistical staff and on-air talent. Beginning in 1964, Roone Arledge was able to transfer this well-drilled cadre, along with the *Wide World* methodology itself, to ABC's coverage of the Olympics, an international event that the vast majority of Americans had previously shown little inclination to follow.

The American Football League was not an instant success—artistically, financially, or as a television attraction. It never really took root on ABC; in fact, NBC—which took over its contract in 1965—can claim the AFL as one of its few success stories in sports programing of the sixties. Still, it was ABC, alone among the networks, that had dared unveil the first utterly self-contained professional sports league that had been formed with the expectation of surviving on television revenues. Other "instant" leagues would soon follow: the American Basketball Association, the World Hockey Association, the World Football League, World Team Tennis. Existing professional leagues were emboldened, if not provoked by alarm, to extend their empires, establishing franchises and building new stadiums in cities where no intrinsic demand for a major-league team had ever made itself known. If the fans weren't there, the TV cameras would be, along with the check for the rights.

The burgeoning of professional teams in America created happiness and pleasure for hundreds of thousands of fans; of that there is no doubt. And there was something irrepressibly American, something close to the country's zany entrepreneurial optimism, about all those ice hockey teams in the red-hot Sun Belt, all those black, Eastern-urban professional basketball players in the white-bread Pacific Northwest, all those blue-collar crowds hooting and whistling for their local WTT squad in Cleveland or Honolulu or Indianapolis—all those Jets and Nets and Sets, those Kentucky Colonels and Condors and Chaparrals, those Boston Lobsters and New England Whalers and Sharks and Fighting Saints; those Detroit Wheels and that Portland Storm and that Chicago Fire and that Southern California Sun.

But underneath the delight and all the sudden local booster pride, there emerged a second mood as the years went on; a sense of hollowness and transience. Sometimes the television money held up in these new instant leagues; more often, it did not. (World Team Tennis lost its TV package almost as soon as the league was formed, in 1974.) Foldings, bankruptcies and mergers became the punishment for failing sufficiently to please television's red eye. By the end of the 1970s, the professional sports map of America resembled one of those endless commercial boulevards that stretch outward from the old central cities; a boulevard chockablock with gaudily colored franchise logos and marquees, each logo a study in stylized good cheer. But many of the franchises were boarded up; many of the surviving ones were starving for trade; the several successful giants were glutted by traffic, and all the customers looked a bit glazed, a bit harried, as though they had still not quite found a place where they wanted to sit down and linger awhile.

Wide World of Sports, the American Football League and the lineal descendants of both proved that, to a very large extent, the paying customers—the turnstile fans—didn't matter anymore. Or, if they mattered, it was largely as ambience, as unpaid, in fact paying, extras in the vast super-studios of the 1970s that had once been known as stadiums.

For by that decade, the center of financial support for virtually every important professional and amateur athletic activity had shifted—from revenues generated by ticketholders at the stadiums and arenas to the rights fees awarded by networks and big independent stations. Automobile racing, rodeos, wrist-wrestling championships and tournament bass fishing were among the few exceptions to this brave new rule.

The American Football League was a "studio" sport in that practically no one watched it (at least in its early years) except on television. The fact that fans showed up in stadium seats at all was a matter of mild astonishment—if not a certain inconvenience to ABC technicians, who tended to charge out on to the various fields of play, still wearing their headset phones and trailing their input cords, to berate the referee for signaling the kickoff before the commercial had ended. ("Aaaaaaaaaaand a *fan* has run out on the field, disrupting the game," Jack Buck would intone into the play-by-play microphone, and silently rub his hand over his eyes.

The AFL was organized—if that is quite the word—in 1959, after a long and intermittent series of other attempts to form a second pro football league, beginning as early as 1926, had ended up in financial pratfalls. ABC did not *create* the American Football League; the league actually more or less thought itself up and then came calling on ABC. But there is no question that the venture would never have made it past the late-night, scotch-on-the-rocks, "what if?" stage had it not been for the guarantee of network television revenues.

NFL afficionados sneeringly called it "The Mickey Mouse League," a singularly appropriate defilement for a league televised by the same people who offered *The Mickey Mouse Club* and *Disneyland*. Its formative years were one long comic opera of slapstick feuds, phantom finances, quick name changes, franchise shifts and wildly undisciplined, high-scoring games played in seedy ballparks before empty seats. One team, the Raiders, played its home games either in Candlestick Park in San Francisco or in Kezar Stadium in Oakland. Team publicity signboards urged fans to "Follow the Raiders," but as Arthur Daley of *The New York Times* sourly noted, it was hard enough to *find* the Raiders, much less follow them. For a few hilarious years, it appeared that made-for-TV sport was an abomination in the eyes of the fans, and that the natural order of the universe would soon reassert itself.

And then the New York Jets drafted a quarterback named Joe Namath, and made-for-TV sports made a seminal turn from Mickey Mouse toward Super Bowl.

If the old Chicago Cardinals had only done what H. L. Hunt's kid *wanted* them to do—let him buy the team—the American Football League would not have been necessary. But no. They wouldn't let the Texas boy in on their game. So Lamar, the son of the Dallas oil billionaire, did what any rejected neighborhood tyke would do—but on a somewhat grander scale. "I got to thinking," he explained years later, "that if there were these other people trying to get into football, maybe we could start our own league."

J. R. Ewing could not have put it better. "These other people" included Barron Hilton of Los Angeles, Billy Sullivan of Boston, K. S. (Bud) Adams of Houston—and a transcendently neurotic, fast-talking entrepreneur, sports owner and sometime radio play-by-play man named Harry Wismer.

Wismer had called pro football games in Detroit and New York, and at one time owned part of the Washington Redskins. The ever-charitable Red Barber reported that Wismer "used to announce on the network that 'there is my friend Dwight Eisenhower,' or 'there is my friend Bernard Baruch,' or any other name that came to mind."* Apparently

---

*Red Barber. *The Broadcasters*. N.Y.: Dial Press, 1970.

one of Wismer's real friends was Lamar Hunt. When Hunt's wealthy playmates decided that not even they could establish a new professional sports league without the guarantee of television revenues, Hunt selected Wismer to be the "point" man in negotiations with the networks.

CBS was out. CBS already carried the NFL. Wismer approached NBC—and was met with politely muffled chuckles. That left one network.

Lamar Hunt decided to play every possible angle in approaching ABC. Hunt knew that Leonard Goldenson had borrowed money from the Metropolitan Life Insurance Company when Goldenson was acquiring ABC. So Hunt prevailed upon a Metropolitan executive named Harry Hagerty to approach Goldenson. Goldenson listened, shrugged, and referred Hagerty to Tom Moore. Moore summoned his redoubtable sidekick, Ed Scherick. Lamar Hunt sent Wismer back into the game. A meeting was arranged at Wismer's extravagant New York apartment.

Now, among Harry Wismer's many neurotic conceits was that he was under surveillance: "they" were keeping an eye on him. So Wismer urged the participants in the meeting—millionaires Hunt, Hilton, Adams, Sullivan, ABC executives Moore and Scherick—to pussyfoot it to his place singly, at staggered times, and to arrive by circuitous routes. On this rational note, negotiations for the TV rights to the American Football League began.

Wismer explained that the AFL would be a "television" league in more ways than one. Its teams would play under rules tailor-made for maximum video effect. Players receiving punts would not have the option of signaling a "fair catch" (no tackling in exchange for no runback). A team would have the option of running or passing for a two-point conversion after a touchdown. And players' names would be printed on the backs of their jerseys. Wismer then told the ABC people that the AFL expected $600,000 from the network for each telecast. Tom Moore, in his deferential, elfin Southern manner, countered that ABC might consider a payment of $250,000.

Harry Wismer leaped to his feet, the absolute picture of violated dignity. He announced that he could not be a party to this level of meaningless bargaining, spun on his heel, and (even though it was his apartment) made a show of storming out.

Unaccountably, given that it was, in fact, Harry Wismer's own apartment, Wismer yanked open the wrong door and stormed directly into his own broom closet. This error took a certain edge off Wismer's high dudgeon. Nevertheless, the evening lay in ruins; there was very little more to say. The participants took their leave—one at a time, presumably, and traveling by circuitous routes—and for a few weeks it seemed that yet another American Football League had fallen by the wayside, or at least into the broom closet.

But the light of reason was slowly dawning on Lamar Hunt. It occurred to him one day that, even allowing for frequently inexplicable Eastern manners, Harry Wismer might not be perhaps the quintessential choice as the spokesperson for the millionaires' group. The Texan turned to another influential New Yorker—an urbane show-business promoter named David (Sonny) Werblin. Werblin and Tom Moore met for a calm, noncircuitous dinner at "21" and reached an agreement on a five-year contract between ABC and the AFL. The network would pay each team $170,000 a year, with escalating clauses. That sum represented survival money for each team. It also represented something even more significant, in the long run. The key phrase here was "each team." In agreeing to distribute ABC's revenues *equally* among the clubs, regardless of individual merit, Werblin and Moore hit upon a TV rights prototype that would later be adopted by the NFL. And when the two leagues merged in 1966 under Commissioner Pete Rozelle, this pooling arrangement would be the cornerstone of a sports dynasty that one observer would call "the perfect socialist system." On the other side of the coin, the networks' commercial revenues from NFL telecasts would establish pro football as the most profitable venture in the history of TV sports—the difference between profit and loss for each network sports division.

The original AFL franchises were in Dallas, Denver, Houston, Los Angeles, Minneapolis, New York, Buffalo and Boston. But it wasn't that simple. In 1960, well before the first nonfair catch of an AFL punt, Minneapolis excused itself from the league and applied for membership in the NFL. This prompted Harry Wismer, by now the owner of the New York franchise, the Titans, to blurt out to Max Winter, the Minneapolis owner, "You know, Max, every time I see you at the supper table, I can't help think how admirably you fill the role of Judas." Oakland, meanwhile, filled the role of Minneapolis. Time passed. Los Angeles moved to San Diego. Lamar Hunt once again took his own football and went elsewhere; this time to Kansas City, where he wouldn't have to look across town and see the Dallas Cowboys. Aging and unwanted NFL stars began to drift into the new league, where they were welcomed—men like George Blanda and Jack Kemp, in what may have been Kemp's first experiment with supply-side economics.

And the games went on. Jack Buck, an ironic and enormously popular announcer out of St. Louis, recalled the strangeness of the early days. "When Scherick hired me, I'd been doing nothing but major-league baseball for years," he said. "I hadn't done football since 1951, when I was a student in Columbus, Ohio. The first AFL game I called—it was the LA Chargers at Oakland—I was so bad that they fired my color man, Jack Denebey. Before the game I'd gone up to the Oakland coach for an interview. He said, 'I don't have time to talk to you. Go down and talk to that man. I do the same thing he does.' He was pointing to Sid Gillman, the LA coach. Gillman told me more than the other guy. He told me to get the hell out of there."

Buck recalled games in which Harry Wismer of the Titans tried to borrow shoulder pads from the opposing clubs; in which coaches directed their teams without the benefit of playbooks. "The AFL could never have played on AstroTurf," Buck remarked, "because they couldn't have drawn their plays on the ground."

Buck announced an AFL game in Candlestick Park in which the wind blew so hard—or so he swore—that a field-goal kicker saw his attempt pinwheel straight down the field, then stop dead and blow sideways into the stands. There were games played in weather so cold that the instruments stuck to the band's lips; games played before audiences so small that the ABC directors would beseech all the fans to sit on the same side of the field, so that the video picture would not look so dismally lonesome. Once, ABC broke off a Titans–Dallas Texans telecast to join *Disneyland.* Perfect.

The ratings never did develop when the AFL was a product of ABC. The telecasts were buried on Sundays by CBS's National Football League offerings; and ABC's own promotional efforts were geared more toward Roone Arledge's NCAA football on Saturdays than the fledgling pro league.

In 1963, Sonny Werblin stepped back into the picture and tried to restore order. He formed a syndicate that purchased the Titans from Wismer's inept and bankrupt group, and renamed the team the Jets. Werblin was a close friend of NBC television president Robert Kintner. Werblin knew that Kintner lusted after a professional football TV package. In 1964 Werblin learned that Kintner had failed, as Kintner and NBC routinely failed, to outbid CBS for NFL rights. (This was the year of Pete Rozelle's $37.6-million two-year coup.)

Sonny Werblin, by contrast, was not quite so dewy-eyed. Not that Sonny Werblin had any illusions about obtaining a $14.1-million jackpot. On the other hand, ABC's existing meager terms set him running off into imaginary broom closets. Werblin was the owner who would very shortly usher in the era of the athlete-as-Byzantine-monarch. So now he had to bankroll his league, but good. He contacted Bob Kintner's new sports president, Carl Lindemann, and told him that NBC could bid on the American Football League—if the bid were $42 million over five years. That amounted to a sum five times greater than what ABC was paying.

When Lindemann's head cleared, he phoned Kintner and asked his boss for permission to write such a check. Kintner granted it. When Tom Moore at ABC was informed of the amount, he simply shrugged and drawled that the AFL people would be out of their minds to refuse such a deal. When it came to a test of big money against big money, ABC was still hopelessly overmatched; the network still had to rely on its wits, nerve and opportunism, conjuring up sports packages where none had seemed to exist.

Sonny Werblin soon had a chance to deploy some of that NBC bonanza in a blitzkrieg assault on the mighty National Football League for the right to sign up the best emerging college stars. A blue-eyed, Roman-nosed, slightly stoop-shouldered Pennsylvania kid who had played some quarterback for Bear Bryant at Alabama became eligible for the professional draft in 1965. Everybody seemed to want Joe Namath— several males included, who were interested in his football talents. Namath was drafted by the St. Louis Cardinals in the NFL and by Werblin's Jets in the AFL. The first major bidding war in TV sports history soon developed. So legendary were Namath's quarterbacking skills that one St. Louis newspaper sports editor, unable to contain his visions of Gateway City glory, pleaded with the members of his staff to send postcards of "wish-you-were-here" encouragement to Namath— signed with their uncles' names, so that it wouldn't look like a campaign.

It is questionable, of course, whether the free-spirited Namath could have found—how does one say it—personal fulfillment among St. Louis's mythological uncles and posh eateries with names like Mrs. Hullings. (Would he have been known as "DeBalivier Boulevard Joe"?) The question was rendered forever moot when Werblin flashed Namath his most winning Broadway smile, and held under it a check in the amount of four hundred thousand dollars. Per year. Such a sum would scarcely cover a modern superstar's agent fees, but in 1964 it was the Louisiana Purchase. Amidst howls that Werblin had turned professional football into a *profession,* for God's sake, Namath put on a green number 12, a pair of white football shoes, and formed—along with golfer Arnold Palmer—the first generation of TV-developed athlete-celebrities.

XIV

BRAVE NEW WIDE WORLD

Ed Scherick invented *Wide World of Sports* for much the same reason that A. Craig Smith had invented the *Gillette Cavalcade of Sports* nearly twenty years before: economic necessity. Like Smith, Scherick felt no particular calling to create some kind of sports crucible for American TV. Like Smith, Scherick was not even a sports fan, his good times with Dizzy Dean notwithstanding. His daydreams were lately drifting toward theater and the movies—*producing* theater and movies, not watching them. His reasons for wanting this show were strategic; they were the reasons of an advertising man.

Like Craig Smith, Scherick wanted a low-budget, regularly scheduled weekly showcase that would attract and retain sponsors. It had to feature events that did not yield to the "blackout" rules that prohibited telecasts of several big-time sports into cities where stadium attendance might be affected. And it had to be on the air all year. As things stood, ABC had no sports presence in the second quarter of its broadcast schedule—the months from April through July. But it was essential to keep ABC's image closely intertwined with sports, to continue the momentum that had been established in the previous fall's NCAA telecasts. Ed Scherick wanted to create an omnibus format that would attract and hold its own following, no matter what the event.

There were two interesting problems connected with this wish. One was that Scherick had no money to spend on such a program. And he could not count on ABC to give him any. ABC was still a relatively poor network; the standing rule for sports was that no event could be purchased and committed to an air schedule unless it had already been sold to advertisers. The other problem was that even if Scherick had the money to spend, it wasn't at all clear what he would spend that money on.

Boxing—the sport that had floated the *Gillette Cavalcade*—was out; it was both oversaturated and in disgrace. Blackouts aside, there was no football in the spring; no basketball—the NBA, an obscure entity outside the East, was just finishing up its season—and the big-leaguers were in spring training. Besides, Scherick couldn't afford events on that level, fifty-two weeks a year.

Ed Scherick thought of the Amateur Athletic Union. The AAU was the national governing body for amateur track and field events. It had been around since 1888, and was one of the oldest sports organizations in America. The AAU organized and sanctioned meets; it kept records and set standards; and it did one other thing: it funneled the best young runners and swimmers and jumpers and javelin throwers into tryouts for the United States Olympic team.

None of which cut a large amount of ice with the great mass of American fans. Track and field was somehow a little *European* for American tastes. The United States had its track heroes; it had its devoted specialist-fans who could pack big stadiums for major events. But in the main, Americans liked to see their athletes square off against one another. *Games* were what Americans related to, and a little blood was not entirely unwelcome. Stopwatches and tape measures were a bit abstract for a country that had, not that many decades before, regarded eye-gouging and cockfighting and bareknuckle boxing as acceptable spectator sports.

In January 1961, Scherick summoned Roone Arledge to his office. The AAU was holding its annual board of governors meeting in New York. What would Arledge think of dropping by that meeting, flashing the old ABC colors, pressing a little flesh and—if the general mood seemed just right, getting the out-of-towners to sign away their TV rights for the cheapest amount Arledge could negotiate?

Arledge thought it sounded just great, and headed off for the convention's hotel headquarters. Scherick watched him leave with mixed feelings. Arledge deserved the assignment because he was a bright, promising and gifted young producer. But the real reason Scherick had chosen Arledge to represent ABC before the stout, heartland men of the Amateur Athletic Union was that—as Scherick said years later—"Roone was a gentile and I was not." In 1961, in the sporting world, those things made a difference. Ask Melvin Allen Israel.

Ed Scherick may have felt a deep private resentment that he could not personally engineer the crucial business deal for his own television show. But Scherick was possessed with a Midas touch in those years. Even in delegating authority, he caused dynasties. Arledge not only consummated a fabulous rights deal with the AAU—fifty thousand dollars for *all* their events—but he also began to form an interest in that organization, and the sports it governed, that led to his eventual obssession with creating ABC's Olympics telecasts.

The next order of business was to line up sponsors. ABC's programing division would not let Scherick's people move ahead with plans for the new show without sponsors. But there was a catch here: without detailed plans for a show, how were Scherick and Arledge to attract sponsors? What was there to say—"We have some AAU track meets we'd like for you to get behind"? Advertisers would want to know why a bunch of skinny men in spiked shoes and no socks would make for great network television each week. What kind of format? What announcers? How did ABC know it would work? Why are you coming to us with this?

Scherick thought he knew all the answers, but in a vague and inexpressible sort of way. Not in any way that would convince an advertising man. And Scherick was an advertising man. Now he would have to try to put pressure on men who thought exactly as he did; tough, shrewd, coldly pragmatic men who understood everything, including romantic visions—especially romantic visions—in cost-benefit terms.

Scherick would speak to these hard people in terms they could comprehend. He gave Arledge a list of agency people and their telephone numbers, and he himself sat down with a similar list. Reduced to its essential thrust, the message he and Arledge delivered was this: we have a new sports show coming up in April, and here is why you will want to advertise on it. If you do, we will let you continue to advertise on NCAA football next fall. It was not exactly "reach out and touch someone," this telephone campaign. And as the winter weeks of 1961 progressed, the advertising community responded with approximately the warmth that the proposition itself implied. Some bristled and refused. Some clenched their teeth and came aboard, because their clients badly wanted to be affiliated with college football. Most decided that they would just wait and see. Among these sponsors was the giant R. J. Reynolds Company.

February gave way to March. A few more sponsors shrugged and tumbled into line. But still not enough. ABC Programing issued a deadline to Scherick: have every commercial minute of this show committed by March 31, or forget about it. The idea will be dropped. By the third week of March, there seemed to be little hope of this coming about.

And then A. Craig Smith and Gillette came roaring back into the picture for one last decisive intervention in the course of American television sports. It was something of an accident, really. No matter. In the end, Gillette was there when needed, and the company helped save the fortunes of *Wide World of Sports.*

Gillette had orginally earmarked about thirty thousand dollars of its advertising budget for a CBS show called *Sports Spectacular,* which ran for a few weeks in the late winter. Gillette's agency, Maxon, even went so far as to notify CBS sales that it would purchase thirty thousand dollars' worth of time. But when a CBS salesman, forever anonymous, heard that a minute of *Sports Spectacular's* time was still available, he leaked the word to a close friend of his at the agency that handled Rise shaving cream. Rise owned an option on that minute, but had decided against exercising it. Hearing that a rival company wanted that time, however, Rise reversed itself, bought the minute—and left Gillette with thirty thousand dollars in its hand and nowhere to spend it.

Gillette took its money to Ed Scherick at ABC. The date of that decision happened to be the last day of March, 1961. On the same day, R. J. Reynolds made up its mind to take a chance on the unnamed, unstaffed, unwritten program. Thus it was that at 4:30 P.M. of March 31, 1961, Ed Scherick burst into Tom Moore's office and shouted, "It's a go!"

The CBS salesman's act of favoritism to his friend at Rise, a thirty-thousand-dollar betrayal, was a godsend to ABC. In 1982, *Wide World of Sports* returned $180 million to ABC's revenues.

Scherick had his fifty-two-weeks-a-year show. Since the first air date was less than a month away, his superiors at ABC indicated that it might be appropriate to add a title, a host, and some working idea of exactly what it was the show would be about.

Chet Simmons hit on the show's title. *Wide World of Sports* was not terribly original; it played off the *Wide, Wide World* umbrella title then in vogue at NBC. But beyond that, it suited Scherick's purposes exactly. His new show would cover the wide world. If ABC could not afford to compete regularly for the high-profile live sporting events available in the United States, then Scherick would steer ABC on an end run around the live-action concept. He would exploit two of the 1960s' newest technologies to aid him in this plan: commercial jet travel and videotape.

Scherick had run the numbers. He knew that it would be far cheaper for him to send a small and tightly organized production crew out across the United States, even across the *world,* covering an eclectic assortment of games and competitions, than it would be to buy rights to established events. Since the rights for these out-of-the-way competitions would be either nominal or nonexistent, the show's budget could absorb the travel costs. Since no viewer would likely have independent access to the competitions Scherick had in mind—AAU events as a base, but also steeplechases, cliff-diving in Acapulco, rodeos, demolition derbies, log-rolling championships—it would be safe to record them on videotape for delayed broadcast, without the audience knowing the results in advance.

After consulting with Tom Moore, Scherick drew up some strict guidelines for *Wide World* events. Among other things, the events had to be "legitimate"—that is, they had to mean something to the participants other than a chance to appear on television. And each event had to be clearly and decisively resolved in the show. No "demonstrations" or "exhibitions" of athletic prettiness. There had to be winners and losers.

So *Wide World* would come cheap. But a crucial question remained: Would anybody watch it? If the American viewing public manifested an overwhelming ability not to give a damn which Mexican urchin could jump off the Acapulco cliffs most adroitly, or which stock car was left running at the end of half an hour of willful collisions, or which cowboy could bind and gag a steer the quickest, all on videotape, for God's sake, and Scherick had no doubts that the American public possessed this ability, well, then, it really didn't matter how cheap *Wide World's* budget would be. Because *Wide World* would be off the air.

The truth was that Scherick had no real idea whether this show would succeed. It was so pasted-together, so absolutely improvised, and the air date for its premiere was drawing so close that he scarcely had time to think about it. Scherick thought, and Tom Moore agreed, that if *Wide World of Sports* had a chance, it would come from the ability of Arledge to invest it with something that was greater than the sum of its week-to-week curiosities and baroque games. Arledge would produce the show. Chuck Howard would assist him. Scherick was still impressed with the unique aura of continuity that Arledge had been able to blend into those NCAA telecasts—that sense of a story playing toward its denouement. Arledge would have to find a way to duplicate that illusion in the vastly more challenging format of *Wide World of Sports*.

And in the meantime, Arledge would have to find himself an announcer.

It was raining in Augusta, Georgia, on a Sunday afternoon in early April, when a steward in the clubhouse of the Augusta National Golf Club announced a long-distance telephone call for Jim McKay.

Jim McKay (his original name was Jim McManus) was covering the

Masters Golf Tournament for CBS television for a fee of five hundred
dollars. McKay had been with CBS for eleven years—hosting local
entertainment shows, sometimes singing, sometimes interviewing
Roller Derby queens, announcing five-minute sports summaries, even
serving as host to a mock-courtroom trial series called *The Verdict Is
Yours,* recording five programs on a given weekend via the new process
called videotape.

But sportscasting was his real love, and the Masters was the best
assignment of his career. If he did well, he might advance quickly up
the CBS ladder—not because the American public would demand him;
the American public wasn't watching; hardly anybody watched golf
tournaments on TV—but because the founder of CBS, William Paley
himself, was watching. Golf was William Paley's idea of a sporting
event. He put the Masters tourney on his airwaves as a favor to his
personal friend, Cliff Roberts, the tournament chairman. So Jim
McKay wanted to do well for Bill Paley. And the final round was just
getting under way. And here came a goddamned long-distance telephone
call for him in the clubhouse.

The call was actually from *two* people—Roone Arledge and Chet
Simmons, both on the line, both yelling at him. They told Jim McKay
that ABC had this new show getting under way and they wanted to
know if he'd like to host it.

Jim McKay looked out the window toward the course. It looked as
though someone was getting ready to tee off. He wanted to get rid of this
call—but he wanted to hear more, too.

On the other end, Arledge and Simmons were yelling at McKay that
they should warn him, the job would involve a certain amount of travel.

"Around the country?" McKay asked, half his attention still on the
golfers outside.

"Around the world," Arledge yelled. Now McKay began to give them
his full attention.

He asked for a certain salary. To his astonishment, the figure was
accepted. He asked for time to think it over; anyway, he had to go cover
the final round of the Masters.

"You've got to let us know," Arledge screamed at him. "We've scheduled a press conference announcing you as the host in half an hour!"

McKay accepted.

Chuck Howard recalled later why the ABC group had decided to
query McKay. "He was more than an announcer," Howard said. "He
was articulate; he wrote his own stuff. Plus," Howard added reason-
ably, "he was available."

Having raided CBS for an announcer, the *Wide World* contingent now raided NBC for the content of *Wide World*'s program segments. What Arledge and his lieutenants needed was a *list:* a master schedule of every track meet, every automobile race, every sporting event of any measurable stature in the United States—and, if possible, in the world. There was, of course, no such master schedule. The nearest thing would be the daily listings in the calendar sections of sports pages around the country. The trouble was that ABC had no library that collected the nation's daily newspapers.

NBC did. And Roone Arledge had the key. It was one of those things he'd just . . . forgotten to turn in when he left the *Hi Mom* show. Arledge placed this key into the palm of Chuck Howard. "If you are caught," he advised Howard, "mention Pat Hernon's name." Chuck Howard became ABC's original mole. He became a graduate student of the nation's sports-page calendars. Each week, Howard would slip into NBC's library at Rockefeller Center, slip out again a few hours later with a list, and return to the home office at Sixty-sixth Street and Broadway. And then, shortly afterward, Howard, Arledge and McKay would board a commercial jet airplane at New York's LaGuardia Airport and head for a city in the United States that was mentioned on Chuck Howard's list. A day or so later, an ABC videotape crew would follow. And a few Saturdays after that, back in New York, Jim McKay would open another segment of *Wide World of Sports,* promising ABC viewers "sport in its unending variety"—a phrase that was altered in the second year to the memorable "The Thrill of Victory, the Agony of Defeat."

Wide World's first telecast featured the Drake Relays from Des Moines, Iowa. Track and field did indeed form the show's backbone for the first several months. Beyond that, the show was a grab-bag, improvised almost from scratch from week to week.

Arledge, Howard and McKay invented *Wide World of Sports* literally as they went along—typically, in the cabin of a jet airplane at thirty thousand feet. Arledge especially thrived on travel; he seemed to function at his peak within a context of simultaneous luxury and stress—the best hotels, the best bars, the best scotch, but also impossible deadlines, tangled logistics, sleep deprivation and, if possible, fierce negotiation.

"People talk about a 'philosophy' of *Wide World of Sports,*" Chuck Howard said. "There never *was* a philosophy, at least not before we started actually videotaping the segments. There was never time for a philosophy. But as the weeks went along it became obvious to us that *where* we were, and *how* we portrayed the participants, were more important to the show than the event being covered."

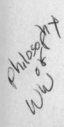

The fact that ABC television had come all the way to Cheyenne, Wyoming, to cover a rodeo, for instance, was of greater interest to viewers than the fact that a rodeo was going on in Cheyenne. But even that novelty would have worn off quickly, had Arledge, Howard and McKay simply structured *Wide World* as a sort of travelogue with muscles. Here, Arledge called once again upon his dramaturgical instincts. He accompanied McKay into Cheyenne saloons, where the two of them sought real-life cowboys to talk to, so that McKay could construct an on-air picture of the rodeo cowboy's lifestyle, the uncertain nature of his hard profession.

It must have been a peculiar spectacle back then in 1961, well before television had domesticated the cowboy bar with lovable commercial pitchmen like Billy Martin and Jim Shoulders—these two hopelessly citified strangers, the button-down, oxford-and-cashmere Arledge (the gold chains and polka dots were still some years away, fortunately), and the natty, five-foot-six-inch McKay, ambling through those swinging doors to make chin music with some rawboned, glint-eyed stalwart of the sagebrush. But somehow it worked. Arledge and McKay didn't come sailing back through those swinging doors. McKay's natural, honest curiosity and reporter's disarming bluntness not only saved their skins, but produced living, flesh-and-blood portraits of plain people striving to be excellent.

McKay and Arledge developed an almost uncanny talent for spotting individuals who might have been ordinary citizens in the eyes of the world, but were heroes in their own community. At Grossinger's resort in the Catskills, the ABC cameras recorded the wife of barrel-jumping Henny Lebell weeping for joy after Lebell broke the seventeen-barrel barrier, a feat thought to be impossible. At East Islip, New York, McKay interviewed the man who had won that city's Demolition Derby two years in a row, and heard the man confide to him tearfully, "I go to church a lot." At Wembly Stadium in England, covering the British soccer championships, McKay was close to tears himself after the Leicester star, one Len Chalmers, suffered a broken leg but was obliged to remain in the game owing to a rule against substitutions. "Poor old Chalmers," McKay kept muttering into his microphone, "poor old Chalmers." "People still come up to me in airports," McKay confessed years later, "and say, 'Poor old Chalmers, poor old Chalmers.'"

The novelty of *Wide World* extended beyond Jim McKay's gift of empathy, of course. In its first year, Ed Scherick audaciously ordered the crew to accompany the AAU's national track and field team to the Soviet Union for its annual meet—even though ABC had neglected to notify the bureaucratic Russians that the cameras were coming. Arledge shepherded some one hundred tons of equipment past the dumbfounded Russians, who then proceeded to infiltrate the ABC remote truck—but only to stare at the monitor screens as their countryman, Valery Brumel, tried to break the world high-jump record.

That dash into Mother Russia was little more than pure brazenness, a typical Scherick testing of limits. The artistry occurred the following year, when the Russian track men came to Palo Alto for a reciprocal meet at Stanford University. As the athletes from both countries filed into the stadium for the opening ceremonies, in two adjacent columns, a Russian and an American linking hands in each rank, a *Wide World* cameraman named Mike Freedman impulsively hurried out onto the track with his "creepy-peepy," and lay down on his back between the rows of advancing men. Freedman pointed his camera upward and produced a striking tableau of the trans-ideologically joined hands as they passed above his lens.

"I was sitting there in the stands; my duties for the day were done and I was just watching," recalled Jim Spence. "When I saw what Mike was doing I began to cry. I knew what those pictures must have looked like." In the Cold War atmosphere of the times, Freedman's impulse was daring, if not politically risky. Would ABC viewers see the *Wide-World*ers as One-Worlders? But it worked. And viewers began to expect images, as well as unlikely heroes, on *Wide World of Sports* that they could never otherwise hope to experience.

Wide World of Sports disproved some of the most deeply ingrained assumptions of commercial video. In an era when live blue-chip events, featuring "name" stars, were held to be the ultimate in network television attractions, *Wide World* established that there was a significant viewer appetite for an afternoon program of videotaped, unheard-of events performed by people whose names were frequently unpronounceable, let alone familiar or beloved. The crucial difference, of course, lay in the *construction* of such a program. Neither CBS nor NBC ever seemed to grasp the essential repertory cohesion nurtured by Roone Arledge, a cohesion that extended beyond Jim McKay and into the technical and production crew. In fact, NBC Sports cast an implicit sneer at *Wide World of Sports* (and later a videotaped series, *American Sportsman,* hosted by Curt Gowdy) throughout the 1960s, by disdaining Demolition Derby coverage and loudly proclaiming itself to be "the network of *live* sports." That was all very well. But it did not address the central appeal of *Wide World,* which had nothing to do with liveness or videotape, but which sprang from the authenticity of the human characters.

As for the contempt lavished by rival networks on the Demolition Derby level of sports competition, it was utterly without merit. No Great Athletic Director in the Sky has ever been discovered to rule that twenty-two padded men crashing into one another on a gridiron was "pure" sport, while several dozen men crashing about in padded autos was "Trashsport." By the mid-1970s, all three networks were wildly engaging in corrupting the *Wide World* prototype—with a clutter of shows such as *Superstars, The Women Superstars, The World Superstars, The Superteams, Challenge of the Sexes, Celebrity Challenge of the Sexes, Dynamic Duos, US Against the World, The Battle of the Network Stars,* and *The First Annual Rock 'n' Roll Sports Classic*—this last, an NBC creation, by the way.

The prototype extended even beyond TV sports. The "reality programing" vogue of the late 1970s, which culminated in such prime-time series as *Real People* on NBC and *That's Incredible!* (with Fran Tarkenton among the hosts) on ABC, was a direct conceptual descendant of *Wide World of Sports.* As with *Wide World, Real People* and *That's Incredible!* focused on relatively anonymous people attempting various tests of skill or nerve. But somehow it was all wrong. A kind of knowing self-mockery, an overwrought awareness of what made for "good video," now permeated the contestants, the human objects of curiosity, on these shows. And in the rare instance in which a contestant revealed a hint of earnestness or naiveté, the quotient of mockery was supplied by one of the consummately aware hosts. A kind of corruption had set in, a corruption of the narcissistic times.

The corruption implicit in these manufactured events did not lie in the unworthiness of the competitions, nor even (in the case of *Superstars,* et al.) in the presence of celebrities as competitors. It lay in the premeditated, coolly disinterested attempt to package an audience attitude along with the packaged event. This phony packaging of attitude would prove to be among the most corrosive elements in American televised sports' progressive decline from excellence.

Wide World offered one further legacy: it established Roone Arledge as the emerging master of ABC Sports. More so even than college football, *Wide World* allowed Arledge to mature as a producer and as an administrator. Characteristically, Arledge exploited these roles with available symbols. The credits for *Wide World* listed him prominently as

"Executive Producer." This was a direct steal from Tom Gallery's on-screen credits at NBC. Gallery was "executive producer" of an entire sports department, whereas Arledge was "executive producer" of only one show. But the ploy served its purposes; it subtly drove home to ABC television executives the point that here was a young programer with specific accomplishments to his credit. Arledge's chief rival for advancement, Chet Simmons, could boast no such title; his chief hope was that, as Scherick's protégé, he had an inside claim on his boss's favor.

The opportunity for successorship came sooner than anyone at ABC had expected. One day in 1964, ABC's vice president for programing, Dan Melnick, announced his resignation. Tom Moore, by then president of ABC television, picked up a telephone and casually relayed that information to the phone-equipped station wagon of Ed Scherick, who was driving home from work.

Ten minutes later, Moore's office door burst open and Scherick stormed in. "I want that job," he announced. He got it.

Jim Spence remembers how strange it seemed that Scherick, who had created and presided over ABC Sports with such fierce passion, never once returned to the department after he resigned from it. "Ed never *once* physically set foot in our office again," Spence remarked. "He just never returned. After all that involvement."

Perhaps Ed Scherick, high-strung and sensitive, nursed an accumulation of affronts—his "phantom" offer to run CBS Sports, his perception that the AAU men would not take kindly to negotiating with a Jew—that corroded some of his accomplishments of the past seven revolutionary years. Perhaps it was nothing more than what he claimed years later: a wearying of sports and a desire to get on with other things. Scherick spent a few more productive years at ABC—he acquired the TV series *Peyton Place,* among others—before moving on to Hollywood in 1967 and founding his own production company, Palomar. Among Scherick's many movie credits for Palomar are *The Stepford Wives, For the Love of Ivy, Shoot the Moon, Raid on Entebbe, Sleuth, The Taking of Pelham 1-2-3, The Heartbreak Kid, I Never Promised You a Rose Garden,* and the made-for-television movie *Little Gloria—Happy at Last.*

Within a year of Scherick's departure, Chet Simmons, too, was gone—to NBC, where he served as Carl Lindemann's assistant until 1977 and then became head of NBC Sports.

Roone Arledge would not become the official president of ABC Sports until 1968, but he informally ran the division for years before that. His reign marked the first effective transition from advertising and public-relations professionals at the helm of TV sports to career network programing professionals. After more than fifteen years, a TV network had finally produced an executive with the talent and will necessary to elevate sports into the mainstream of the medium.

This is hardly to suggest that advertising and public relations professionals would no longer influence events. In the same year that Roone Arledge arrived at the threshhold of dominance in television sports, 1960, the man who would become his coequal in sports television assumed his own seat of power.

XV

THE COMMISSIONER

lvin Ray "Pete" Rozelle was in many eerie ways a perfect analogue of Arledge. The two men's careers complemented and reinforced each other like two powerful, antipodal currents of electricity: as Arledge pushed television farther into the realm of sports, Pete Rozelle, as the commissioner of the National Football League, was pushing sports farther into the province of television.

Even the two men's personal styles and temperaments seemed to express their curiously symbiotic destinies. Arledge, the Long Island born Easterner, favored the flamboyant chains-and-open-collar display of the West Coast mogul, and affected a West Coast kind of *hauteur* in ramming his program concepts through the network bureaucracy. Rozelle, the born-and-bred Angeleno, dressed in the natty, button-down uniforms of the Wall Street corporate animal, the subtle flecks of sky blue in his burgundy ties just matching the blue of his tailored oxford shirts. Whereas Arledge was short, fair, blown-dry, possessed of a cleft chin and tending toward plumpness, Rozelle was tall, deeply tanned, combed, beset by a receding chin, and imperially slim. Whereas Arledge exhorted, cajoled, inspired and occasionally fulminated, Rozelle simply gathered his power quietly, thoroughly; then dictated.

One was a TV programer with a knack for orchestrating sports events. The other was a sports executive who programed the networks as if he owned them. It was inevitable that their orbits would intersect. This did not happen for nearly a decade. When it did, the strict separation between sports and other discrete areas of American television, most notably prime time, began to disintegrate, multiple millions of new revenue dollars were generated—and a top-secret scheme was hatched between the two that in 1982 came within hours of robbing CBS television of the very National Football League telecasts that CBS had popularized more than twenty years before.

Like Roone Arledge, Rozelle seemed to have some mystic power of timing. Whereas Arledge managed to arrive with the advent of videotape, jet travel and satellites, Rozelle had the occult intelligence to attend Compton Junior College in Los Angeles—just the campus that a professional football team, the Rams, would pick as its training site after moving to LA from Cleveland in 1949. Student Rozelle volunteered to be a gofer for the Rams' public-relations man. Years later, after college, Rozelle took advantage of this relationship: he became public-relations director of the Rams himself. In 1957, when he was thirty, the Rams made him their general manager. Two years later Bert Bell, the National Football League commissioner, died of a heart attack while attending a Philadelphia Eagles game. The league named an interim commissioner, and in January of 1960 the owners met in Florida to elect a permanent one.

Rozelle, then thirty-three and unknown to most of the owners, again benefited from timing. Seven owners were dead set on electing Marshall Leahy, an attorney for the San Francisco 49ers. Four others were dead set against him. One owner abstained. A three-fourths majority was required. It was a hung jury. After seven days and twenty-three ballots, the owners turned in frustration to the young, innocuous general manager from Los Angeles. The man who seemed at pains to offend no one became the NFL's new commissioner.

But Rozelle's unctuous manner was calculated. From the very outset, Pete Rozelle grasped an overmastering truth that had eluded the old men, the Old-World franchise owners who were his clients: television. Rozelle knew quite a lot about television, and he would soon learn a lot more. Already he could envision the financial growth curve; it pointed at the moon. Television, Rozelle saw, was the NFL's future, not just a timely revenue supplement to turnstile receipts. Rozelle's intuition told him that football actually read better on the small, selective videoscreen than it did in the stadium—unlike, for instance, ice hockey, which had far greater visceral impact as an arena sport but which somehow lost its sense of velocity and collision on TV.

Rozelle's mission was to harness the NFL to television. This harnessing, he saw, would require a closed system, an airtight conduit of authority that must flow from the commissioner's office and be interrupted by no one, not even an owner, no matter how compelling that owner's case might be for individual enrichment.

Rozelle established his will to impose that authority quite early in his regime. In his first year of office, not even old enough to run for President, and having revealed no previous hint of aptitude for inside Washington politics, Rozelle brought off a ringing conquest of the United States Congress. He lobbied successfully for a bill that sanctioned collective TV contracts between a network and a professional sports league. This bill was indispensable to Rozelle's grand design for empire. It meant that he could strike a TV bargain that would be binding upon each and every team in his league. Before Congress's action in 1961, TV contracts were arranged team by team; clubs in the largest cities could generally expect higher TV receipts than their counterparts in, say, St. Louis and Cleveland. No more. Henceforth—at least in the National Football League—the commissioner would take care of the negotiating, and the commissioner would distribute the spoils equally among his constituent franchises. There would be no fat-cat NFL teams, but the important thing was that there would be no paupers—no rot eating into the bottom of the league. The NFL under Pete Rozelle would be more strictly organized than McDonald's. Pete Rozelle was in fact quietly constructing a perfect model of socialism—television was the cornerstone of the model, and in order properly to harness television Rozelle needed to tread with consummate delicacy around the shoals of antitrust law. The 1961 act of Congress was the first step in what would become a lifelong obsession of Rozelle's: the license to do exactly as he thought best for his league, and for network television, too, for that matter—unchecked by Congress, or network presidents, or public opinion, or even by renegade owners within his league.

Perhaps anticipating the challenges to come, the young Rozelle dared yet another audacious act in his first year. He fired a preemptive shot across the bow of the NFL owners' luxury liner. The shot was calibrated to graze the oldest and most venerated owner of them all, the formidable George "Papa Bear" Halas, the founder of the Chicago Bears.

Halas had provided Rozelle with a pretext. After his team had lost an important game to the San Francisco 49ers, Halas fumed in public that "incompetent officiating" had been the cause of the Bears' downfall. Halas went further. He demanded satisfaction. He wanted this new young commissioner, this Rozelle, to lop off some zebra heads. Halas wanted the firing not only of the errant official himself, but of the NFL's supervisor of officials.

George Halas could not have done Pete Rozelle a more timely favor. But Rozelle could benefit only if he played the incident with utter precision. His course of action was fraught with danger. The NFL owners would be watching him, measuring him. An error of just a few degrees would cost him his own job; compliance with the powerful Halas would humiliate him and stamp him as a puppet.

Rozelle did not respond publicly to the Halas ultimatum. Instead, he picked up his telephone and called the old man in Chicago. Quietly, but without the faintest trace of deference in his voice, Rozelle instructed George Halas to report to NFL headquarters in New York. Halas went livid with outrage. He told Rozelle he would be damned if he came to New York. Rozelle tonelessly repeated his command. Halas fulminated. He offered Rozelle a compromise. He would agree to meet the young man for a few minutes at LaGuardia Airport. Rozelle, polite and firm as an Internal Revenue Service field auditor, repeated the conditions: George Halas would report to NFL headquarters in New York.

George Halas did, in the end, as he was told. In the same blandly professional, somewhat impersonal tones, Pete Rozelle told Halas never to create a public controversy like that again, and levied a fine. And then Pete Rozelle saved himself from the poisonous enmity of the men who had hired him by managing a discreet touch of redemption: he saved Halas's face by keeping the incident utterly out of the newspapers.

Rozelle was to unsheathe his iron fist again and again. In 1963 he suspended and fined two of the league's most popular stars, Paul Hornung of Green Bay and Alex Karras of Detroit, for placing bets on their own teams. The punishment shocked the press and the fans; it seemed rather draconian. But Rozelle was not interested in matters of personal compassion. He was interested in protecting his league and its affiliation with television. Rozelle had seen what the presence of gamblers and the rumors of "fix" had done to boxing just eight years before: they had destroyed boxing's TV connection. That would not happen with Pete Rozelle's league. Five years later, the fist came down again. Rozelle wrung tears from pro football's greatest star and one of America's first TV-made sports celebrities, Joe Namath, by handing the demigod quarterback an ultimatum: get rid of your financial interest in the bar called Bachelors III or get out of football. "Bars and the like attract persons who could cast suspicion on professional football," he said primly, no doubt speaking over Namath's head and outward toward the great Sunday-afternoon, Family TV-watching electorate. "I will not allow the suspicion of evil to exist."

As things developed, "the suspicion of evil" was to prove the one quality that the master of quality control could not control. The NFL never managed to shake itself free from the embrace of professional gamblers. NFL point spreads became classic focal points of illegal betting. And rumors of player involvement with oddsmakers continued to dog the league over the years. But at the same time, a parallel phenomenon was revealing itself, and it caused no end of wonder: *America didn't care!*

The Family didn't seem to mind one bit whether or not the good old bearded quarterback for that hell-raising West Coast team knew any gamblers or not. (Why, wasn't another bearded TV star, a good old country singer, making a big hit with a song called "The Gambler"? Didn't CBS have Jimmy "The Greek" Snyder in its NFL-coverage family?) And as the curve of public apathy increased, the curve of Rozelle's crusade against "evil" looped downward. A prime canon of marketing is: Don't fix it if it isn't broken.

Likewise, Rozelle never managed to look or sound very convincing when he was goaded into answering charges that the NFL was shot through with racism, or that drug use was out of control among players, or that his game officials, and the very rules they were paid to enforce, sanctioned violence and brutality. But then, Rozelle did not really have to look or sound convincing. He was not accountable to the people asking the hard questions, the press and the civic reformers. Pete Rozelle was accountable for the continuing financial prosperity of the National Football League. And the manipulation of network television continually to further that end seemed, quite often, to be the only pursuit that Pete Rozelle was really interested in.

Like Roone Arledge, Pete Rozelle permitted few close friendships. Those he did allow seemed always to mesh conveniently with Pete Rozelle's professional considerations. Carl Lindemann believed himself to be a personal friend of Rozelle's. When he was head of NBC Sports, the two men played tennis together once a week at the Midtown Tennis Club, and Lindemann was always on Rozelle's elite guest list for the mammoth party the commissioner threw every August at his country home in Harrison, New York. ("This party is for the *world*," a regular guest once remarked. "He has lawn tents flown up from Washington that look like TWA terminals. He has a couple of society orchestras— Peter Duchin, Lester Lannin. It's like *The Great Gatsby,* except that Gatsby couldn't have afforded it." But after Lindemann left NBC Sports to accept a slightly less senior position at CBS, Rozelle did not so much as send him a card of good wishes. And the invitations to Rozelle's August party ceased to arrive.

As the years went on, Rozelle's circle of intimate friends coalesced around a group of four: Herb Siegel, chairman of the board of Chris Craft and an astute media man; Jack Landry, the senior vice president of marketing at Philip Morris, the fourth-largest national advertiser in America and owner of Miller Beer, which flooded NFL telecasts with commercials in the eighties; David Mahoney, chairman of the board of Norton Simon, the silk-stocking Park Avenue public-relations company; and Bob Tisch, president of Loew's. All of these men, Jack Landry in particular, contributed immeasurably to Rozelle's encyclopedic knowledge of the network television business, particularly the ever-shifting realities of its internal economics, and to his knowledge of how those economics could be stretched to just the edge of the diminishing-returns line when Rozelle negotiated for rights contracts. In return, the four men got good seats at Rozelle's football games and invitations to his August party.

Congressman Jack Kemp was another fairly close friend of Rozelle's. Presumably this friendship took root after the merger of the AFL and NFL.

There was one other man who had every reason to consider himself Pete Rozelle's dear friend. Bill MacPhail, the soft-mannered, affable gentleman-president of CBS Sports, had known him from the early days, before Rozelle had ever thought of becoming NFL commissioner. Bill MacPhail's network established the National Football League on television. Bill MacPhail introduced Pete Rozelle at Toots Shor's and stood drinking scotch with him into long amber evenings—although Rozelle measured his scotch carefully, sipping only enough to appear convivial. Bill MacPhail flew off to Florida on business-pleasure trips with his old pal.

And it was Bill MacPhail whom Pete Rozelle repaid by singling out CBS as the network he bore down upon the most relentlessly, year in and year out, to push back the outward tolerance for rights payments, using perhaps the most aggressive ploys and stratagems in the history of broadcast negotiations.

Recall that Bill MacPhail cited his "chemistry" with Rozelle as one factor in the commissioner's 1962 move to block an upstart NFL rights bid by the Hughes Sports Network. But Rozelle never hinted at any such sentimentality. He insisted that he acted on the grounds of pure reason: Hughes Sports, he believed, could never generate the kind of promotional momentum necessary to build a massive audience for its telecasts. Therefore, the ratings would be lower, the ad revenues would be sparser, and the rights for NFL telecasts would have to be negotiated more cheaply the next time. Chemistry? Rozelle was more concerned with practical math.

Here are some better examples of Pete Rozelle's respect for tradition, form and ceremonious duty. In January 1964, CBS signed a $28.2-million, two-year contract with Rozelle that was, at the time, the talk of the industry—CBS had been paying $4.6 million a year until that time. The drastic increase was explained partly by the fact that the networks were bidding for the first time on the right to telecast *two* games each Sunday instead of one. Nevertheless, few people in sports or television could imagine how any contract could ever rise significantly above that historic deal.

That $28.2-million figure had been the product of a bitter internetwork war that was laced with intrigue: ABC, which had somehow managed to put together an astonishing offer of $13.2 million, later had reason to believe that a spy within its ranks tipped the figure to CBS at the last minute, allowing MacPhail's network to counter with its winning figure.

At any rate, there would almost certainly be no bidding war in 1966–67. ABC had since regained college football, and NBC had taken over telecasts of the American Football League with a five-year, $36-million contract. Who was left to bid for the NFL against CBS?

Pete Rozelle knew who. Pete Rozelle fully intended to witness another "historic" increase in rights for 1966–67, even if it meant bidding against CBS *himself.* In November 1965, Pete Rozelle informed CBS television that if he did not receive a figure in the price range he had in mind, the National Football League was prepared to telecast its own games.

Rozelle was not kidding, not bluffing. Over a period of months, acting in secret even from his old Toots Shor pal Bill MacPhail, Rozelle had put together a meticulously detailed master plan for a National Football League network. It was all there: the schedule of AT&T long-lines charges for intercity connections; the names and qualifications of available on-air talent, engineers, cameramen, sound men, producers and directors—all the personnel and spare parts for a network, financed mostly by CBS's rights money from 1964. If Pete Rozelle had wanted to rescue CBS from an upshot network four years before, he seemed in no great hurry to repeat his heroism now.

CBS was outflanked, outgunned, outsmarted. It seemed that the fellow they'd hired for his inside connections wasn't quite as connected as they'd thought. In a year when it was unopposed by any other network, CBS forked over a humiliating twenty-five percent increase; it agreed to pay the NFL $37.6 million for two years of regular-season games, plus $2 million for rights to each NFL championship game in 1966 and 1967.

But Pete Rozelle was not yet through with Bill MacPhail and CBS. In June of 1966—before either of those $2-million championship games had aired on CBS—Bill MacPhail picked up his office telephone and heard the bland voice of his old friend Pete Rozelle on the other end. "Got a pencil handy?" Rozelle asked by way of opening pleasantries. And as MacPhail grew progressively rigid with shock, Rozelle proceeded to dictate the terms of the impending merger he had arranged, again, in utter secrecy, between the NFL and the American Football League.

No one in sports had suspected that any such maneuver was in the works, although it certainly made sense: bidding wars for college football talent in the post-Namath years were costing each league a combined $7 million yearly in draft choices alone. MacPhail's concern was more immediate. The merger meant that his $2-million championship telecasts, the prime showcase event in CBS's NFL schedule, were now reduced to subsidiary contests. One of the terms of the merger was a championship game between the top teams in *each league*—an attraction soon to be known as the Super Bowl.

"Why didn't you notify me that you were planning this?" MacPhail demanded angrily of Rozelle.

"Because," came the unemotional voice on the line, "it was our business and nobody else's."

In the pen stroke that ordained the merger, of course, Rozelle created the context for the event that would come to stand as the single, overweening embodiment of televised sport, with all its forced grandeur, its obsessive self-worship, its celebration of excess, its general rube trappings of synthetic classicism that seemed so ingrained into its transient, tradition-starved age.

Pete Rozelle even *named* the Super Bowl (the cautious owners would have been satisfied with "World Championship Game"), and he applied its identifying Roman numerals like some proprietor daubing gold leaf onto the shingle of a mock-Edwardian surf-and-turf house, and then stepped back to watch the popular culture play out its inevitable role in the ensuing folk-passion drama.

The Super Bowl quickly became more than just another TV sports extravaganza; it became a symbol for America's values and for America's lack of values. While sportswriters and TV columnists wrestled each January for the proper ironic distance to mitigate their awe over the statistics (the ever-more staggering prices for Super-broadcast rights, for Super-advertising per minute, for total Super-advertising income, estimated expenditures on Super-equipment, estimated expenditures by the Super-crowd, and so on) the nation's academic elite were straining equally hard for the proper semiotic context. "Methodologically," proclaimed one, "it draws on a variety of communications-related disciplines to achieve a balance between Anglo-American emphasis on empirical data and Continental interest in philosophical implications."* (This same academician brought a stopwatch to Super Bowl III and determined that with a live attendance of 71,882, a TV audience of 95 million, an advertising rate of $240,000 per minute and a copy total of more than 3 million words sent out by newsmen, the actual on-field playing time amounted to seven minutes.)

The first Super Bowl game, in January 1967, was actually transmitted by both NBC and CBS—a curiosity that underscored the event's actual impact as a contest of *networks,* not of teams. In succeeding years NBC and CBS alternated coverage, but always with an eye toward topping each other's previous performance: for Super Bowl XVI in Detroit, in January of 1982, for instance, CBS employed twenty-three cameras—eight more than NBC had used in the previous year, and incidentally eleven more cameras than CBS itself had needed to cover the 1980 Republican National Convention. The extra hardware brought the market value of CBS's Super-Bowl equipment to $10 million, up from NBC's previous high of $6 million, and swelled the network's actual budget for the event to $2 million, up from its own high of $1.3 million in 1980.

Buried in all these statistics was the interesting fact that neither CBS nor NBC actually *needed* to pay out that kind of cash, since each network had an exclusive on the game in alternate years. What it all meant was that the two networks were waging their own private Super Bowl, their own internecine war of excellence—or excess—on terms that only the television industry itself could fully comprehend.

All in all, the Super Bowl was one of Pete Rozelle's better impulses.

As cold, even brutal, as Rozelle's behavior toward MacPhail might seem on its surface, it was not, in Pete Roselle's value system, anything personal. Rozelle was not a cruel, sadistic person. He was a professional in the discipline of public relations, trained and temperamentally inclined to advance his client's interests to the exclusion of nearly every other consideration. Bill MacPhail and CBS were hardly Rozelle's only marks. His welcoming gesture to the incoming AFL owners was an $18-

---

* Michael R. Real. *Mass-Mediated Culture.* Englewood Cliffs, N.J.: Prentice-Hall Inc., 1977.

million "joiner's fee." And as the combined twenty-six-city empire began to jell as a kind of secular Sunday heaven on America's television
screens, Rozelle extended his authority to the cities themselves: he
encouraged a spate of taxpayer-financed stadium building that enhanced
his teams' aura of luxury and importance, and conscripted even the
ordinary American citizen, football fan or no, into his revenue-making
legions.

Before he could safely engineer the AFL-NFL merger without fear of
ambush from his nemesis—antitrust litigation—Rozelle even had to
make his second conquest of the United States Congress. The commissioner wanted an act of legislation that specifically exempted the merger
from challenges under antitrust statutes. Moreover, he wanted it fast—
before members of Congress returned to their districts to campaign for
the November elections.

Once again, Rozelle lobbied with the surehanded instincts of a Washington mole. He ignored the most superficially obvious target of his
persuasions, Congressman Emanual Celler of Brooklyn, because Celler,
as chairman of the House Judiciary Committee, was known to oppose
any shortcuts around antitrust hearings. Instead, Rozelle turned his
charm upon Senator Russell Long of Louisiana. Senator Long represented a constituency that was panting for an NFL franchise. He, as it
turned out, shared Rozelle's philosophies regarding antitrust.

Long wielded his own lobbying skills in the Senate, many of whose
members were acquainted with the hospitality afforded by the ownership of the Washington Redskins. The Senate passed an antitrust exemption by acclamation, tacking it on as a rider to one of President
Johnson's crucial anti-inflation bills. It was an end run, and Congressman Celler never caught up with the play. In 1967, the commonwealth
of Louisiana received a brand-new professional team, hand-delivered to
the city of New Orleans. The team was felicitously named the Saints.

As for Rozelle's dear old friend Bill MacPhail, within a few years of
his mortification in the mid-sixties, CBS top management gently removed him from further contract negotiations with the NFL commissioner. So much for connections.

With the merger of the National and American football leagues,
Rozelle extended his manipulative influence to two of the three major
networks. NBC, which had telecast AFL games, became the television
arm of the unified league's American Conference, while CBS retained
rights to the older, NFC teams. For interconference games, the visiting
club's network would retain coverage rights.

The merger boosted NBC at once into the National Football League business, but at a competitive disadvantage with its ancient enemy. For once, it appeared that CBS had emerged a winner from some facet of a Pete Rozelle production. The AFL cities, aside from New York, were mostly America's secondary urban tier—and even New York's vast market was partly claimed by the Giants. In 1970, Rozelle nudged three original NFL franchises—Pittsburgh, Baltimore and Cleveland—to join the American Conference, but even with that shift, NBC labored under an inherent TV market shortfall, compared to CBS. There was no third entity in pro football coverage, of course. At least, not yet.

If there is one person, besides Rozelle himself, who might be credited with establishing on ABC the transformational program form known as *Monday Night Football,* it is Johnny Carson. Carson, who brought so many powerful and disparate personalities together on his NBC *Tonight Show,* was the catalyst who finally steered Pete Rozelle and Roone Arledge onto the same orbital path. It did not happen on Carson's famous desk-and-sofa TV set. Carson was not even aware that he was a dynamic in any such convergence. But the effect was the same as if Carson had sat the two men down next to Ed McMahon and started them talking.

By 1968, the two largest networks, CBS and NBC, as corporations, had not yet overcome their historic indifference toward sports as a first-rank programing element. The latest of many impresarios to stumble up against this leaden reality was Pete Rozelle. Beginning in about 1967, Rozelle started to lobby each network to create a climate of enthusiasm for his next great dream for extending his empire: live NFL football telecasts in prime time.

From the start, Rozelle's bargaining options were limited. There was the matter of which prime-time night. Saturdays were too valuable for any network to disrupt. Fridays, the logical choice, were strictly off limits: the defiant NCAA had already put the networks on notice that any television competition with traditional Friday-night high-school games (the feeder system, of course, for college football) would be met with a massive mobilization of harsh public opinion. The midweek nights were out; they would distort the competing teams' practice schedules too radically. That left one evening—Monday.

In September 1968, at Rozelle's urging, NBC decided to experiment with a couple of prime-time pro football telecasts. NBC's Monday schedule was built around feature-length movies. Not perhaps the most creatively uplifting TV fare, but a reasonable antidote to CBS's formidable lineup of *Gunsmoke, Lucy, Mayberry, R.F.D., Family Affair* and *Carol Burnett.* Somewhat tepidly, NBC's highest management agreed to test Rozelle's novel notion.

Johnny Carson exploded.

An item in the September 7, 1968, *New York Times* announced:

> Johnny Carson said yesterday that he would not appear on the *Tonight* show on Monday because the National Broadcasting Company planned to pre-empt a part of his regularly scheduled 90 minutes to televise a professional football game.

Carson, then in his seventh year at NBC, was among the network's most potent revenue-earners; the *Tonight Show* gross revenues were running at nearly $28 million a year. He was, perhaps justifiably, worried that any shifting about of his show's starting time would threaten his viewers' habits and erode the program's aura of anchoring importance. "Just this week," Carson complained to the *Times,* "I found out that somebody at NBC sold a football game for Monday night and they want me to cut down on my show. I won't do the show any night any more unless it starts at 11:30."

NBC had committed a horrible gaffe. It had already contracted for the game; there was no backing out. But how to placate the gold-plated Carson? Improvising wildly, network officials tried to substitute a taped rerun of an earlier *Tonight* program following the game. Carson's lawyers blocked the move. And so, in an almost unprecedented concession for commercial TV, the NBC Network canceled all of its programing scheduled for after the game (which ended, by the way, at 12:06 A.M., thirty-six minutes beyond Carson's normal starting time).

After that humiliating experience, NBC was effectively out of the Monday Night football business. Rozelle next took his plan to CBS, where he met with even less cooperation: William Paley was not about to dismantle one of the strongest single-night lineups in prime-time history for some damn males-only football game. That left one network.

It would be quite tidy and symmetrical to report that ABC immediately leaped at the chance once again to thumb its nose at stodgy network caution, and plunge into a bold, radical programing gamble, which would be of a piece with ABC's swashbuckling history. But this time it did not happen that way; not exactly, at least. Even ABC sounded a cautionary note, and Pete Rozelle had to dip again into his black bag of bargaining devices.

By 1968, both Tom Moore and Ed Scherick were gone from the

scene. Roone Arledge ran the Sports division, but he didn't run the network. And the first faint signs of caution were beginning to seep into ABC's corporate persona. On the instruction of ABC Television Network president Elton Rule, who had replaced Tom Moore, Arledge turned Pete Rozelle down.

Bill MacPhail at CBS could have told Arledge what would happen next. Back came Rozelle, a few days later, silken and blandly correct, with some disturbing information for Mr. Rule. If no major network accepts a Monday Night football schedule, Rozelle reported politely, we are prepared to sell a similar package to the people at the Hughes Sports Network. And most of the stations that transmit such a network's NFL feed would be ABC stations.

A classic American motion picture would, within a few years, forever capture this philosophy of negotiating with the phrase, "making them an offer they can't refuse." And like most of Rozelle's other "offers"—even the ones that stretched CBS's forbearance so direly—this one proved amply enriching to all concerned. *Monday Night Football* premiered on ABC on September 21, 1970—the first regular-season telecast featured the telegenic Joe Namath and his New York Jets against the Cleveland Browns—and quickly prodded something in America's unconscious memory: the ancient, simple hunger for *drama*. Drama had never been among television's most signal accomplishments, and for very good reason: the evocation of drama has always been a peculiarly individual enterprise, a spontaneous eruption of one artist's vision; and television, from the first, had been collectivist at its very roots. Storytellers had never been near the buttons and levers of managerial power in television; their services had always been delegated by the businessmen whose overriding mandate was not to create drama, or anything else in particular, but to avoid losing audiences. By 1970, that mandate had led to the presence of a thick new bureaucratic layer between the network command chain and the creative people who supplied entertainment product, a layer that consisted of market research.

Hollywood production studios were responding to the dictates of companies that offered a saturation of "scientific" formulas for creating successful shows: demographic studies and audience preview tests and "Q" profiles that measured a star's "likeability," and detailed analyses of program "components" that had succeeded or failed in the past. It is unlikely that any network executive who came to power after 1970 ever understood why his prime-time series were accepted or rejected, at least in terms of their connection with the natural human appetite for dramatic expression. The late novelist and philosopher John Gardner defined dramatic expression, variously, as "a benevolent vision of the possible which can inspire and incite human beings," and as "a game played against chaos and death, against entropy."

Monday Night Football brilliantly surmounted television's built-in obstacles to these dramatic qualities. It did not require the stultifying presence of jaded, formula-deadened Hollywood scriptwriters and producers, because the players on the field became their own characters and improvised their own narrative destinies. Of course, football players had been doing just that for as long as the game had been played; for fourteen years, under the eyes of CBS and, later, NBC. But CBS's and NBC's eyes were fixed and formalistic; their cameras recorded mainly the statistical progress of the game. This austere technique, or lack of technique, goes far toward explaining why professional football was perceived as a dehumanized, corporate-militaristic allegory on the older networks, and why, through ABC's prism, it became a parable of the personal and the grand.

Roone Arledge's unique position with *Monday Night Football,* as a sports programer in prime time, allowed him to impose a personal vision that his rivals could not even summon, much less impose. Arledge was uniquely equal to the task. His dramaturgical instincts for story line were seldom used to better advantage. At its outset, *Monday Night Football* became almost a redemption for the culture at large.

The program made its debut in an epoch marked by the gunning down of students by National Guardsmen on college campuses; by the continuing slaughter and maiming and psychic wreckage of young American men in Southeast Asia; by a President who felt constrained to protest, perhaps not in strictest accuracy, that he was not a crook. In the chaotic, inverted reckoning of those times, *Monday Night Football* offered a benevolent vision of the possible; it offered a game played against chaos and death, against entropy. It offered a kind of "reality" without the consequences of reality. It intensified the passions of mythic conflict, but it withheld the horror and guilt of America's exposure to living-room war: the images of torn bodies, the grief over slain, wasted heroes.

On *Monday Night Football* the heroes arose again and again from the brilliant green field in their gleaming helmets that caught the stadiums' fiery floodlights, and director Chet Forte's twelve probing, peering, insistent cameras zoomed in and in for lingering portraits of their handsome, charged faces beneath the helmets. If the three networks have been accused of prurient dwelling on the faces and long legs of beautiful cheerleaders, Arledge's corollary dwelling on the male athletes' sexual appeal has received almost no comment—but it helped attract women to *Monday Night Football,* and women provided its margin of ratings success.

And through it all, far above the battle, came the sacraments of the most perfectly selected cast of correspondents ever created for broadcast: Keith Jackson, and later Frank Gifford, issuing terse, telegraphic bulletins from the field of combat; Don Meredith, slicing through the tension with the timeless wry humor of the battle-savvy grunt; and, to put it all into some final Olympian perspective, his very voice and cadence redolent of something that mere words could not approach (though his words were seldom "mere"), was Cosell, sports' Matthew Arnold, at large upon the ether as Rozelle's armies clashed by night.

Monday Night Football was hardly drama in any exalted sense of the term. It was never intended to be. The progressive story line in any given game was random, uncontrolled by a serious or complex vision, and frequently overstated by announcers. Nor, in the end, could *Monday Night Football*'s visual and charismatic finesse compensate for any of the troubling societal tendencies that some experts were attributing to professional football's obsessive appeal: the legitimization of gambling and drug use, the ever-expanding pressure on college, high-school and even grade-school youngsters to live up to pro football's prototype.

But as a step forward in televison programing, *Monday Night Football* was seminal. Roone Arledge's genius and Pete Rozelle's genius had finally fused, and the product was state-of-the-art television covering state-of-the-art sport. As the cameras covered not only the game on the field but also ABC in the act of covering the game; and as Cosell, Gifford and Meredith described not only the facts of the play on the field but the story line that evolved from the play, the viewer began to feel connected to something that was larger, more luxurious, intimate, important and real than anything else, more so even than the progressively dissolving society around him. People came to these telecasts who had never even watched football on TV in any other form: most significantly women.

America unleashed its gratitude for *Monday Night Football.* In its first season, it drew an average share of thirty-one percent of the audience—nearly one-third of all Americans watching television, and well above the twenty-four share ABC had said it would need to survive. Movie attendance fell off drastically on Monday nights. Bowling leagues switched their nights to Tuesdays. Restaurants and bars either accepted a decline in customers or installed large screens tuned to the game. Years passed, and the frenzy continued. ABC's own public relations department proudly reported that, in 1979, Miami–Dade Community

College's south campus introduced a course entitled "Understanding and Enjoying *Monday Night Football.*"

It was inevitable that the hot fandango between Rozelle and Arledge would provoke trembling lower lips at the other networks—the two were so unnervingly made for each other—and in January of 1972 the first open snufflings were heard.

Robert D. Wood, then president of the CBS Television Network, penned a tearful, three-page "Dear Pete" letter obviously designed to remind the wayward commissioner of where his domestic responsibilities lay.

> I don't think I have to point out to you that CBS supported the NFL before anyone else was interested in telecasting professional football. Nor do I think I have to point out to you that CBS provides the NFL with virtually half the money it gets for rights to its games. In the light of our long relationship . . . I think it is only fair to tell you some of the things on our mind as we consider the question of [picking up] our option.

What Robert Wood had in mind was Rozelle's unmitigated gall in sneaking special little trinkets and bonbons over to his new little flame, in the form of especially attractive team matchups—at the expense of CBS.

"Let us consider the nighttime NFL schedule of the last two seasons," Wood wrote, struggling manfully to keep a lid on his emotions:

> In each of these seasons, we expected that for the 13 [Monday Night] games, each of the 26 teams would appear on one occasion. Instead, we found that in 1970, five teams did not appear at all on prime time television while five other teams played twice on Monday nights.

And on in that vein. The letter was laced with hard evidence—names, dates and winning percentages—and also with what can only be described as rather elephantine attempts at veiled threats ("why does it make us wonder about the desirability of picking up our option without assurances that this will be corrected?")

Whom did Wood think he was kidding? Pete Rozelle worried about CBS picking up its option? Pete Rozelle understood far better than Robert Wood how far CBS could be bent without breaking off from the NFL. The answer was all the way to the profit line, and the profit line could be pushed up and up and up almost infinitely, as CBS Sports salesmen relayed Rozelle's merciless pressure to the willing advertisers themselves, increasing rates.

Almost ten years from the date of Robert Wood's tear-stained letter, in the early months of 1982, Pete Rozelle would bend CBS Sports across his gabardined knee to a degree that made all past profiteerings look, by contrast, like the fond benevolences of a doting philanthropist.

It began at the NFL owners' meeting in Phoenix in February. Ed Garvey, the NFL players' representative, had leaked word to the press several days previously that Rozelle's combined contract demands for the five-year period beginning in autumn 1982 would exceed $2 billion. At a press conference during the owners' meeting, a reporter asked Rozelle whether that figure was within any reasonable bounds of accuracy. To the stupefaction of everyone in the room—the gathering included several network sports executives—Rozelle replied rather blandly that yes, it was.

"That was our first inkling of what we might expect," recalled a senior executive at CBS Sports. "We all agreed that when Pete came to us this time, we would take a very hard-line stance against him."

Similar vows of solidarity had been made, and broken, many times over the years at CBS. This time would be different, but only in the *degree* to which the vow was broken.

Now came Rozelle's campaign of terror. If Roone Arledge was the supreme adapter, Rozelle was the supreme negotiator. Few leaders in American business, and perhaps politics as well, have understood power, weakness and options as well as the NFL commissioner. Over the years, Rozelle had taken to negotiating with the three networks separately—starting with the one least involved in revenue payments (ABC) and working methodically upward, toward CBS. And now, in the early months of 1982, Rozelle began his grim circuit.

One of Rozelle's unsettling mannerisms at the negotiating table had been his habit of tapping a gold-plated cigarette lighter on the table's surface—*tap . . . tap . . . tap . . .* as the bargaining went on. During conversational lulls, this *tap . . . tap . . . tapping* would fill the room, further unraveling the nerves of the network people, who were jumpy enough in Rozelle's presence as it was. Now, as Rozelle started to make his rounds, the CBS people had to just sit and wait for the tapping to come, ravenlike, to their door. Some of them must have heard it in their sleep.

As the CBS executives waited, they heard rumors. A CBS secretary came to work one day and reported that she had spotted Pete Rozelle and Roone Arledge talking intensely to one another in a nondescript coffee shop in the Upper East Side of New York, not one of the fashionable restaurants where "everybody" went and where confidences quickly turned into rumor.

Then word came that Rozelle had finished his talks with ABC and had moved on to NBC. *Tap . . . tap . . . tap . . .*

Rumors of a price began to make the rounds. It was an astounding figure. Hard on its heels came a story, somewhat tentative, that NBC had rejected the price. Could CBS be sure? If that figure was a harbinger of what was coming their way . . .

And now, finally, the tapping was at CBS's door. "He hit us with a number that was absolutely *staggering*," recalled a CBS Sports executive. The division's president, Neal Pilson, uttered the equivalent of "Nevermore." And the decisive negotiating battle of the latest network–NFL war was engaged.

It lasted for weeks. But the dimensions of the struggle quickly became apparent to CBS. All the figures that had been leaked from ABC and NBC were true. From ABC, Rozelle had managed to extract a five-year commitment of $680 million (Ed Noble had bought the entire ABC Network for $8 million in 1943). In return, Rozelle awarded ABC its long-sought entree into the Super Bowl telecast rotation, beginning in 1985. And that was the *smallest* of the contracts. Rozelle's price from NBC had topped the $700-million mark—and NBC's Sunday-afternoon schedule was generally agreed to be weaker than CBS's because of the differences in market size.

Pilson and his aides were utterly determined that this time, no matter what Rozelle had managed to gouge out of the others, CBS would hold its ground this time. A 100-percent increase over the last contract—well, that was one thing. But Rozelle was demanding a leap of *150 percent,* and that was too much. For one thing, CBS was not at all sure that its advertisers, so bottomlessly bountiful in the past, could support this kind of commitment. Rozelle wanted more than $720 million.

Back and forth it went . . . *tap . . . tap . . . tap . . .* until Rozelle tired of the game and, as he had invariably done in the past, produced his secret weapon. This time it was like a laser gun in what until then had been a clash of broadswords.

We'll take the NFL off CBS, Rozelle blandly informed the television men gathered around the table.

It was unthinkable. No one who heard it could believe the words had been uttered. CBS without the National Football League? It would be like Washington, D.C., without the White House and Capitol Hill. But in the stricken silence that followed, Rozelle calmly outlined the system by which it could be so.

That secret coffee-shop meeting between Rozelle and Arledge had in fact been a summit of sorts. The deal that went down pledged Roone Arledge to accept a Sunday schedule of NFL games if one of the other networks were to fail to meet Rozelle's figures. Then Rozelle had gone to NBC and promised two things: one, that the $700-million fee would be reduced proportionately if CBS somehow succeeded in striking a lower bid; two, that if CBS held too firm, and Rozelle broke off the bargaining, NBC would accept the slate of NFL games that CBS had traditionally carried.

In other words, NBC would take CBS's games, and ABC would take NBC's games. The National Football League would lose nothing; it simply would not gain as much as it might have. And CBS? It would be back in the business of the Sunday-afternoon ghetto.

CBS agreed to pay Pete Rozelle's price. And thus the historic $2-billion NFL-TV football deal of 1982 was hammered out. *Tap . . . tap . . . tap.*

"This thing has gotten very, very unpleasant," a CBS man remarked several months later. "It has become a system of 'pay or else.'" He noticed that too.

Other network TV executives noticed something else interesting about that $2-billion combined contract, especially in light of the NFL players' strike that delayed the 1982 football season for five weeks and played havoc with the networks' budgets, particularly CBS's. They recalled that among the many arguments Rozelle had summoned on behalf of his numbing increases was that his league needed an extra reserve of revenue to bankroll itself against the likely demands of the NFL Players Association, which had been threatening a strike in 1982 for several years.

But several executives saw the deal as having produced exactly the opposite effect. "It *caused* the strike," insisted one. "When those players read about $2 billion in the paper, there was no way they weren't going to harden up and try for their share."

Thus the convergence of Pete Rozelle and Roone Arledge, inevitable from the moment each of them took his place in the TV sports firmament, generated not only the single most significant programing breakthrough since *Game of the Week*, it also generated the richest single financial package in television history. Clearly, Pete Rozelle and Roone Arledge were the two dominant figures of TV sports' age of ascendancy.

A question then intrudes: which was better?

It is a meaningless question, of course. The two men's roles were complementary; therefore, impervious to comparison. And yet, within the value system of two such men, for whom competition and conquest are everything, there must be some mutual appraisal; some hidden, last-tag standards for measuring personal best.

And given Pete Rozelle's apparent fanaticism for imposing final authority, for leaving his network adversaries with absolutely no ground to fall back on, the remark of a CBS vice-president might provide an insight as to which man had the all-encompassing edge. "I wonder how Pete felt," he mused, "when Roone went on from there and bought the United States Football League?"

XVI
THE CREATION OF COSELL

e was Arledge's fantastic votary, a self-invented, self-absorbed, self-perpetuating and frequently self-contradictory force of nature whose inescapable shadow would tinge nearly every single facet and development in television sports coverage over the ensuing two decades, a presence who would simultaneously serve as the conscience and the scourge of his profession, an unapologetic ego who could seemingly inhabit several mutually canceling personas at once, and whose maverick proclivities often tended to beggar even the celebrated mavericks, Arledge included.

He was a man who needed no further introduction. A man whose ascension, in early middle age and against high odds, to the calling of his destiny was a virtual parable of ABC itself.

In the winter of 1954, a young magazine writer named Ray Robinson took a long taxicab ride from his Manhattan office out to a neighborhood liquor store called the Wilmont in the far reaches of Brooklyn. The liquor store was co-owned by the New York Giant baseball stars Willie Mays and Monte Irvin. Ray Robinson had scheduled an interview with Irwin for a men's adventure magazine called *Real*.

Robinson found Irvin waiting for him at the liquor store, as arranged. But the ballplayer was not alone. Hovering near Irvin was a tall, pale man with slightly stooped shoulders, who stared quite baldly at Robinson through hooded eyes beneath brows that arched and dropped like declarative sentences.

"We all went to the back of the store and sat down," recalled Robinson. "I realized that I'd have to interview Monte in the presence of this guy. He was Monte's lawyer, and Willie's, too. So I spent a couple of hours getting my story, and this guy kibbitzed. At the end, he was complimentary—sort of. And then he just abruptly demanded, 'You want to give me a ride back to Manhattan in your car?' I told him I'd never owned a car in my life."

The two men ended up sharing a taxicab back to midtown. And on the way, Ray Robinson sat and listened in politely restrained disbelief as Howard Cosell calmy foretold, in a voice that struck Robinson as that of a burlesque barker, his coming glory as a sports broadcaster.

"He unfolded his ambitions for his life," Robinson remembered. "There was no doubt in his mind that he would reach the absolute top of the field—because most of the sportscasters already there were what Howard called 'sons of the wild jackass.' As I think back on it, he was incredibly prescient. It was eerie. He *knew* it was coming. He said, over and over, that sports on television was going to be the most important thing in the country. His refrain was that he couldn't miss, *if only he got the opportunity*."

What made it all so eerie, in retrospect, to Robinson, was that at the time, Cosell's dream seemed so wildly beyond the limits of hope. The fellow spinning out this most ardent of American Boy fantasies was then thirty-four years old, an age when most men had submitted themselves to whatever fortunes their lives had foreordained. Cosell's own fortunes were not that bad. Recently discharged from the Army with the rank of a major, married to the woman he would tenderly romanticize for the rest of his life (the former Mary Edith Abrams, whom he called Emmy), set up as a thirty-thousand-dollar-a-year Wall Street lawyer, a Phi Beta Kappa who had majored in English literature at New York University, Cosell could look forward to a life of influence and ease that for most Americans was a distant ideal, impossible almost to imagine. Robinson was astonished to learn, on top of all this, that Cosell was already into broadcasting—albeit in a fringe, dilettante sort of way. He was the host of an obscure, fifteen-minute, noncommercial and nonsalaried Little League show on ABC radio on Sunday mornings. The job had grown out of Cosell's legal work in incorporating Little League baseball in New York. Cosell mediated questions asked of professional athletes by kid ballplayers. (Later research revealed that Cosell also *wrote* the questions.) This bit of amateur dabbling hardly qualified as sportscasting. Sportscasting was a young vagabond's game, not a mature, urbane, Phi Beta Kappa lawyer's.

And the voice was all wrong. Unmistakably New York and gratingly nasal, two qualities that were not exactly in high vogue among the great heartland audience, it seemed to possess a further, eccentric denti-lingual will of its own: it rose and fell in cryptic disregard of all inherent rhythm and stress; it paused precipitously between consonants as if to gather itself before pouncing like a wolverine upon the next syllable. It had none of Mel Allen's clarion country lilt, or Red Barber's formal precision, or Dizzy Dean's playful yawp or Lindsey Nelson's melodic urgency—all the great broadcasters, it seemed, were Southern. Cosell's voice, as Ray Robinson listened to it in that taxicab wending back from Brooklyn, was freighted with the ancient woes and sad knowledge of Brooklyn and of the *shtetl* back beyond Brooklyn—for there was another impediment to Cosell's dreams. Cosell was a Jew. Unlike Mel Allen or others who had neutralized their Semitic qualities through the dropping of a last name, the adoption of a laundered American-pie accent, or some lucky blind roll of physiognomy, Cosell made no attempt to alter, modify, or even make a comedic point of his Jewishness. It was simply there, a part of him for others to take or leave; and in 1954, the prevailing social inclination would be to leave it. But more than that, Cosell's Jewishness seethed inside him; it was a powerful motivating force, and Ray Robinson, a Jew himself, saw that at once, and understood the probable consequences, and privately reduced Cosell's chances of fulfilling his dream to zero.

Robinson miscalculated Cosell's chances, of course, but he hardly misread the consequences. To say that Howard Cosell was hazed for his Semitic origins throughout his career is to make an understatement. The matter of concealing Jewish attributes became a particular avenue of attack. "How can a guy who wears a hairpiece and changed his name from 'Cohen' pretend to 'tell it like it is?'" was a favorite taunt—hurled most prominently in recent years by David Halberstam, writing in *Playboy* magazine in 1982. Asked that question directly, Cosell would reply that the name change actually restored his family surname, the Polish spelling of which was *Kassell*. His grandparents, fleeing Jewish persecution in Eastern Europe, were unable to clarify the family name to impatient United States immigration officials. "And the officials simply did what they always did in a situation like that," said Cosell. "They wrote down 'Cohen.' My father, Isadore Martin Cohen, always yearned to have the original family name restored to us, and I carried out the legal change as a fulfillment of his wishes."

The hazing, and the pointed slurs at Cosell's identity, went far beyond the "tell-it-like-it-is" taunt. And they arose from sources far more public and institutional than the daily dose of hate mail that Cosell received. In December 1972, *Parade* magazine's pseudonymous Walter Scott, the magazine's resident advisor to the gossip-lorn, printed the following cryptic letter from one "Ann Emmett, Detroit, Mich.":

Howard Cosell, the ABC-TV sportscaster—is it true that in the old days he used to announce on the radio under the name of Father Coughlin?

The letter was manifestly someone's idea of a cruel joke—whether the perpetrator was "Ann Emmett" or someone within the ranks of *Parade* who set up the question as a device for allowing Scott to reveal that "Howard Cosell used to be Howard Cohen but never Father Coughlin." Father Coughlin was the rabidly bigoted "Radio Priest" of the 1930s; among his more notorious opinions were that Jewish money had started the Russian Revolution and that (in 1938) the Jews were getting what they deserved at the hands of Hitler. The association of Cosell's name with Coughlin's, even on the pretext of denying the association, was not *Parade* magazine's noblest moment.

Robinson and Cosell became friends. Robinson—who would one day become executive editor of *Seventeen* magazine—hired Cosell as a columnist for *Real;* the column was called "Cosell's Clubhouse." At the same time, the lawyer-cum-sportswriter began to plead with Robinson for an introduction to Don Durgin, then the head of ABC radio. Robinson thought this odd. Cosell was on ABC radio, however tangentially, while Ray Robinson's acquaintanceship with Durgin was distant—he knew the man only through a mutual friend who had worked with Durgin years ago in the mail room of the advertising firm Foote, Cone & Belding.

But it wasn't really odd at all. This was Howard Cosell at his most characteristic, at once bristling with bravado and wracked with the darkest self-doubts. Show business, politics, sports and other public professions are laced with this personality trait; a classic internal-combustion machine that often produces compulsive success; people who embody it are familiar American archetypes. But at the height of his extraordinary, flawed celebrity, Howard Cosell somehow failed to fit that archetype. He never struck anyone as a man hobbled by insecurities. Perhaps that was because he suppressed that side of himself so thoroughly under his facade of high dudgeon; perhaps it was because, as Cosell always bitterly claimed, his chroniclers in the print press were so blinded by resentment of his flamboyant success that they always saw him in terms of caricature, and never as a whole person.

That caricature was inevitably a price of American fame, and that at least some of the caricature was roughly good-natured never registered with Cosell. He came of age at a time when "the Jewish Problem" was a dominant preoccupation in America. His autobiography—or the first of his several autobiographies; he is sportscasting's Proust—broods frequently upon his Brooklyn childhood experiences vis-à-vis such horrors as "the Catholic kids from Saint Theresa's parish. Running from them, hiding from them; they were always after the little sheenie."* He is a self-admitted hypochondriac. Such a personality is blind to the generalities of caricature. Every reference is personal and barbed.

Cosell's profound self-doubts explain something else that many observers of his career have found puzzling: his apparent shift, somewhere in the mid-1970s, from being a crusading gadfly, a plain-truth-spouting champion of sports' dispossessed, to being a first-name-basis confidant of sports' ruling classes—exchanging his sword of vengeance for a Montechristo cigar.

Again, the contradiction is more illusory than real. The behavior of Howard Cosell from those first drafty afternoons in the back rooms of ballplayers' bars in Brooklyn has consistently been the behavior of a man conditioned to view himself as an outsider, a man possessed of an unquenchable desire to *belong*. Such turbulent forces of temperament do not necessarily produce bad work. In the early 1960s those forces impelled Cosell into the orbit of another outsider, the embattled young Odysseus of boxing, Muhammad Ali. As an American outcast because of his controversial religion and his exemption from military draft on conscientious-objector grounds, and as a worldwide icon because of his surpassing physical beauty, his humor and his very persecution, Ali must have been the fulfillment of Howard Cosell's most fervent escapist dreams. In Ali, Cosell—still a fringe broadcaster himself in those years—could romanticize the outsider's state. Cosell's outrage on behalf of Ali was no less real for all that. His single-handed championing of the deposed champion from 1967 through 1970 was the summit of Cosell's career.

When that outrage began to seem mellow after *Monday Night Football* made Cosell a genuine first-rank American star—or, if not mellow, at least a little contrived, a little selective—his detractors renewed their vitriol. They sensed that Cosell had jettisoned his once-useful image as an angry social critic, a "tell-it-like-it-is" type of guy, and had taken up with the overlords. Their suspicions were fueled by Cosell's cameo appearances spoofing himself in movies and TV situation comedies, by his brief fling as host of a TV variety show, *Saturday Night Live with*

---

*Howard Cosell. *Cosell*. Chicago: Playboy Press, 1973.

Howard Cosell, which ran from September 1975 until January 1976, by his presence as host of the gimmicky "Trashsport" series *Superstars,* and mainly by his obvious pride in the cultivation of intimacies with franchise owners, show-business celebrities and politicians. For a brief time in the mid-seventies, Cosell terrorized his friends with serious talk of running for the Senate from New York.

The suspicions were partly justified. Cosell had found a new frame of reference among the powerful, the monied, the adored. Given his lifelong insecurities, his wish to belong, this shift was inevitable. But—and here is the essence of Cosell's particular video genius—he had made the shift without abandoning his ground as a gadfly. He was both privileged, indulgent insider and fiery, reformist outsider.

This capacity to inhabit two powerful but mutually exclusive personas at once was not unknown among American folk pundits—Mark Twain spent his most productive years torn by the conflicting wishes to lampoon the mannered pretensions of the Gilded Age and to be a leading light of that age; he managed both—but it does require an unusual blend of positive and negative charges. It also makes for endlessly fascinating television, TV being a medium ideally suited to absorbing contradictions and leaving a rich yield of raw personality. No sportscaster ever left a larger residue of his personality on the medium than Howard Cosell.

Cosell finally got what he wanted from Ray Robinson. Robinson arranged a lunch for Cosell and Don Durgin, the ABC radio chief. Durgin was not impressed. Like Robinson, he couldn't get past the voice. But Durgin's programing assistant, a man named Ray Diaz, held out. Diaz—perhaps recalling the improbable success of another man with an "un-announcerly" voice, CBS's World War II legend Elmer Davis— argued that Cosell might in fact be a hit because of his strong inflections, especially in New York. It was a shrewd notion, but highly unorthodox in those days of the golden throat. Nevertheless, Durgin relented, a little. He offered the thirty-thousand-dollar-a-year lawyer a six-week tryout to do several five-minute sports pieces each weekend, at twenty-five dollars a spot. The thirty-thousand-dollar-a-year lawyer jumped to accept.

And then Howard Cosell, the outsider who was too insecure even to approach the head of ABC radio without the help of an intermediary, revealed the opposite side of his complex nature. Now he became a stalking panther of the dugout, the locker room, the ring. He had purchased a tape recorder, a huge and primitive portable model called a

Magnemite, which he was obliged to strap across his back by means of a thick nylon sling. Almost staggering under the weight of this ponderous metallic cube, Cosell set out to rewrite the conventions of broadcast sports reporting, and to invent himself as an airwave personality in the process.

The self-invention was no casual matter. Cosell started with the voice: if it was his biggest handicap as a prospective broadcaster, he would turn it into his strongest weapon. Instead of trying to round out his voice's abrasive edges, Cosell sharpened them further. By studying the rehearsal methods of several actors who lived near him in a Manhattan development called Peter Cooper Village, notably Karl Malden and John Forsythe, Cosell found the technique for exaggerating his natural tonal shifts, his abrupt harsh stresses and his elliptical slides into hushed monotone. The result was one of broadcast history's most inspired creations—a voice that was virtually a finished character in and of itself. It was a voice that would become instantly recognizable and endlessly parodied, a voice that sounded like parody itself and yet commanded a certain offbeat authenticity that melded with the airwaves' inherent staginess. As he achieved the status of a star, Cosell inexorably made this voice his own. And yet, in a strange sense, it belonged to the airwaves even more than to him: as he spoke to a few people gathered in a room, the shifts and stresses would inevitably sound melodramatic, too big for the occasion, the contrivances almost embarrassingly apparent. But on the air, after a while, the voice seemed utterly at home.

Next came the content. Here Cosell would have his answer for the "sons of the wild jackass," the existing sports journalists for whom his lip curled in contempt. The bare, statistical, hits-runs-and-errors approach to radio sports reporting of the 1950s bored and offended Cosell, but it also filled him with a gleeful anticipation, because it left untapped such a wealth of potential interviews, feature profiles, commentaries and what are called, in broadcasting, "actualities"—the voices and the background sounds that compose an aural environment for a story in the making.

Ray Robinson was in on the very beginning. "He asked me to go to Florida with him in the spring of 1955," Robinson recalled. "He was going to interview ballplayers in spring training for the radio show. I spent two or three days closely involved with him, and then I simply couldn't take it anymore. It wasn't just that he never did define my role in helping him, or that he never paid me for my time. It was that even then, Howard knew everything—or at least he thought he did."

If Robinson was exasperated, the players themselves were amused and intrigued by the tallish, pale man bent sideways under the weight of his unwieldy tape machine who invaded their clubhouses and pestered them with questions that the regular sportswriting crowd never dared or even thought to ask. Professional athletes have always been a surprisingly blunt, candid lot—at least until the age of media-saturation prompted many of them to regard their statements as highly marketable commodities, if not auditions for broadcast careers of their own—and they responded to Cosell's blunt questions. As for Cosell, he began to feel as though he belonged. There is this terribly revealing remark, obviously intended as self-flattering, from his first biography: "Some of the local announcers laughed at me. But not the professionals. I learned quickly that they respected a man who worked. 'You're like shit,' (Yankee catcher) Ralph Houk told me. 'You're everywhere.' " *

Cosell began a regular sports commentary, *Speaking of Sports,* on ABC radio in 1956. He even made it to the ABC Television Network—to the extent that there was an ABC Television Network in those days—with a nightly report called *Sports Focus.* And for seven years, beginning in 1959, Cosell covered heavyweight championship fights for ABC radio, contributing prefight and postfight interviews, blow-by-blow reporting and between-rounds commentary. He covered New York Mets baseball for two years, teaming with Ralph Branca, the former Dodgers pitcher. (The pair heaped such wickedly satirical scorn on the team, underscored by fervent indignation at the organization's inept management, that they were soon dispatched.) He was the sports reporter for the local WABC radio news from 1961 through 1971. He formed his own production company and turned out critically acclaimed documentaries on the legend of Babe Ruth, Vince Lombardi, Grambling State University and Mickey Mantle, focusing on Mantle's poignant obsession with death.

Howard Cosell had arrived. He belonged. Or did he? Within just a few years of his breakthrough into ABC radio, there arose a fresh reason for him to activate the old insecurities. For five years, beginning in 1959, Cosell was denied access to appearances on ABC television. "Locked out," was the phrase Cosell used. Roone Arledge, his eventual rescuer, went farther. "For reasons I never fully understood, and don't now, Howard was blackballed," Arledge declared in 1982.

The man in the middle of the controversy was Tom Moore. Moore did not see eye to eye with Cosell from the moment he arrived at ABC. He

---

* Cosell. *Cosell.* Chicago: Playboy Press, 1973.

canceled *Sports Focus,* put out the word, through Ed Scherick, that Cosell was not his idea of an on-air personality, and embarked upon ABC's historic network TV sports buildup while Cosell watched, in agony, from the exile of radio and local TV.

Moore himself admitted, quite blandly, years later, that "I must say, I never expected that Howard would make it" on television; yet he insisted that this was purely a professional evaluation and had no factor of ethnic prejudice. Moore added, candidly, that Cosell's chances were not enhanced by the fact that Cosell was a close ally of Jimmy Riddell, an ABC vice-president who opposed the Moore-Scherick relationship. Riddell believed that ABC should develop its own sports department rather than contract from an outside agency such as Scherick's Sports Programs, Inc. Tom Moore believed that Jimmy Riddell should mind his own goddamned business, and ostracizing Riddell's pal Howard Cosell was one way for Moore to put Riddell in his place.

So Cosell—now a man in his forties—stewed, enduring an exile not all that different from Ed Scherick's own deferred aspirations. To his credit, he turned the exile into an extended experimental period for developing other, off-screen video skills. It was during this time that Cosell produced his string of documentaries. Also during this time, Cosell met a kid whose name was then Cassius Clay.

The relationship began in August 1962, when Cosell interviewed the up-and-coming young Clay on his radio show, asking Clay to predict the winner of the Floyd Patterson–Sonny Liston bout. Clay managed to predict both men as winners, in a manner similar to Cosell's own fondness for overstatement. Several months later, following Clay's own victory in England over the British champion Henry Cooper, Cosell coaxed Clay into a live interview on his local New York sportscast. Clay stunned the WABC viewers. Instead of respectfully muttering modest responses to Cosell's questions, under the ancient code of unwavering banality, he began to rant about Sonny Liston as "the Big Black Bear, the Big Black Bear." He wanted Liston, this unknown kid was yelling; he'd knock him out; it would be no contest, not a chance.

In that unrehearsed moment, the Act took its essential form. Cosell and Ali would embellish it over the years, in good times and bad—on the radio from the Fifth Street Gym, where the young fighter trained; from ringside in Miami, where he stopped Liston and became an instant national figure; from a press conference in Miami the next day, where he announced that he had become a Black Muslim and that his name was now Muhammad Ali; from a succession of arenas in Lewiston, Maine, Toronto, Britain, Frankfurt, Madison Square Garden, the

Astrodome and other outposts as Ali fought matches as fast as the promoters could make them, in anticipation of his reckoning with the United States Army and the New York State Boxing Commission.

Sometimes the Act was mock-confrontational, with Ali threatening to "whup" Cosell; sometimes it was mock-racist, with the two men throwing rather alarming slurs at one another; sometimes it was subdued, as with Ali's announcement that he had turned Muslim; sometimes it took on an almost father-and-son quality, with Cosell upbraiding the champion after one of Ali's episodes of cruelty in the ring, against Floyd Patterson or Ernie Terrell. Always, the Act was weirdly fascinating. It differed from anything else on radio or television. It violated norms; it was anarchy to people's conditioned responses. (Could anyone imagine Lindsey Nelson jiving with Willie Mays? Chris Schenkel trading insults with Jim Brown?) And there was the delicious, outlaw thrill of never knowing for sure that Ali was not going to grab the nervy, toupeed announcer by his bow tie and throttle him.

But Ali's reckoning was never far in the background. It came on April 28, 1967, in Houston, where Ali declared his conscientious-objector *Ali* status before a United States Army recruiting officer. By this time, *H.C.* Cosell and Ali had catapulted one another into pop-cultural celebrity-hood. Tom Moore had left ABC. And Howard Cosell had been plucked from network exile by Roone Arledge.

Turning Howard Cosell into a star may stand as the single most weirdly, inexplicably prophetic stroke of all Roone Arledge's experiments at ABC Sports. There simply were no precedents. Arledge was conferring a caustic sensibility upon a subject that had always called forth hearty enthusiasm, a "How-about-that?" kind of joy. Granted, Howard Cosell had proved himself as a "sports journalist." But the American viewing public had revealed no churning hunger for sports journalism. The fact was that no available indicators existed to assure Arledge that Cosell would be anything but a bizarre, temporary curiosity for ABC Sports—if not a fiasco. The closest that Arledge himself ever came to explaining his intuition, many years later, was that he saw Cosell fulfilling a Dorothy Kilgallen role within an announcing team—Kilgallen having been a similarly quaint irritant on several radio and TV panel shows of the 1950s.

Given this vacuum of plausibility, there inevitably arose darker interpretations. Some journalists and TV production people who knew both men came to believe that Arledge enjoyed a certain Svengali-like control over Cosell; that he instantly foresaw everything, the controversy and the ratings value of the controversy; that he shrewdly encouraged Cosell's more extreme affectations until Cosell, bemused with his own success, could no longer tell the difference between his real-life persona and his on-screen persona. Such a theory, of course, rests on a view of Cosell as a kind of innocent. And whatever diverse and complex traits defined Cosell's character, innocence was not noticeably among them.

Cosell's first "real" TV network exposure—discounting his *Sports Focus* appearance back in ABC's age of obscurity—came in 1965, three years into the Act, just as Arledge was consolidating his own presence at ABC Sports. And if Arledge was struck by any early prophecies of Cosell as the ultimate antistar, he never mentioned them. His early interest in Cosell, Arledge claimed, was purely practical. "I was very impressed with the fact that, at a time when ABC didn't have the major events on the scale of CBS and NBC, Howard had more access to athletes than just about anybody," Arledge said. "So I was determined to break down the blackball against him. In 1965, we had a Saturday-afternoon major-league baseball package that was not successful. I kind of snuck Howard onto the network by letting him interview ballplayers on our pregame show. He did a helluva job. This was still a time of the golden-throated announcer and the ex-jock; that was the tradition. Nobody ever criticized anything, nobody *ever* asked an athlete a difficult question. Howard stood all that on its head. So then I got him into boxing."

"Getting him into boxing" meant, essentially, transferring the Act with Ali onto *Wide World of Sports*. It took a bit of doing. By the early 1960s, boxing was a closed-circuit TV event. Entrepreneurs such as Irving Kahn, the founder of TelePrompTer, had been paying promoters for the exclusive rights to distribute live championship matches directly to movie theaters equipped with large TV screens; and the networks, still smarting over the scandals of the late fifties, were not exactly distraught over the competition.

So ABC and *Wide World* could carry only a few selected examples of Ali in the ring. Most of these were on a videotape-delay basis. The lone exception was Ali's September 1966 fight against the German Karl Mildenberger from Frankfurt—the first live color sports event to be transmitted by satellite. What *Wide World* showed was Ali the personality—bantering with Cosell, reciting his poetry, demonstrating the "Ali Shuffle." This, after all, was the kind of thing that *Wide World* had been designed to do: to focus on the humanity of sports participants. *Wide World* became the chief conduit for presenting Ali, and, by extension, Cosell, as characters in their own peculiar, half-comic, half-desperate continuing drama.

Cosell had no obligation to plead Muhammad Ali's case over the airwaves after the events of 1967, which saw the New York State Boxing Commission strip him of his championship, an action that was quickly adopted by every other state in America. The hate mail and the sarcasm from the press, two sources of torment that wounded Cosell out of all necessary proportion throughout his career, could have been cut to a trickle had he simply kept quiet about the issues.

So why did Cosell continue to make waves about the manifest fact that Muhammad Ali had been denied due process of law—denied his means of making a living without a jury trial on the merits on his case? In light of his later, donnish behavior that betrayed a relish for the trappings of vested power, Cosell's militant crusade for Ali might be viewed as crass publicity-seeking opportunism. At the other extreme, the extreme Cosell himself advanced, it might be viewed as the idealistic impulse of a man trained in law and driven by an unquenchable civil-libertarian fire.

why back ali

Or it could have been something far more elemental, and far more revealing, about Cosell's unorthodox but inescapable attraction as a video force. It could have been a primal hunger to belong, a hunger that attached itself to charismatic Ali in the years Ali was a romantic outsider, but that could transfer itself with no apparent sense of contradiction to the *inside* of sport, and celebrity, and ruling-class power, when those conduits opened up. It was like nothing so much as the hunger of television itself, randomly searching for and consuming content, first this idea and then that, with not the slightest regard for serial logic.

And that may have been Howard Cosell's ultimate secret. He *was* the medium, personified.

XVII

ARLEDGE'S OLYMPICS

If college football introduced Roone Arledge's idiom for TV sports, and if *Wide World* proved that he and his technical assistants could create an audience for televised competitions for which no inherent mass interest had previously been detected, and if *Monday Night Football* proved that he could transplant a sporting event into prime time and sell it successfully as pure programing, then Arledge's Olympics telecasts combined all of these revelations into a unified theory of video, the implications of which reached well beyond the boundaries of sports.

So intensely did Arledge's blend of personal intimacy and technology burn itself into his Olympics telecasts that, in most years, they stood as more than mere records of a sporting event: each was a document of its social epoch. By 1972, in Munich, the Games had become such a meta-center of worldwide communications that a brigade of Palestinian commandos paid them a macabre compliment—turning them into a live TV theater of terrorism in which eleven Israeli athletes and coaches were snatched from their compound, taken hostage and later slaughtered in the crossfire of a nighttime shootout. Four years later in Montreal—in the heart of what Tom Wolfe called "The Me Decade"—the glittering, preening boxer Sugar Ray Leonard was unloosed upon the Culture of Narcissism. And in 1980, a nation frustrated to distraction by its apparent paralysis in the face of Soviet and Iranian aggression threw itself into a hysterical binge of patriotism after the United States hockey team defeated the Russians at Lake Placid.

For all the artistic prestige, the awards and the industry dominance that it was to harvest from Olympics coverage, ABC came to the Games in a remarkably offhand way—almost, in fact, as an afterthought.

"We got 'em because we could have 'em practically for nothing," remembered Julius Barnathan. "It was the old story at ABC. In the early sixties, we didn't have anything going for us—not until we got college football and *Wide World*. It was *Wide World* that pointed us to amateur sports, and gave us our first expertise on Olympic-type events. Why'd we go after the 1964 Games in Innsbruck? Because we could have 'em practically for nothing! For peanuts! Especially after they flopped so bad on CBS on 1960. Nobody wanted to touch 'em after that."

There were good reasons for this apathy besides CBS's artistic fiasco. Until the Olympics, American TV sports had been just that—*American* TV sports. Producers, directors and technicians had not been obliged to cope with incompatible electronics systems or to negotiate their requirements through interpreters with supercilious and uncomprehending functionaries from alien cultures. Who needed it? And for what—a glorified track meet that Americans never cared about anyway?

Arledge and his people had some experience in the demands of international logistics through *Wide World of Sports*. But nothing *Wide World* ever attempted had compared to ABC's first Olympics, the 1964 Winter Games at Innsbruck, Austria. For them, Arledge would have to mount a full-blown transcontinental expeditionary force with manpower and equipment for a twelve-day operation in a country not accustomed to the nuances of television. The early omens were not promising.

There was the dinner Arledge had in Innsbruck with one Professor Wolfgang Friedle, the head of the Austrian organizing committee. Arledge talked to Professor Friedle nearly nonstop throughout the meal, explaining ABC's technical needs in the most minute and exacting detail. Professor Friedle nodded and listened in silence. At the end of the meal, a hoarse and still hungry Arledge arose and extended his hand and bade farewell to Friedle. The professor bowed. "It wass certainly a pleasure meeting you," the Austrian recited haltingly. "Hello."

As a television event, the Innsbruck Games would compare to ABC's later extravaganzas as a Coronet educational film on tooth decay compares to *Star Wars III: Return of the Jedi*. It was not even presented live. A film of each day's events had to be air-lifted each day from Austria to New York, where it was edited and broadcast the following day, on an hour-long "highlights" program at 10:00 P.M. Communications satellites were in orbit by 1964, but they were not yet synchronized with the earth's rotation to provide a continuous relay target for a TV signal. So ABC was obliged to follow a jet-age version of crossing the Alps by elephant, with Arledge in the role of Hannibal.

The result was a fairly primitive documentation of an Olympics, by today's standards, but in 1964, the Innsbruck telecasts created a freshet of excitement. They were judged superior, artistically, to NBC's subsequent coverage of the Summer Olympics from Tokyo. And with excellence inevitably came competition. The larger networks began to sense that ABC was in the process of staking out yet another neglected sports event as its own, and there was a renewed determination that ABC would not own this particular event, not at a discount price, anyway. No longer would Olympics telecast rights be sold for peanuts. Arledge managed to secure both the Winter and Summer Games for 1968—but not before he agreed to commit $2 million of ABC's money for Grenoble and $5 million for Mexico City. That was expensive in those days. But suddenly, for Roone Arledge and ABC Sports, money did not seem to be an object.

Arledge's parent network was not yet wealthy on the scale of CBS and NBC. But it was no longer impoverished, either. The days of being required to line up sponsors before bidding on an event were gone, for the most part, although a certain informal sounding-out process was maintained. Arledge's production budget at Grenoble was half again as large as his winning bid: $3 million worth of color cameras (forty of them; the downhill skiing alone took twenty-five); engineers and production crew (250 of them); eighty thousand feet of camera cables, not to mention an assortment of helicopters and snowmobiles. It wasn't "For Men Only."

Grenoble marked the first extended satellite coverage of an Olympics. Early Bird, the first "synchronous" satellite, had been locked in orbit above the Earth since 1963. The Winter Games from France provided a striking showcase of its power to flatten out and condense the planet.

So did Peggy Fleming. The regal young figure skater, a *Wide World of Sports* discovery four years previously in a dark and dingy Cleveland ice emporium, won a gold medal and captured the American romantic fancy even as Arledge's shrewd cameramen captured her own cool elegance. Fleming's performance at Grenoble symbolized, in many ways, all that was positive and transcendent in the marriage between television and sports. It showed millions of viewers a superb young athlete at the very moment of idealizing her excellence—in an unfamiliar form of competition that was at once difficult to an almost superhuman degree and free from all connotations of conquest, pain, or neurotic vulgarization of self. And it was a performance that touched off a nationwide flurry of imitation. In the course of a few minutes' exposure spread over a few days, Peggy Fleming on television resurrected the sport of ice skating from its status as a passé pursuit and made it fashionable once again—for participants as well as for new fans.

The Summer Olympics of 1968 in Mexico City were the Games of social rebellion. They unfolded in the most convulsive year in postwar history, within weeks after the assassinations of the Reverend Dr. Martin Luther King, Jr., and Senator Robert Kennedy, and within days before the riot-smeared Democratic National Convention in Chicago. Their site was a city steeped in the desperation of the Third World. Just a few weeks before the Games began, Mexican police had gunned down hundreds of students in the course of quelling civil demonstrations.

Arledge brought to this treacherous site the apparatus for what was then the largest TV sports venture in history. ABC would feed forty-four hours of events back to the United States. The volume of information, the sheer data, to be contained in those forty-four hours would surpass anything television had attempted until that time.

Arledge had determined that his announcers would be equal to that flood of information. It would not be enough for an ABC on-air man simply to report the statistical results of a given competition. He must be able to tell the viewers something about the competitors; to reveal some telling wisp of character, or an imitation of story line. This was the formula that had worked so well for Jim McKay and *Wide World of Sports:* the personalization of athletes who had no previous connection with the audience. But *Wide World* had focused on only a handful of competitors each week. The Mexico City Games would attract some sixteen hundred.

up close + Personal

No matter. Roone Arledge would see to it that his announcers knew their subject matter.

This was where Dick Ebersol came in. In the winter of 1967, Ebersol, then a student at Yale, had applied for a job with *Wide World of Sports.* He had seen a *Wide World* crew in action two years earlier, covering Le Mans, when Ebersol was a student at a boys' school near the site of the French auto race course. "I said to myself, 'That's what I'm gonna do,'" he recalled. Arledge had barely acknowledged Ebersol's application at the time, but something must have stuck in his memory— perhaps the fact that Ebersol was fluent in French. Four months afterward, a telegram arrived at Ebersol's living quarters in New Haven.

Ebersole first research

Dick Ebersol's first assignment for ABC Sports undoubtedly made the four-month wait seem worthwhile; it certainly seemed to suggest that an interesting career lay ahead. His mission was to travel about the world. In the course of those travels, he would be collecting information that would form the basis of two book-length manuscripts. The first would be a detailed history of each modern Olympics since the Games were reintroduced in 1896 in Athens, Greece, all the national results, as much anecdotal material as Ebersol could muster, and the results of the competition within each Olympics event.

That would be the easy part. The larger duty in Ebersol's global mission—salary, $125 a week plus expenses—would be to compile a biography, with anecdotes, of each of the sixteen hundred athletes headed for Mexico City. "I suppose that I traveled the equivalent of two times around the world," Ebersol said. "The hardest part was Russia. I never did make it inside the Soviet Union. But I was able to set up a correspondence with some of the athletes, and that was the beginning of a network that got me in touch with the rest of them. I ended up getting most of what Roone had asked for."

Most of Arledge's charges generally did.

But no one assumed that the telecasts from Mexico City would be harmless exercises in anecdotes. These were the Games of social rebellion. No one doubted that there would be trouble, and Arledge's network took the necessary precautions. Although Mexico City was in the same general time zone as the United States, Arledge's nervous superiors decreed that the bulk of coverage would not be live; it would be delayed on videotape. "They gave us the worst hours the network had," Arledge recalled.

But ABC's corporate caution was just one source of the restraining pressure that came down on Arledge and his crew. The other source was the International Olympics Committee itself. The president of the committee was an elderly martinet named Avery Brundage—intransigent, power-obsessed, ferociously sensitive to matters of image and public relations. (Brundage would endure his most appalling ordeal at the 1972 Games in Munich.) It was Avery Brundage who dispensed broadcast rights to his Games, and it was Brundage who expected those games to be covered with the proper discretion and grateful respect. If trouble erupted on the fields of competition—as it almost certainly would—Arledge would be caught in a pincer: on one side, his own network; on the other, the man who could freeze ABC out of Olympics coverage for the next decade.

The trouble came toward the end. Two black American sprinters, Tommie Smith and John Carlos, finished first and third in the two-hundred-meter run, with Smith setting an Olympic record. The athletes mounted the reviewing stand—and struck an attitude of protest: heads bowed, fists clenched and brandished aloft, feet bare.

It is reasonable to doubt that any network would have ordered its cameras turned away from such a gesture. Reasonable, but not conclusive. (CBS had been panning dutifully away from fights on NFL playing fields for years.) The test of ABC's—Arledge's—nerve would lie in how the network performed following the incident. Would the coverage proceed as though nothing had happened? Or would Arledge order some kind of journalistic follow-up? There were no precedents.

Arledge was not a creature of precedent. He dispatched Cosell to find the record-setter, Smith, and interview him on-camera. The task was formidable: Smith and Carlos had vanished, leaving no trace. A token search for them might have let ABC off with a face-saving alibi. But Cosell probed through the night, calling on every contact he could think of, until at last he tracked Smith down in a hotel room across town. He badgered the grudging Smith into explaining the symbolic components of the protest. The interview aired. Brundage was outraged—he expelled Smith and Carlos from the Games—and the Americans who had tuned in to ABC expecting to watch a sporting event received, instead, a glance into the caldron that was their own society.

"No network," Arledge said years later, "had ever gone on the air, having bought the rights to the Olympics Games, and defied the Olympics Committee. It just wasn't done."

A self-serving reflection, perhaps—but true.

Now came NBC's turn: Sapporo, Japan, site of the Winter Games of 1972. Here was the opportunity that NBC's sports department had coveted for years: a chance to outperform ABC at ABC's own specialty and forever quash the claim—fast attaining the status of a folk myth— that ABC was unmatchable in sports coverage.

Instead, NBC stumbled into a series of blunders that very nearly sealed the myth. What NBC managed to establish was an embarrassing statistic: that in nearly two decades of snubbing sports as a serious program form, the big networks had produced not one vice-president or executive producer capable of mustering an overall coverage plan to fit the internal logic of a major sports event. (Harry Coyle, the brilliant NBC baseball director, might have qualified as an exception, had he been a top management man, rather than a magnificent technician.)

NBC sallied forth to Sapporo with one monomaniacal goal in its corporate mind: to cover the events from Japan live. *Live* was virtually a one-word manifesto with NBC Sports in those days. NBC was the network of live sports. The stress on "live" was in part an elephantine attempt to damn ABC by implication. It sought to draw attention to the fact that *Wide World of Sports,* one of ABC's most prominent offerings, was on videotape.

So NBC covered Sapporo—live. Which meant that the major big-audience events, such as the downhill skiing, hit the airwaves at 11:30 P.M. From midnight until 2:00 A.M., NBC filled time by rerunning tapes of the preliminary competition—not too compelling, given that the final winners had just been seen live. The elementary lesson that Carl Lindemann and Chet Simmons had failed to absorb from Arledge was that "live" (or tape, or film, or picture-postcard, or any other technique) meant nothing to the audience as an absolute value. Arledge's genius lay in how he adapted technology to suit strategic programing needs.

But a second NBC mistake at Sapporo made its live coverage emphasis look like a stroke of divine inspiration. Because it was impossible to cover two or three simultaneous events live, NBC designed a sort of anchor-room studio in Sapporo, in which the principal correspondent, Curt Gowdy, sat and reported the results of various events back to the United States.

The overmastering problem with this studio, as quickly became apparent, was that it didn't *look* like Sapporo. It didn't look like anywhere. It looked like a goddamned TV studio. So there sat Gowdy, halfway around the world, amidst some of the most stunning topography and architecture on the face of the earth, reading off the medalists and the point standings like some Eyewitness News anchorman in Tulsa.

Sapporo, in certain ways, was Roone Arledge's finest hour. The ordeal was especially painful for Gowdy; it was an unworthy showcase for that superb professional's talents. Gowdy's was one of the voices that defined and established the craft of television sportscasting, and it is possible that, over three decades, his voice was heard more than any other on television's airwaves. The former University of Wyoming basketball star, whose first on-air assignment was covering a six-man football game in 1942 for five dollars, distinguished himself at all three networks. In addition to his NCAA football partnership with Paul Christman for Arledge in the sixties, Gowdy covered six Olympic Games, several Super Bowls and World Series, and was the host of ABC's *American Sportsman* for twenty years. It is possible that Gowdy's longevity worked against him in the latter stages of his career. He became the target of mocking reviews by certain critics who affected to find his approach outdated—a curious, if not spurious complaint to make in the 1970s, which saw a wholesale influx of sportscasting "talents" whose training and even grasp of basic grammar betrayed a general slovenliness.

It was in Munich, in September 1972, where televised sports intersected most hideously with the darker currents of global competition, where TV sports' very success at engaging the human imagination produced its first harvest in human blood. That ABC was the transmitting network was sheer coincidence. But given ABC's predominant role in shaping sports as a solid-state metaphor for twentieth-century life, the coincidence has its inescapable irony.

At 4:00 A.M., Munich time, on Tuesday, September 5, the eleventh day of the Games, the ABC Sports production crew completed its three-hour satellite feed of videotaped events to a ground station in Raistag, Germany, from whence it would be relayed by four satellites, one over the Indian Ocean and three over the Atlantic, to a receiving station in Maine, there to be flashed on land lines to ABC in New York for distribution across the network.

It had been, until then, a triumphant telecast of a triumphant Olympics—"The Olympics of Joy," as Chancellor Willy Brandt proclaimed them. These were the Games that would lift Munich, and West Germany, once and for all above their quarter century of shame, the legacy of Nazism. The mood had caught the imagination of nearly everyone, athletes, fans, television crew. The first week had been idyllic: blue skies, radiant sunshine, the police in pastel uniforms. The American and German television technicians who worked the events together formed deep emotional bonds; there was champagne in paper cups at the close of a work day, and toasts to the futility of war.

A young ABC producer named Doug Wilson had even managed to render, in a rare, haunting video image, the quintessence of the humane spirit that pervaded the first week. Wilson was in charge of the unilateral (that is, exclusively American) cameras covering the gymnastic competition inside the Sport Hall. Wilson and Gordon Maddox, the expert commentator, had begun to notice a small, frail-looking Russian gymnast, her blonde hair in colorful bows, named Olga Korbut. Korbut should not even have been at Munich. She was an alternate, and had joined the Russian team only after the regular number-three gymnast injured her wrist. But something in Korbut's character, her transparent joy at doing well and despair at failing, alerted Wilson and his crew. True to ABC's insistence on story line, the Americans turned their attention away from the eventual gold medalist, the great Ludmilla Tourischeva, and began to follow young Olga about. Soon, print sportswriters filing stories about the gymnastics leaders began to receive bewildering communiques back from their United States copydesks: "What about Korbut?"

Near the end of the competition, Korbut failed. She slipped on the uneven bars. As she padded past the ABC cameras, her eyes were shiny

with tears. Wilson ordered an extreme closeup of her face. The result-
ing image sent a shudder of empathy throughout America. It fixed the
sport of gymnastics in the American consciousness, as Peggy Fleming's
pristine elegance had fixed ice skating four years before at Grenoble.

The Olympics of Joy: in planning since 1968, with construction costs
at $450 million, crowned by a modernistic, eighty-thousand-capacity
Olympic stadium and a terraced Olympic Village that could house
twelve thousand athletes and team personnel. After the Games, this
village would become a sophisticated housing development, the very
symbol of optimism. The Press City stood adjacent to the Olympic
Village: a behemoth of a building that contained the needs of four
thousand journalists and twenty-five hundred radio-TV technicians,
plus film laboratories and transmission units. The Press City would
become a school after the Games.

A cyclone fence separated the Press City from the Olympic Village.

At 5:00 A.M. on September 5, Roone Arledge and Dick Ebersol
walked down a hallway in the Press City and through a doorway that
exited upon a loading dock. On the far side of the loading dock stood the
cyclone fence. Under the light of a descending full moon, the Olympic
Village glowed a dull metallic gray, its jagged contours filling the sky.

Arledge had just spent an hour with his closest aides—Ebersol,
Chuck Howard and Jim Spence—going over telecast plans for the coming day. Howard and Spence had fled to catch a few hours of sleep, but
Arledge, who seemed never to require sleep during the course of an
Olympics, had coaxed Ebersol to stay on for a few more minutes.
Arledge said he wanted to talk over "some business things," but as the
two men stood on the concrete surface of the loading dock—a surface
broken only by the shapes of a few large garbage cans several feet
apart—Ebersol had the impression that the florid little man, so often
inaccessible to those who requested his time, simply wanted a bit of
companionship. The two men stood in the cold morning air, looking at
the moon, for nearly five minutes. Ebersol remembered that Arledge
rambled somewhat on the subject of nature, and then of art—two topics
that fascinated Arledge, and about which he could talk extremely well.

Finally, Ebersol, pleading fatigue, excused himself and started for his
room. Arledge remained alone on the loading dock for a few final moments. Then he left.

No one will ever know how soon after that the dark forms began to
emerge from behind the nearby garbage cans. No one would ever be able
to say with certainty how many more minutes the eight terrorists, members of the Black September Movement, would have granted the two

Americans before murdering them en route to their grisly rendezvous with the Israeli athletes in nearby Building 31. Ebersol always believed that his and Arledge's lives had been spared by a matter of minutes. The dawn was nearing.

For the next twenty hours, ABC Sports in Munich converted itself into a para-news organization. It was a technically superb but somehow eerie transformation, considering how intertwined were the aims and the fortunes of ABC and the modern Olympics.

Never before had Arledge's video instincts been so resoundingly validated. The very fact that ABC was able to transmit live pictures of the terrorists as they occupied the Israeli compound was a product of that instinct. One of the conditons that Arledge had routinely demanded in his Olympics negotiations was the right to use unilateral cameras—that is, ABC-controlled cameras that were electronically independent of the worldwide pool feed. As soon as the terrorist attack became known, German officials ordered that the worldwide feed be shut down. They forgot about the autonomous American contingent, which acted with an almost catlike swiftness as soon as the news broke.

Within minutes after he had stood sleepily and unsuspectingly in the path of the terrorists' assault route over the cyclone fence, Arledge was whipping his array of producers, cameramen and reporters into ad-hoc coverage units. An associate film producer named John Wilcox and the ABC News correspondent Peter Jennings, who was actually on vacation, taking in the Games as a spectator, rushed into an obscure entrance to the Olympic Village before German officials had time to tighten security. Wilcox had grabbed a hand-held camera. Once inside, he and Jennings fanned out, Wilcox positioning himself less than fifty feet from Building 31. His pictures would be the most dramatic and intimate of the coverage.

Another primary feed came from an ABC camera, outfitted with a long-range lens, which was set up on a high bridge adjacent to the Press City. This camera could home in on the rooms where the doomed hostages waited with their captors.

Howard Cosell arrived with a clutch of reporters and photographers at an entrance to the village. By Cosell's own account, he stripped off every article of clothing that bore an ABC insignia and, because he happened to be wearing Puma tennis shoes, somehow convinced a guard that his group consisted of shoe salesmen and workers in the village. The ruse worked. Once inside, Cosell found and interviewed the best friend of Moshe Weinberg, the Israeli wrestling coach who was the first victim of the gunmen.

In the principal anchor booth, Jim McKay stopped being a sports announcer and began improvising the role of news anchorman. For hours, McKay assimilated the wisps of information making their way out of the village and processed them into a coherent narrative of the unfolding horror. "My father once told me," he remarked at one point, "that our greatest hopes and our worst fears are rarely realized. Tonight, our worst fears have been realized."

When it was finally over—when the macabre event had played itself out in a blaze of nocturnal crossfire at a military airfield some twenty-eight miles from Munich, in which all the remaining Israeli hostages were slaughtered—ABC found itself covered with glory. Arledge's producers, announcers and cameramen shared twenty-nine Emmys for their work at Munich. Ratings figures showed that more than half of America's households had watched at least part of the coverage. Senator Ted Stevens of Alaska read an effulgent tribute to ABC into the Congressional Record. Writing in *The New York Times,* critic Les Brown observed that "The achievement carries a special significance in the world of American television, as another milestone in the emergence of a full-fledged third network force."

Les Brown could not have known then how chillingly correct he was. A "full-fledged third network force" indeed was emerging at Munich, and in certain ways that were not apparent on the TV screen. For even as he was orchestrating his network's brilliant coverage of the terrorist attack on Olympic Village, Roone Arledge was moving on an entirely different plane of action: the gritty plane of business, of iron-fisted bargaining as opportunistic and self-serving as ABC's camerawork was grand.

Never mind terrorism and murder. Never mind the complexities of commanding 250 technicians and 16 color cameras and 18 videotape machines. Never mind the immediacies of covering 6,500 athletes as they participated in 195 events. Life went on. There were other fish to fry. In particular, there were the *next* Olympics to think about: the 1976 Winter Games in Innsbruck and the 1976 Summer Games in Montreal.

Roone Arledge wanted these Games for ABC. Innsbruck would be no problem. It was Montreal he coveted; he could not afford to let Montreal slip from ABC control and into the hands of CBS or NBC, both of which lusted for the chance to wrench the Games out of ABC's dominion.

And so, at the height of his preoccupation with the athletic and sociopolitical convulsions in front of his ABC cameras, Roone Arledge plunged into a swift and brutal campaign to seal off any rival claims for

Montreal in 1976. So sudden and so discreet was his maneuver that years passed before his rivals were able to understand completely how he had done it. As a chapter in ABC's long and sometimes savage struggle upward into parity, the ploy ranked with Tom Moore's and Ed Scherick's fabled decoy move against Tom Gallery and NBC—in the force of its consequence, if not in sheer charm.

It was the first major application of what became known as the "Arledge closure."

As to the competitive importance of the Montreal Games, the record leaves no doubt. All the networks understood their value. As early as 1970, CBS Sports vice president Bill MacPhail had written a letter to the mayor of Montreal requesting information about whom MacPhail should contact "to indicate our enthusiasm for obtaining the rights." And in 1972, NBC deployed its two chief sports executives, Chet Simmons and Carl Lindemann, to Munich with a similar goal. "We had one thing in mind," recalled Lindemann, "and that was to negotiate for Montreal like crazy."

But upon arriving in Germany, and seeking out the Canadians, who had also showed up there, Simmons and Lindemann were surprised to find their efforts rebuffed. "They told us," said Lindemann, "that there would be no discussions about future rights until these Games had been completed. They said they were only in Munich to observe, not to discuss."

Nevertheless, the two NBC men persisted. A week passed. The Canadians remained intransigent. And then a rumor began to make the rounds at Press City: a rumor that the Canadians had struck a deal with ABC. The Canadians would not confirm the rumor. "Do not be concerned," Paul Desrochers, a member of the Canadian Olympic organizing committee, told Carl Lindemann. "We will be in touch with you." Angry and confused, but helpless, Simmons and Lindemann returned to New York.

In October of 1972—a month after Munich—CBS renewed its efforts to enter the bidding. Television network president Robert Wood wrote to Gerry Snyder of the Canadian committee reaffirming CBS's enthusiastic interest and proclaiming his willingness to come to Montreal and state his network's case. Snyder wrote back, acknowledging the letter and promising to set up such a meeting.

In November, the Wednesday before Thanksgiving, NBC began to smell smoke. "It was decided," recalled Lindemann, "that I would get my ass up to Montreal as quickly as possible." Lindemann took along the general counsel for NBC, a man named Corey Dunham. They were granted a meeting with Paul Desrochers, whose first cryptic words were: "Where have you been?"

Dumbfounded, Lindemann sputtered, "Waiting for your call! Like you instructed us in Munich!"

Desrochers proffered a Gallic shrug. "Ah," he said, "a great deal has happened since then."

Simmons and Lindemann were able to get nothing further from the Canadian, beyond a vague suggestion that negotiations were still open. They flew back to New York on Friday afternoon, the day after Thanksgiving.

The following morning, Saturday, Lindemann received a call at his home from Marvin Josephson, the president of International Creative Management, the prestigious consortium of literary, talent and business agents. "What I am about to tell you will be upsetting," Josephson began. "ABC and the Canadian Olympic organizing committee have a deal for the Montreal Games. And we have been retained to sell the overseas rights."

The subsequent uproar was fierce—and futile. Both CBS and NBC charged that the Canadians had foiled all their attempts to submit competitive bidding, while allowing the networks to believe they were still in the running. No matter. ABC had the Games.

"What happened," said Lindemann, "was that when Arledge met with the Canadians at Munich—and they did meet—Roone recognized that the Canadians wanted some fast bucks. He offered a unilateral bid of $25 *million*. Ten percent of it immediately. At that time, that was an *enormous* amount of dough." ABC's total investment at Munich, for rights and production, had been only $13.5 million. "And then he hit 'em with the 'Arledge closure.' He said, 'But you've got *only twenty-four hours* to make the deal. I don't want you going out and shopping around for a better bid. Make the deal now, or we withdraw it.'

"So Roone had it all nailed down by the time he left Munich. And the Canadians carried out the charade that things were still open for another six weeks. They did it to save face, I guess, and to present the illusion that things were on the up and up."

Arledge's numbing stroke paid its dividend. True to the legacy of similar audacious blitzes by ABC Sports in the past, it sent waves of prosperity through the entire network.

Montreal was an elegant video dance, a television sports masterpiece. It stood out all the more brightly in contrast to the cluttered, over-hyped cacophony of events that had come to characterize TV sports in the seventies. Working from a scattered array of venues—there were events, often simultaneous, from as many as twenty-four separate sites—Arledge constructed his montage of live pictures from a bank of thirty-two monitor screens, shifting from boxing at a gymnasium to a swimming event to archery to rowing with a deceptive sense of effortlessness. Arledge interspersed this live coverage with what was by now an ABC Sports trademark, dozens of "up close and personal" vignettes of the competitors. These vignettes helped establish Sugar Ray Leonard, among others, as an American celebrity, and generated a fresh climate of fashionability for boxing.

These vignettes, and Arledge's new style of "whip-around" skipping from event to event, amounted to something more: they were a dress rehearsal for *ABC World News Tonight,* as the evening newscast would look within a year, when Arledge took it over. ABC Sports subordinates who watched him operate at Montreal vividly remember an incident at the start of the Games that upon later reflection seemed to stand as a clear demonstration of Arledge's journalistic designs.

"We had put together this special two-hour program, a preview of the upcoming Games," recalled Peggy Brim, "and it had taken *weeks* to produce. Two days before air Roone looked at it and decided it was all wrong. He tore it apart. Changed it utterly. It seemed like an insane thing to do at the time. But it wasn't insane. Germinating within him was a whole vision of what this Olympics was going to be. It was to be *live,* it was to be *journalistic.* What he threw out was a more traditional, a 'this-is-what-we-have-coming-up' type of show. It didn't have the tone, the mood to be the frontispiece for this new vision: live, now, present-tense, an absolutely vivid assurance that *we will be there,* everywhere, as it is all transpiring. Our people all over the city of Montreal. He was roughing out his vision for ABC News."

The vision became manifest on June 1, 1977. On that date, Arledge accepted from Fred Pierce, president of ABC television, the dual presidencies of ABC News and Sports.

Once again, Arledge's timing was impeccable. In many ways, 1976, his best year in TV sports, was his valedictory year. With the single, monumental exception of Olympics telecasts, he was never again to involve himself as deeply in sports programing as he had before. The reasons were not hard to understand.

By 1976, Arledge had spend sixteen years of his life supervising the video coverage of games. In that time, he had seized a category of programing that had been dismissed as banal, even somehow faintly disreputable, by the ruling lords of network television, and he had advanced that programing category to such a refined and intensely stylized form that it took on the power of a popular-culture mythology against which people measured themselves and their response to the society.

Now the cycle had completed itself, at least as far as Arledge was concerned. By 1976, his best and most creative work lay years in the past. Even his Olympics extravaganzas, which grew in size and in virtuosity with each new telecast, were more or less refinements of a principle he had established, alongside Scherick, with *Wide World of Sports* in 1961. By 1976 the other networks had learned how to imitate Arledge's video look—often with the help of former Arledge protégés, such as Don Ohlmeyer at NBC. And Arledge, in his turn, was showing signs of boredom with it all. He seemed less interested in creating new esthetics than in experimenting with power itself: now vindictively "punishing" the National Basketball Association by scheduling the successful Trashsport series *Superstars* against it on Sunday afternoons (the NBA had sinned by signing with CBS instead of renewing with ABC), now slapping down $94 million to raid NBC for major-league baseball—in a four-year deal that gave ABC rights to Monday night games, the All Star Game, the playoffs and the World Series in alternate years, now plucking the Kentucky Derby and the Preakness away from CBS, now swooping in for yet another Olympics deal (the 1980 Winter Games at Lake Placid) that left his rivals howling once more about "private and noncompetitive practices."

All of these expenditures, by the way, raise an interesting question: where did all of Arledge's bargaining money come from over the years? For a poor network (even granting the relative nature of "poor" as applied to network finances), ABC had always been able to flash a very serious roll of money when it craved rights to a sporting event. If Arledge's quick promise of $25 million stunned the Canadians in 1972 (not that it helped much in the end; Montreal ran up a $1-billion deficit on the '76 Games), they should only have known what lay ahead in 1984: Arledge would commit nearly *ten times* that amount for Los Angeles. More to the point, ABC's winning bid of $225 million didn't just beat runner-up CBS. It beat CBS by a margin of $75 million.

How was it possible? There were several reasons. *Wide World of Sports* was the first big one. Despised and ridiculed by its rivals for showing anonymous competitors doing silly things on tape, this low-budget, highly rated program became a cash faucet for ABC Sports. By the 1980s it was gushing out $180 million a year in gross revenues. This gave the sports division a little mad money to spend when the itch struck.

Another reason had to do with ABC's good luck in betting on the American economy. Most rights deals—Olympics deals in particular—are made several years before the money is actually paid. "ABC just kept betting on the economy to go up," said a rival programer, "and they were correct every time."

But the most important reason involved a simple, elemental willingness to spend. A certain riverboat-gambler instinct is built into ABC's corporate personality. The network staved off oblivion in its early years by taking long risks. Many of those risks involved sports. ABC was emotionally wedded to sports investments to a degree that neither CBS nor NBC could comprehend. Thus, while the bigger networks maintained a self-indulgent "country-club" atmosphere *within* their sports departments, pampering their staffs and corporate friends with the best hotels and buffets and limousines at the site of a sporting event, these same networks turned conservative when it came to the crucial matter of competitive bidding. Sports executives at both CBS and NBC recite endless stories of incidents when their pleas for just an extra million or two dollars—which might have put their network ahead of ABC in their quest for a prestigious event—were primly turned down by their division superiors as "not profitable."

Arledge never had any trouble persuading his division head to commit money to sports. Arledge was the division head.

The 1960s would stand as the most brilliantly productive of Arledge's career. These were the years in which he had functioned most purely as a video artist, seizing an all but discarded program motif and rehabilitating it with a narrative voice of its own, an intensely intimate visual look, and perhaps most important of all, a charged sense of its own urgent distinctness from anything else on television.

College football, *Wide World of Sports,* the Olympics, *Monday Night Football:* these were the canvases onto which Arledge had poured his inventive genius. The idioms he created for each, and the fundamental idiom that informed them all—take the game to the fan, saturating the fan in a universe of *game* that radically transcended the experience of a fan sitting in any stadium—would continue to discharge energy well into the 1980s, with no apparent lessening of force. A new generation of network and cable programers would forge successful careers by imitating Arledge's precepts, and some would even find ways to streamline the expense involved. But no one would prove the idiom obsolete.

"He pushed the whole industry," said Don Ohlmeyer, the most effective of several Arledge protégés to import the master's techniques into a rival network—in this case, NBC. "He changed the perception of television."

But what lay ahead for Arledge would be less rewarding. The grinding demands of administrative duty would sap more of his energies as the possibilities for artistic innovation inevitably diminished. The 1970s would not be a sterling decade for TV sports. They would be a messy, cluttered decade, a time for the American middle class to release a self-indulgent impulse that it had held in check through years of social preoccupations. TV sports, even as its forms were spreading through the rest of television, would fall prey to the hidebound interests of trend-wise entrepreneurs who wanted to blend it with slick packaging formulas that were shooting through prime-time entertainment programing. To the extent they succeeded, TV sports would become mannered, overdone—even actively deceptive. Before the seventies were over, most of Arledge's attention would be focused on the fresh challenge of news, but he could not escape accountability for some sad excesses committed in his old division.

There was one further aftershock of Arledge's golden cycle: TV sports affected society. Even at its esthetic peak, and without any deliberate intent, TV sports sent powerful signals into the culture that made a difference in the way people thought and behaved. Some of the differences were innocuous. Some of the differences were not.

XVIII

COLLEGE SPORTS FOR SALE

I f there was one supreme illustration of how the crossed wires of American sport and American television sent high-voltage shocks through American society, it was in the matter of college athletics.

The collegiate example is doubly compelling because it underscores a separate but closely related truth about TV and sports: that television's conquest of the sporting world was seldom a one-way process. In nearly every important instance, the degree of exploitation was at least mutual. Further, the ground rules that governed the exploitation were as often as not dictated by powerful barons, not within the colonizing networks, but within the athletic kingdoms being colonized. This was certainly true in the case of the National Collegiate Athletic Association.

No casual reader of newspaper sports pages over the last quarter century could be oblivious of the ever-soaring dollar value the NCAA and various bowl-game committees placed on telecast rights for college football and basketball games. Nor could anyone fail to connect this soaring dollar value—$11 million for a Rose Bowl telecast, $1.1 million for rights to a national regular-season football telecast involving "major" teams—to an ever-descending morass of pressures upon schools to *get* that money: pressures that by the 1980s had mired many of America's best-known universities in a slough of recruiting scandals, illegal payoffs to athletes, an almost reflexive lowering of scholastic standards for ballplayers, an endemic climate of para-professionalism at several dozen football and basketball "factories," and an abiding mood of shame, furtiveness and bitter cynicism hovering about college games—games that at one time had stood as a celebration of youthful vigor and joy.

TV money, and its misuse, had widened a schism that had always existed between the college athletic program and the rest of the college campus—to the point that certain teams, sequestered in their lunarlike facilities and feasting on the carcasses of beef supplied to them by adoring booster clubs, had about as much to do with ordinary campus life as an army of occupation has to do with the life of a conquered city.

This is not to suggest that the NCAA or any other governing committee had deliberately funneled television's limitless millions into a corrupt conspiracy for circumventing the amateur structure of college athletics. In fact, the NCAA worked doggedly with a staff of sixty-three overwhelmed investigators to cover more than seven hundred schools, ferret out the misuse of money and publicly punish the violators. Nor was network television an indictable co-conspirator. It was merely purchasing a product.

The wellsprings of the greed were legion. Countless coaches, athletic directors, boosters, athletes and athletes' parents bore personal accountability for the dollar-obsessed defilement of college sports. But in the end, the evil was institutional: like petrodollars gushing into a small, historically impoverished Middle Eastern emirate, the tele-dollars gushing into college athletic departments imposed a new socioeconomic system upon an outmoded structure. The structure failed.

"The rights costs to college football were growing faster than the TV package itself was improving," said Chuck Howard, ABC's longtime producer of college football. "The ratings would stay flat—good, but flat—from year to year, but the cost of rights would shoot up 100 percent, 180 percent. Every time a new deal was struck with the NCAA, people would say that the network that did it was crazy. In the sixties, that network was almost always us. The reason we could afford to pay those incredible rights costs was that we could pass the burden along to the advertisers. The advertisers didn't mind. They loved being associated with college sports—partly because advertisers are sports fans themselves, and partly because of the *exclusivity*. There was only one show in town where college football was concerned, and that was ABC."

Those rights packages didn't hammer themselves out, of course. They were the handiwork of collegiate officials just as determined, in their own way, to exploit the fantastic wealth inherent in college sports telecasts as were the networks.

The most relentlessly successful of these officials was a former United Press International sportswriter named Walter Byers, the executive director of the NCAA. Just as the National Football League was fortunate to produce a negotiator of Pete Rozelle's merciless brilliance, the NCAA was lucky, in a dollars-and-cents way, to generate its own iron-willed, tactically shrewd autocrat-genius of the bargaining table. Byers's success at revolutionizing the TV value of college football paralleled Rozelle's success at enriching the pro game. (The NCAA did not concern itself with negotiating rights to regular-season basketball games—only championship tournaments—so football was Byers's main area of concern.)

Walter Byers would never attain the mass-public recognition power of Pete Rozelle, a figure whom Byers regarded as a natural adversary, a competitor for the TV-football dollar. Not that Byers ever wanted that kind of recognition. He would dash up several flights of stairs, cowboy boots clicking, to his office in Shawnee, Kansas, rather than share an elevator with someone who might try to get chummy with small talk. When Walter Byers talked, it was likely to be big. He was a living expression of college sports' collective self-image. He was Kansas City–born, a product of America's middletown grass roots and damned proud of it. In 1952, the year after he was first elected executive director, he moved the NCAA's head offices from Chicago to Shawnee, a suburb of his home town, as a defiant statement of contempt for big-city sensibilities. A small man, clear-eyed and with strong lines etched into the jaws of his roundish face, Walter Byers enjoyed watching the big TV boys from the East come 'round to his small town as though it was the center of the universe.

"Byers would have been good at the United Nations or negotiating with the Russians," one network producer observed dryly. "He was particularly skilled at playing Roone Arledge off against Bill MacPhail. He's the one man responsible for the enormous escalation of TV dollars into collegiate sports, and I don't suppose that's a bad thing, in itself. But what it led to was this: a situation in which the only way a school could participate in this windfall was to *win*. A football team had to go 8-of-10, 9-of-10—it had to be a *glamour* team to get the networks' attention. The ability to get on national television became paramount in college sports, and there you have the root of all the corruption."

The pressure to produce big winners, and the rule-breaking that went with it, did not start with TV money, of course. The buying of college football teams was a matter of controversy in the 1920s and 1930s. But by the mid-1980s, the escalation had reached such a pitch—CBS Sports president Neal Pilson estimated that television would pour half a billion dollars into college sports over a five-year span—that some form of corruption was all but unavoidable at most schools.

It is fairly safe to assume that Walter Byers never expected to be pushing that kind of temptation around.

He assumed his executive directorship of the NCAA in 1951, and continued in it through the 1980s. But although his duties in this official capacity were significant, it was as a member of a twelve-member committee that he never chaired that Byers forged his most lasting accomplishments: the NCAA's television committee. The committee had been created as far back as 1952. In that era Notre Dame University, a football powerhouse, was America's college team, just as the New York Yankees were America's major-league baseball team. College administrators, sensitive to the impending age of TV sports, were concerned that the networks might focus almost exclusively upon Notre Dame and its opponents, unless some collective safeguards could be established to forbid such concentration of coverage. It was the TV committee's mandate to devise the safeguards.

Byers may never have chaired the TV committee, but he was always its shrewdest and most influential member, particularly vis-à-vis the networks at negotiating time. When the committee struck its first deal, with NBC in 1952, it felt grateful to accept a payment of $1 million, for one year, and to extract an agreement from the network that no college would appear on the air more than once a season.

But as the years went on, the committee's list of conditions became longer and bolder. Not only did the price of telecasts shoot up, but the networks also had to agree, in effect, to do things the NCAA's way. For instance, the TV committee insisted on the right to approve all network play-by-play men. Byers's influence was clear in this matter. He felt that any reference, no matter how indirect, to professional football was tantamount to free advertising for a competitor's product. The networks indulged this blatant editorial interference until the mid-1960s, when Roone Arledge at ABC publicly repudiated it and declared that ABC would decide on its own announcers. But even Arledge's manifesto did not entirely satisfy everyone that Byers had been faced down.

Writing in the December 14, 1970, issue of *Sports Illustrated,* Frank Deford summed up the prevailing skepticism when he observed that, "Like most well-paid TV announcers, neither [Bud] Wilkinson nor [Chris] Schenkel has any heart for venturing real opinions or honest criticism. Speaking of old speak-no-evil, Chris Schenkel has attained new heights. Now he sidesteps naming the player who commits an atrocious foul when it is obvious to all in the stadium."

Whatever the precise degree to which Arledge enforced his "pick-our-own-announcers" dictum, it is clear that he was Byers's classic foil: the one network sports chieftain who could stand face-to-face with the hardbitten little Midwesterner, conceding the necessary points, perhaps, but in the end extracting as much for his side as Byers got for his. Arledge even learned to play some of Byers's better-known ploys, and to turn them deftly to ABC's advantage.

It was just such a psychological gambit, in fact, that enabled Arledge to recapture college football for ABC in 1965, after seeing the rights wrenched away by CBS and then NBC following his own triumphant performance in 1960 and 1961.

"In 1965 we are out of pro football because NBC has taken the American Football League away from us," recalled an ABC insider. "CBS is Mr. NFL, and the college rights are going to be up for grabs; so there's a good chance that ABC will come away with nothing major in TV sports. We're looking at disaster. Roone seized the initiative in a brilliant way. He called up Walter in Shawnee. He said to him, 'Look, you shouldn't even put the NCAA contract out for a bid. You should give it to us and I'll tell you why. If CBS or NBC wins the bid, you'll be second-class citizens behind their pro telecasts. You'll get their leave-behinds: their second-best announcers, producers, technical directors. With us, you'll be the main guys.' Walter flew out to New York and they closed the deal in a hotel room. It was tremendous. Walter took all of what Roone had to say and then he added, 'OK, hear this: I want a shitload.' And Roone said, 'I'll fill your pockets.' And that," concluded the ABC insider, "was the start of our exclusivity in college football."

But not without a few additional Byers strings. Another curious staple of college football telecasts that had Byers's imprint upon it was an NCAA rule that required a brief prepackaged film promo spot limning the ivy-shaded virtues of each competing school whose team was competing on a Saturday-afternoon telecast. Particularly in the late 1960s and early 70s, when much of that venerable collegiate ivy was being singed by SDS firebombs, these paeans had a certain surreal quality that tended to compromise the objective authority of the network carrying them. But paeans were what Walter Byers and his committee wanted, and paeans were what they got.

The popularity of college sports on TV continued to increase, and the networks were rewarded for their paeans: The money rolled in.

But for all of Walter Byers's shrewdness, there was one fundamental oversight. It was an oversight that his archrival, Pete Rozelle, had been careful not to commit. Eventually, this oversight would lead to the unraveling of Byers's empire.

Two decades after the young Roone Arledge composed his romantic homage to the TV coverage of "enthusiastic college kids—the pride of America, not hard-bitten old pros," the very success of Arledge's vision had helped nourish a generation of thinly veiled professionalism that mocked his very words.

Clemson University, the national football champion of 1981, stood in national disgrace in 1982: assailed with 69 charges in an NCAA bill of particulars that listed more than 150 rules violations dating to 1977. The charges included offering young athletes cash for enrolling at the university, cash to spend on cars and clothes and TV sets, cash for such fleeting achievements as "Specialty Teams Player of the Week," cash to pay phone bills and dental bills and airline ticket bills. "There emerges," wrote Dave Kindred in the *Washington Post*, "a picture of a big-time operation running out of control. It seems every Clemson football player had a hand out, and if a booster didn't come across with money, then a coach did."

In 1982, the Clemson scandal was by no means the only symptom of decay. From Florida State University, there emerged a lacerating glimpse into the abuses of "big-time" (as the newspaper phrase invariably had it) college basketball. James Bozeman, Florida State's team captain and an all-America candidate, went public with charges that the university improperly administered medical treatment to injured athletes, prescribed drugs irresponsibly, forged the scholastic transcripts of certain incoming players, supplied answers to athletes in correspondence courses, used the sexual enticements of female students to lure prospective recruits, encouraged illegal summertime team practices and, inevitably, paid its student-athletes under the table. The charges were about standard for a big-time athletic factory.

For his troubles, Bozeman received several crank telephone calls from Florida State fans and boosters, including two death threats. A supporter of Bozeman's requested protection from the United States attorney general. "We did not want to ask the Florida attorney general," the ally explained, "because he is a member of the Florida State Booster Association."

In 1982 alone, seventeen schools were on probation under NCAA rules for violations that included improper recruitment, extra financial aid to players, falsification of grades and transcripts, illegal out-of-season practices and even lying to the NCAA investigators. Another thirty-five schools were under active investigation. The University of San Francisco dropped its historically acclaimed basketball program (it had produced the great Boston Celtic Bill Russell, among others) after a series of recruiting embarrassments. UCLA, the college synonymous with basketball championships, was scrambling to deal with charges that overzealous boosters were providing cars and discounted apartments for star players.

Two societies, separate and unequal, were polarizing the campuses: athletes and civilians. The academic revulsion for the situation, long held in silent check, was starting to find expression. One horrified Ivy League president, Howard R. Swearer of Brown University, finally made public a proposal that many of his colleagues had made in bitter, private jest. Writing in the February 21, 1982, *New York Times,* Swearer quite seriously called for "associating a professional or semi-professional team with a university. The regulatory and enforcement burden and the temptations for illegal and unethical practices would be dramatically eased. . . . The clear separation between the academic and the athletic purposes of a university would be beneficial to both."

How had it all been allowed to come about? The "institutional" evil of big TV money was one factor, but human venality played the active role. Often that human venality expressed itself through booster clubs.

Before the bar graph representing TV income took a turn toward the vertical in the mid-1960s, the central administrative figure in most university sports programs was the athletic director. Typically, the athletic director was neither a career academic nor a trained business manager. He was more likely to be a beloved coach, now emeritus, promoted to a desk job from which he could look out over the campus like a sort of living statue—Old A. J. (Hut) Hutchings, inventor of the split-W formation back in Ought-Eight and winner of more Southeast Seven conference titles than any. . . . "A lot of these guys were 'club members' who went to a couple of meetings a year and played golf the rest of the time," was the way one network producer of college sports coldly put it.

Not all athletic directors fit that description, of course. A good number were smart, sensitive and honorable professionals. But when Roone Arledge began to take the fan to the game (not the game to the fan), their sealed-off world was forever ripped asunder.

The explosion of TV rights revenues in the mid-1960s corresponded with an explosion in college costs. As the price of a college education spiraled upward, the value of athletic scholarships soared, and so did athletic-department budgets. In 1982 Michigan State University, a fairly typical Big Ten school, spent $1.7 million on athletic scholarships. Coaches' salaries increased—not always to the level of Jackie Sherrill's $1.7 million at Texas A&M, but substantially. In 1972, ath-

letic departments were shaken by a side-effect of the feminist revolution. The United States Department of Health, Education and Welfare
created an act, Title IX, that forbade sex discrimination in any educational institution receiving federal funds. With women's participation in
college sports more than doubling itself in the 1970s, this meant that
athletic directors would now have to spend millions of dollars in that
area—which they once could ignore with impunity.

More money, but more costs. More TV exposure, but more pressures
on recruitment to obtain that exposure. More rewards for making it in
the "big time," but more retribution for falling short. The track had
suddenly become very fast indeed—not to mention crowded. The A. J.
(Hut) Hutchingses of the collegiate world scarcely even knew which
direction to face, let alone run. Into this widening vacuum of expertise
stepped the members of the friendly local booster club.

Booster clubs had been as much a fixture of American college-town
life as Kiwanis or Rotary clubs for decades. Composed of former players,
alumni and just plain fans, they constituted one example among dozens
of grass-roots civic pride: booster clubbers would buy up group seating
blocs for home games, sponsor award banquets where the head coach
regaled them with coachly wit, paste their season schedules in their
shop windows and their GO TIGERS stickers on the bumpers of their
cars.

Not all boosters were *outré*. Not all of them had the team nickname
engraved into their upper front teeth or wore the old school red-and-
white to bed and to the shower. Many boosters were rational, respectable citizens. Others, who might never have thought to go out and stage
a fund-raising for a new biochemistry lab, or donate a side of beef to the
philosophy department, began to espy a certain philanthropic opportunity in the growing befuddlement of the athletic department. These
activist boosters began to raise and distribute money on their own. The
more responsible universities subjected these people to strict budgetary
accounting procedures. Many schools did not.

What happened at Oklahoma State University in 1978 was in many
ways typical of booster-club excess. The existence of a secret booster
club, organized to pay OSU football players from a "slush" fund of
several hundred thousand dollars, became public knowledge. Revelation
came not through any zealous investigations by the local media nor
through any outraged disclosures by athletes or coaches or faculty. Revelation came because a rival flouter of recruiting regulations, a Tulsa
businessman, became incensed over the way the secret club was han-
dling things, and blew the whistle.

And if a college coach somehow managed to withstand the pressures of a corrupt booster club, or alumni association, or board of trustees, or even in some cases the local press, he still might have to confront one last special-interest lobby on behalf of breaking the rules: the college athlete himself.

"Kids come in here knowing the going rate," said one athletic director of a large and reputable Midwestern football school. "They know what everybody else is getting in cars, apartments, cash, grade considerations. They come in expecting what the market will bear. There's a big, functioning grapevine out there [in the high schools of America]. We have to be ready to deal with that. We hold back on the car, the kid takes his ball and goes someplace else."

It could hardly be otherwise. Football and basketball on television had in some ways come to stand for college life in the imaginations of young boys and their parents, and football had the greater hold on the greater number. Its squads were larger—a college football team might dress upwards of eighty players for a home game, compared to ten or eleven in basketball—so it gave the illusion of being a more accessible sport for aspiring players. Its marching-band pageantry and layers of self-glorifying ritual sank deep into white, middle-class America's collective memory; it was an ancient game, the game most richly expressive of formalized warfare. Finally, beyond the college ranks beckoned the pros, so enshrined by TV.

By the early 1970s, TV football, professional and collegiate, had formed a paradigm for values and behavior that penetrated down to the very roots of society. As early as age seven, an Amerian child could step into the football culture, if his parents were inclined to push him over that line. Outfitted in professional-style polyurethane helmets and uniforms, trussed up in hip and kidney pads, mouthpieces, face guards and cleated sneakers, small boys could be found hurling themselves at one another in Pop Warner leagues (nearly six thousand teams around the country), in Khoury leagues, in American Youth Football leagues, in the leagues of Football United International and in dozens of other ad-hoc outfits, scampering obediently through their pro-style offenses and their flex defenses while their coaches, of varying ranges of expertise, compassion and TV-nourished megalomania, brandished their pro-style clipboards on the sidelines. Pigtailed moppets, meanwhile, spiffy in pleated cheerleader microskirts, high-kicked their heroes to junior euphoria.

Small wonder that by the time these juvenile gladiators reached high school—many of them veterans of such midget-scale "postseason" extravaganzas as the Junior Orange Bowl in Miami, the Junior Liberty Bowl in Memphis, or the Piggy Bank Bowl or the Honolulu Bowl, or at the very least, of kids'-league banquets with trophies rampant and their likenesses reproduced on placemats—small wonder they knew a thing or two about the realities of making the collegiate big time. They'd been in the big time virtually since they were toilet-trained. They had seen recruiting violations in the fifty- to eighty-pound divisions.

There were other indications that the realities of big-time TV college football did not conform to the idealistic sweetness of those little packaged paeans Walter Byers liked the networks to air at halftime.

Asked what he thought was his most significant contribution to the art of telecasting college football, ABC's Chuck Howard thought for a long time and then said, "The postgame show."

Why? "We had an obligation to refine and upgrade the postgame show," said Howard. "There were always people around the country with an interest in other games, other scores."

What kind of people would those be? "Bettors," said Chuck Howard. He went on: "In order to be a complete service to the viewer, we have spent the last ten years refining the postgame score operation. In the early days, it was just a matter of some guy reading scores off a wire-service ticker. Then we started picking out two or three key games a week and flashing their scores. Then we assigned Bill Fleming to do the job. Postgame scores were Bill's sole function. The telephone company would come and erect a separate phone booth in the pressbox for the job. Bill would hire six or seven local kids and he'd oversee their efforts to get an update on, say, the Notre Dame game. Then our graphics people would type up the score and get it on the air. Now, we use a computer line that feeds on a telephone company line and reaches us wherever we are in the country. We have nine people in our studios calling around for scores. We can keep tabs on sixty-five to seventy games a week. We earmark about thirty of those as crucial, and we get those scores on the air as soon as we can during our live telecast. We're like an early edition of the Sunday paper."

Chuck Howard was a decent man—in fact, a man of rather singular honor among network television professionals. In constructing an elaborate facet of sports coverage that would gratify the wishes of bettors, Howard was being relatively restrained. His telecasts never mentioned "point spreads," they never employed the services of a tacit tout on the order of CBS's Jimmy "The Greek" Snyder or NBC's Pete Axthelm for pro football telecasts. (CBS coyly explained that Snyder was on for his "entertainment value.") Howard even stopped short of most American daily newspapers, which routinely printed "Latest Line" or other odds-making sports columns, for the delectation of the seventy percent of American men and fifty-five percent of American women who indulged in illegal sports betting.

But there it was: a matter-of-fact acknowledgment that a great portion of America's interest in sports had to do with America's chance to make money off sports. And that even in the putatively pure arena of college athletics, part of television's mandate was routinely to expedite the transactions.

Indiana University's basketball coach, Bobby Knight, probably summed up the overall ethical climate best. "Right after the gambling information," Knight suggested, "you ought to list whores' phone numbers. Call Cindy at 555-4410. Twenty-five dollars an hour. Then list her strengths and weaknesses."

On September 15, 1982, Walter Byers's fundamental oversight finally produced the shock wave that many athletic directors had been quietly predicting for years. A federal district judge, Juan Burciaga, in Oklahoma City, ruled that the NCAA was "a classic cartel," and that only an individual college—not a collective association—had the authority to sell TV rights for its football games.

The judge was ruling on a lawsuit brought by the University of Oklahoma's board of regents and the University of Georgia Athletic Association. The two schools, chafing at their inability to get on the national airwaves as frequently as their power and prestige might allow, had contended that the NCAA restraints amounted to a violation of the Sherman Antitrust Act. In 1983, the judgment was upheld by the Tenth District Court.

Byers might have deflected such a ruling had he taken the preventive steps that Pete Rozelle was careful to take early in his regime with the NFL: that is, to lobby Congress for an exemption to antitrust rulings.

It was an expensive mistake to make—it stood to invalidate a combined network rights deal worth $281.5 million, and a cable contract with Ted Turner's broadcasting system worth an additional $18 million.

But then, perhaps it would lead to the fulfillment of Brown University President Howard Swearer's sardonic vision. If television were able to negotiate individually with the football and basketball "big-timers" of the college ranks, the day might not be too far off when the super-universities would field their own professional teams.

XIX

THE DECADE OF HUSTLERS

The Sunday afternoon of May 14, 1972 marked the onset of the most explosive, wildly uneven, ethically troubled and dollar-obsessed decade in the long progression of TV sports.

The onset was deceptively lyrical. On that balmy afternoon in Dallas, NBC Sports transmitted a championship match between two elegant Australian tennis professionals, Rod Laver and Ken Rosewall. The match stood, in the estimation of experts, as the greatest of all time. The event was the grand finale in a professional tennis tour called World Championship Tennis—something of a television creation in its own right. WCT, founded four years previously by the Texas millionaire sportsman Lamar Hunt, had become "major" in 1972 when it secured a contract with NBC to carry eight tournament finals on Saturday afternoons.

Now, in this era when people still spoke occasionally of "color" television and when the sight of tennis players in gaudy television blues and yellows and scarlets still drew startled comments, a national audience of 21.7 million viewers watched as something hauntingly dramatic began to shape itself in the public consciousness. As the afternoon progressed, it became clear that tennis would never again be a remote "club" sport played and watched by the effete upper crust. From now on, tennis was the stuff of *arena*.

For three hours, thirty-four minutes, Laver and Rosewall dueled like master fencers, trading their spin serves and slashing backhands and stretching, almost magisterially precise volleys. The last two sets were decided by "tiebreakers"—the scoring adaptation that had made tennis a feasible television sport by curtailing the potential for endless unresolved play. Nevertheless, the match became marathon. It spilled deeply into NBC's regular program schedule; producers feverishly improvised contingency schedules as the two artists drew out their hypnotic duel.

Finally, as announcer Bud Collins shrieked superlatives into his microphone, the aloof lefthander, Laver, prevailed. His winner's purse came to only fifty thousand dollars, a pittance by the standards of only a few years later—but Laver had touched off a multi-million-dollar bonanza.

The mysterious fusion that had welded TV with pro football at Yankee Stadium in 1958, with ice skating at Grenoble in 1968, and that would join it with gymnastics at Munich later on in 1972, had now flashed at Dallas. An instant tradition had been created. Tennis, in the blur of Laver's and Rosewall's rackets, had become a mass-audience TV sport.

"Big" tennis was part of the largest shock-wave cluster in the long-deferred, but always implicit TV sports boom. There had been earlier, isolated detonations: the American Football League back in 1960, the American Basketball Association in 1967. By 1970, expansions of existing leagues had enriched the pop-cultural vocabulary with such neo-nicknames as Blues, Mets, Nets, Jets, Astros, Capitols and North Stars. The number of major-league franchises for baseball, basketball, football and hockey stood at eighty-seven—more than twice the total at the decade's beginning.[*] Most of these new teams owed their existence at least partly to the promise of television revenues.

But 1972 was television's true breakout year in sports, however erratic the yield. In certain ways, it was an expression of the times. Something in the nation's collective civic consciousness was about to snap. In 1972, the American people re-elected a President amidst harrowing rumors that his fund-raising committee had tried to tamper with the Democratic campaign. In that same year, another presidential candidate had been shot down in Maryland and the Democratic vice-presidential nominee had withdrawn from the ticket following disclosures that he had undergone shock therapy for depression. This was the era of the Pentagon Papers, the massacre at Attica State Prison, the phantom "light at the end of the tunnel" in Vietnam, the saturation bombing of Hanoi and Haiphong; the year in which wire-service photographs from Southeast Asia showed naked children streaming down a road in tears, fleeing napalm. By 1972, American society was heading into the final, most tortuous throes of what a new, appointed President would call "our long national nightmare."

People behaved as though they wanted to blot the hideousness of

---

[*] William O. Johnson, Jr. *Super Spectator and the Electronic Lilliputians.* Boston: Little, Brown, 1971.

political and military reality from their minds. A massive unclenching from social awareness was gathering momentum. By 1974, when it was all over—when Vietnam and Watergate were formally laid to rest—America would plunge itself into a prolonged binge, a compulsive orgy of self-absorption, celebrity-worship, pouty posturing, attitudinizing, luxury drugs and therapeutic jingoism. In 1972, the party had already started. Television was ready with its own array of stimulants. NBC and CBS were finally onto the secret that ABC had had to itself for a decade. Sports on TV *sold*. In keeping with the times, sports on TV were fast becoming a kind of disposable, transient sensation, like a disco hit or miracle diet. The gratification of this whim would take on an ever-increasing rush of reckless frenzy until it foundered, eight years later, in the shambles of the Moscow Olympics of 1980.

The man who flashed the most entrepreneurial money, slapped together the most garish string of new instant professional sports leagues, and ultimately left behind the most wreckage of any 1970s promoter was a smallish, slightly built young Southern California lawyer with the name of Gary Davidson.

In 1972, Davidson and his partners were organizing the World Hockey Association to rival the established NHL. At the same time they were already laying the groundwork for what would become, briefly and absurdly, the misbegotten rival to the NFL, the World Football League. Davidson and his friends had concocted the American Basketball Association back in 1967. The ABA, with its red-white-and-blue balls, three-point perimeter and pin-the-tail-on-the-donkey franchises (the Utah Stars, the San Diego Sails, the Virginia Squires) was in fact the Davidson group's most enduring creation. It hung on for nine years, vainly seeking a network television contract while its teams scrambled from city to city or simply folded (by 1975, only three of the original eleven franchises remained), before its six surviving teams merged with the NBA in 1976.

Davidson and his friends lost money on the ABA, but by 1972 they had gained a certain cold-eyed worldliness that would serve them well in this disposable decade. Along with his partner and fellow Californian, a public-relations professional named Dennis Murphy, Davidson turned a profit on his new hockey league before the first puck was tossed down on the ice. The two men achieved their wealth by charging a finder's fee of $25,000 for ten of the WHA's new franchises. The other two they kept for themselves. Then Davidson sold his San Francisco franchise for

$215,000 just before the first player draft meeting—and assumed the *presidency* of his own new league.

As for fan incentives, Davidson and Murphy by 1972 had advanced somewhat beyond the peppy idealism of red-white-and-blue basketballs. "We'll let 'em [the hockey players] fight," was Murphy's pledge to *Sports Illustrated*.

But it was with the World Football League that Gary Davidson truly captured the spirit of the decade. In addition to barbarizing the rules a little—prohibiting a "fair catch" or a punted ball was one piquant touch—Davidson once again saw to it that one person who would not lose money on the World Football League was Gary Davidson. Repeating his ploy with the WHA, he kept a franchise for himself, Philadelphia, then sold it immediately to a group of businessmen for $690,000, then awarded himself a no-cut contract as league commissioner worth $100,000 a year. He also cut himself in on ten percent of the WFL's television revenues over a projected ten-year-period.

That period never materialized. The WFL did not fare nearly so well as did its commissioner. The stumbling block was television. The WFL began its existence in 1974 under an agreement with TVS, an independent sports network, that guaranteed each club a net of $100,000. But despite a startup in July (to get the jump on the NFL) and the innovation of midweek games (to fill up a presumed wasteland of pro football gratification between Monday and Sunday), the World Football League was in ruins halfway into its second hideous season.

Its Nielsen ratings in most cities had been weak. Its live attendance figures, sportswriters soon discovered, often included many thousands of fans attending on discount tickets or on outright "freebies." Players went unpaid for weeks, some of them actually subsisting on charity donations handed out by wealthy fans. Davidson himself became a casualty of all the confusion; he resigned his post as commissioner after an indignant Tom Origer, owner of the Chicago Fire, threatened to fold his team if Davidson did not step down.

The excesses of the decade to come were all there in the WFL's smoldering ruins: overproduction, overconfidence in television's ability to deliver fans for a sporting attraction automatically, an arrogant presumption that *anything* with "sports" written on it would make money in the overheated, hero-starved caldron that was the popular culture of the 1970s. The Washington Ambassadors, the Birmingham Americans, the Detroit Wheels, the Jacksonville Sharks, the Philadelphia Bell—all those hopeful jaunty nicknames faded like cheap mascara from the sporting world's public face, to be remembered only by a few bewildered fans and the star-crossed players themselves.

But there would be no shortage of main-chance promoters to rise in Davidson's place as the video sports goldrush of the seventies swarmed on.

Within months of the Laver–Rosewall tennis masterpiece on NBC, the networks were a-thwack with the sound of fuzzy yellow ball on catgut. A sport of individuals, tennis was a video-closeup natural for the emerging Culture of Narcissism. Glowering, temperamental new stars such as Jimmy Connors and Ilie Nastase quickly gained the status of cult antiheroes; their odd mixture of privilege and petulance fit perfectly with the angry national mood.

By March of 1976 the networks were saturating the public with no fewer than seventy tennis "classics"—up from seven just five years before. The economics were irresistible: CBS could buy delayed-tape rights for, say, the Marlboro Australian Open for as little as fifteen thousand dollars. Production costs were minimal. And for certain matches, a network could charge sponsors as much as fifty-five thousand dollars a commercial minute—the same rate it charged for an NFL telecast.

Perhaps no sport more thoroughly embodied the video promiscuity of the 1970s, or suffered from it more grievously, than tennis. Television's lack of a coherent design in tennis coverage soon became hilariously obvious. A viewer could tune in NBC and find a match between Arthur Ashe and Stan Smith, switch away to ABC during a commercial break—and find a match between Arthur Ashe and Stan Smith. Two separate matches. Both on videotape. In 1976, *Sports Illustrated* gloated over the following absurdity: on a Saturday afternoon in July, NBC aired a Chris Evert–Evonne Goolagong match from Wimbledon that was actually twenty-five hours old; on the following day, ABC showed the same two competitors in a match that had been played several *months* before, at Hilton Head Island, South Carolina. The screen had become a time-warp of tennis clutter.

The excessive onslaught even produced its own cockeyed grandeur. Billie Jean King, a bona fide prodigy since the early 1960s, established her mass-public status as the figurehead of women's tennis—through a typically bizarre promotional charade: her defeat of the aging tennis hustler Bobby Riggs at the Houston Astrodome in September 1973 in what was ballyhooed as a final reckoning between the forces of male chauvinism and feminism. In a setting awash with dancing girls, bands, and wild-eyed spectators decked out in costumes beyond the ken of *Let's Make a Deal,* and crowned by the authenticating presence of Howard Cosell at the ABC microphones, King arrived at courtside in a glittering

Egyptian litter borne by a flounce of semi-naked men, and presented Riggs with a live pig. It was consistent with the era that this event was masterminded not by a TV network but by a show-business promoter, Jerry Perenchio.

But for sheer opportunism, the "Battle of the Sexes" was hardly at odds with the general ethos of TV tennis. After all, the decade's most important women's tournament tour was sponsored by a tobacco company. In return for this gallantry, the company required that the tour be named after one of its cigarette brands. America's top women tennis players thus became accomplices in the company's baldly unapologetic scheme to get around the 1970 congressional ban on TV cigarette commercials. In the 1950s, a popular TV tobacco commercial featured a tap-dancing woman whose upper body was covered by a giant mock-up of a cigarette package; only her busy bare legs were visible. In the 1970s, on the women's tennis tour, this image was metaphorically updated. The cigarette brand's slogan was "You've Come a Long Way, Baby."

And then there was the brief abomination known as World Team Tennis. Concocted in 1973, boasting sixteen original franchises, eight of which quickly folded, and flashing such gimmicks as multicolored courts, substitutions and byzantine schedules (one year Cleveland played half its home matches in Pittsburgh), WTT could be accused of many faults. Diabolical shrewdness was not among them. Not even the TV networks of the seventies were prepared to absorb the WTT's level of blithe vulgarity. Denied any real chance of big television revenues, the league survived just long enough to witness the general TV-tennis craze collapse under its own weight, much as TV boxing had collapsed in the 1950s—with a scandal. (A WTT franchise known as the Golden Gaters did manage to get twenty-five percent of its games broadcast on *radio* one year, prompting *Sports Illustrated*'s William Leggett to wonder whether the listeners' ears tended to go from side to side.)

TV tennis's eventual scandal was one that humiliated the most august network of them all, CBS. It was a scandal that summed up all the banal promotional greediness that was corroding sports' bright promise as the best and highest use of television.

On February 2, 1975, CBS telecast a tennis match between Jimmy Connors and Rod Laver in Las Vegas, Nevada. The match was part of no established tournament or professional tour. It was, in fact, a confrontation dreamed up and packaged for CBS by a consortium of outside promoters—companies called Trans World International and Tennis Championships, Inc. The Connors–Laver match was trumpeted as "The Heavyweight Championship of Tennis"—a designation that had no meaning apart from its promotional cachet.

"Tennis Championships, Inc.," was in fact a man named Bill Riordan, a former manager of Jimmy Connors. The president of Trans World International was a man named Barry Frank. At one time, Frank had been a vice president of sports at ABC. Now he was a professional concocter of television-oriented sporting "events": his other creations included *Challenge of the Sexes, Superstars, Battle of the Network Stars, Celebrity Challenge of the Sexes, Games People Play.* A little over a year later, Barry Frank would become vice president in charge of CBS Sports.

The "Heavyweight Championship of Tennis," won by Connors, was a ratings success. America was at the peak of its tennis frenzy. Tennis-related industries had grossed $1.25 billion in 1974. The *fines* levied against some of the top men's players—eight thousand dollars against Ilie Nastase in the Canadian Open—surpassed the winning purses of tournament champs just a few years before.

CBS was delighted and surprised with the ratings outcome. CBS Sports was then in the throes of managerial uncertainty. Bill MacPhail, the gentle steward of that division for so many years, had resigned in 1974. The network replaced him with a rising star from its news division ranks, a thirty-seven-year-old corporate soldier named Robert Wussler. Wussler had joined the company in 1957; his first notable service had come as a skiing cameraman at the Squaw Valley Olympics. Since then, he had directed special events for CBS News and established a classy local-news department at the network's important owned station in Chicago, WBBM.

Sleek Robert Wussler, smart, glib and jovial, was headed for big things: the CBS Network presidency for sure. Beyond that, who knew? Perhaps the head of CBS News, still the primary jewel in William Paley's crown. It wasn't beyond comprehension that one day Bobby Wussler could be running CBS's entire corporate show. But first there was this stop in CBS Sports.

Wussler was not a sports man. But in the imperial design of CBS, Inc., that was not important—that was *still* not important. What mattered was the grooming of talent for larger things; and how convenient it was that a spot at the top of one of the divisions had opened up. Let this fellow Wussler cut his managerial teeth down there in Sports for a while, then move him up and along. That was CBS's standard drill.

The CBS chieftains had not learned anything from the years of Mac-Phail being eaten alive by Pete Rozelle. They scarcely imagined what a snakepit of greed, a speculator's paradise, they were dropping Wussler into. But then, they had scarcely imagined several years before that

Dizzy Dean was broadcasting on their airwaves.

One of the first things Bobby Wussler bought as head of CBS Sports was the "Heavyweight Championship of Tennis." Its early ratings success pleased him. He also liked the cut of this Barry Frank's jib. Wussler ordered up some more "Heavyweight Championships of Tennis." Maybe running a sports department was not all that complicated after all.

The next "Heavyweight" match would be between Connors and John Newcombe, on April 26, 1975, from Caesars Palace in Las Vegas. To sweeten the audience interest, the gambling casino would kick in $250,000 in prize money—winner-take-all.

Since Connors had won the first match, and was Bill Riordan's property, Riordan became the sole promoter for the Connors–Newcombe exhibition, and of the two "Heavyweight" matches that followed.

Connors defeated Newcombe, and again the ratings were sensational. Wussler was on a roll. He asked Riordan to produce yet *another* "Heavyweight" match, and the promoter complied: on February 28, 1976, Connors met and defeated the Spaniard Manuel Orantes. Again, the viewing audience was huge. It seemed that CBS Sports had tapped into a continuing series that might prove as popular in its own way as *All in the Family*.

In the self-congratulatory glow that surrounded these triumphs of sports packaging, no one at CBS seemed to notice, or feel any concern for, a small inaccuracy that had crept into the network's promotional language for these last two exhibitions. On-air announcers as well as press releases had begun to refer to the matches as *winner-take-all*.

The winner was not taking all. In each "Heavyweight" match, both players were guaranteed certain minimum purses in advance. For instance, at Las Vegas, loser Newcombe pocketed $280,000—more than the announced winner's "all." And the winner, Connors, in fact amassed a total of nearly half a million dollars, the extra cash coming from the TV rights money and other sources.

In any case, no one gave the winner-take-all claims a second thought. They were four more syllables in an ocean of hype, nothing to be alarmed about. And while the small deceits that would blossom into scandal took quiet root, the two principal victims moved quickly toward what seemed to be the fulfillment of their professional dreams.

In April 1976 Wussler moved up, as predicted and planned, to the presidency of CBS television. His successor at CBS Sports, at Wussler's own suggestion, was the Trans World International packager, Barry Frank. "The appointment fulfilled my dream of running a network sports department," Frank admitted a few years later.

This was to become the first publicized instance in which television coverage of tennis prompted the payment of "guarantee" money to top players, assuring them of rich rewards regardless of their performance. In the ensuing years, as the ratings value of tournament tennis became tied ever more closely to the participation of a few superstar players, many tournament directors around the world took up this practice—officially outlawed by tennis associations—of offering "guarantee" or "appearance" money to the stars. The inevitable scandal broke in the summer of 1983. Author Michael Mewshaw,* after traveling on the men's tour for several months, produced an account of a sport that had virtually self-corrupted in pursuit of TV riches. "Appearance money" had so flagrantly overshadowed prize money, Mewshaw reported, that players frequently either lost on purpose or covertly agreed to withhold their peak performances, all toward the end of hurrying off to the next tournament and its guarantees.

One of the problems of running a network sports department in the 1970s, as executive Barry Frank soon learned, was that you just couldn't trust what the damned promoters were selling you. The fourth "Heavyweight" tennis exhibition—as offered to Frank by sports packager-promoter Riordan—would feature Connors against Ilie Nastase in Puerto Rico on March 5, 1977. A few weeks before the match's air date, Frank happened to pick up a CBS Sports press release on the event—and was shocked to the roots of his corporate sensibilities to discover the match was being promoted as "winner-take-all."

As he recalled the incident, Frank sent the release back to the promotion department with an instruction, scribbled in the margin, to delete the phrase "winner-take-all."

"On the day of the match itself," Frank recalled, "I am sitting down in a bar in Houston, Texas, where I am attending an affiliates' meeting, and I hear on the television set Pat Summerall describing the match as 'winner-take-all.' I jump up and run to a telephone and put a call through to Puerto Rico and reach our director in the truck. I tell them to cut it out right now, and I go back to my drink. When I see Bob Wussler a couple of days later, I ask him whether we should run a correction. Wussler says no, forget about it. Which I do. I being the guy, remember, who *blew the whistle* on the whole thing."

Once again, the matter seemed forgotten—until two months later,

---

*Michael Mewshaw. *Short Circuit*. N.Y.: Atheneum, 1983.

when Neil Amdur, writing in *The New York Times,* broke the story that CBS had improperly advertised three of its "Heavyweight" tennis matches as being winner-take-all. The following November, Wussler found himself standing before a House communications subcommittee that was holding hearings on the question of whether all the major networks, in their competitive zeal, had been manipulating sports events and purposefully deceiving their viewers. Besides the spurious "winner-take-all" matter at CBS, the subcommittee sifted through a veritable grab-bag of possible TV sports abuses and excesses.

There was the question of exclusive contracts between networks and boxers, such as ABC's arrangement with Sugar Ray Leonard and CBS's with Howard Davis. Did this constitute "owning" the fighter? There was the problem of predominantly black colleges and universities in obtaining network TV exposure in sports. There was the disclosure that officials of the Sugar Bowl had asked ABC to step in to try to persuade the University of Pittsburgh to accept a Sugar Bowl berth—had Pitt's acceptance been influenced by promises of future regular-season appearances on ABC? Roone Arledge, testifying, said certainly not.

But the subcommittee's most stinging rebukes were reserved for CBS—and Wussler. A staff report maintained that, contrary to Wussler's repeated denials in testimony, the executive knew that the winner-take-all claim was fraudulent, and that he disregarded any opportunity to correct the misstatement. Wussler also denied that CBS paid the athletes directly. This conduct, said the staff report, "cannot be excused, considering the weight of evidence, by suggesting that it was all a mistake."

As damning as the phony winner-take-all claims proved to be for CBS Sports, they were not the only transgression within the "Heavyweight" matches, as it developed. An FCC staff member, reviewing the videotapes to compile the number of times announcers voiced the false claim, started to get intrigued with all the mentions and visual depictions of Caesars Palace Hotel—the "pops," as they are called in the industry—as well. The investigator rewound the tape and began to count the "pops." He counted some fifty-seven, all without any announcement that a promotional consideration had been paid by Caesars Palace.

On March 16, 1978, Robert Wussler resigned from CBS. His stated reason was that he would form his own production company—a standard disclaimer for TV executives forced to depart their positions under inconvenient circumstances. A short while later, Wussler was named president of WTBS, Ted Turner's "Super Station" in Atlanta.

Wussler's director of sports at WTBS was the very man he had replaced as the head of CBS Sports just four years earlier, Bill MacPhail.

Barry Frank fared a little better. Banished from CBS Sports, he returned to Trans World International and resumed the packaging of sporting events for network television. By 1983, Frank was able to dismiss his earlier dream of running a network sports division; he had a better thing going back at TWI.

"I can influence the content of TV sports from here better than I could inside a network," Frank declared. "I deliver cans of tape to CBS and NBC on about thirty different kinds of events—ABC still produces all their own stuff. My company represents the TV rights for World Figure Skating, Wimbledon, the Masters, the U.S. Open, plus all kinds of skiing, diving, gymnastics—you name it. I'd say that about ninety percent of the stuff we sell to CBS and NBC we produce ourselves. We deliver them a can of tape and they put it on the air. *Events.* That's what people want to see and we can do them at network-level quality. I wouldn't be anywhere else."

It seemed, as the 1980s got under way, that things had not changed so much after all since the days when Edgar Scherick was putting sporting events together from his ad agency, Dancer Fitzgerald & Sample. Except that now the packages were in color.

With Wussler's departure, the presidency of CBS Sports went to a caretaker replacement, Frank M. Smith, Jr., who held the job until 1980. Then Smith stepped aside for Van Gordon Sauter, yet another CBS non-sports executive on his way to the head of the news division. Sauter, a Falstaffian man who affected a bushy gray beard, tweed jackets and an office that resembled the captain's quarters on the *Pequod,* did not know much about sports and he did not claim to. But in his brief tenure, Sauter managed to stabilize the troubled division, largely by committing gigantic investments to the traditional, time-honored competitions—he spent $180 million toward long-term contracts for college football and basketball—instead of to the frivolous, synthetic concoctions of doubtful legitimacy.

Sauter's successor was the horn-rimmed Neal Pilson, a Yale Law School graduate and longtime business-affairs specialist. Pilson continued the task of restoring dignity and credibility to a division that had in many ways suffered the brunt of TV sports' entrepreneurial orgy of the 1970s.

ABC's scandal came in boxing.

Like CBS, ABC was burned because it accepted a prepackaged event from an outside promoter. In this case, it was the fraud-soaked United States Boxing Championships, designed and delivered to Roone Arledge's sports division by the flamboyant boxing baron Don King.

In the speculator's paradise that network sports had become, Don King was Promotion personified. He had the contacts, he had the cash, he had the flash, and he had about him a mesmeric aura of authentic suppressed violence: big and bulk-shouldered like a boxer, King had once served a prison term for beating a man to death.

King's very appearance suggested *video;* he looked like a man caught in the convulsion of some orgiastic electrical charge, like a human transmitter. His hair actually stood on end. His eyes bulged. He wore tuxedoes and capes of white ermine and sky-blue velvet that seemed to give off sparks. He had promoted seven of Muhammad Ali's title bouts and had an office in the RCA Building and smoked cigars that looked like shotgun barrels. Don King was a force. But in 1976 Don King was a force in distress. Muhammad Ali, his ticket to promotional Valhalla, had gone over to a rival promoter, Bob Arum. Don King would soon be wearing seersucker suits and sensible shoes if he did not soon get another scheme together.

He began to muse over an old dream of his, a massive boxing tournament on television, a tournament that would create champions right out there, live, in full view of the world. Fighters in all weight divisions, competing over a series of several weeks—a repertory cast of gladiators. Yes, that was the dream to pursue. And King knew just the man who could make it real.

Even before the 1976 Summer Olympics, Roone Arledge liked King's scheme well enough to purchase it. But the United States Boxing Championships did not gain real momentum in ABC's plans until the wondrous crop of young American champions began to emerge at Montreal. With Sugar Ray Leonard, boxing connected with the new celebrity culture. Now a televised tournament began to seem almost fated; it would be only the preliminary to something even more grand, more combustive. Did people want to see international boxing champions on TV? Why wait for the Olympics to come around every four years? Why not instigate them—in the swashbuckling ABC tradition of old? Why not create a television-sustained, professional, continuing worldwide boxing Olympiad? An American Football League of the ring?

However, Arledge made a terrible miscalculation in accepting Don King's boxing tournament. It was one breakthrough too many. It nearly ruined him and his sports division.

It wasn't as though Arledge naively trusted Don King; Arledge was hardly that credulous. But the assurances of independent controls that King's people provided were enough to deflect Arledge's better judgment. King had invited the reputable Jim Farley, chairman of the New York State Athletic Commission, to serve as an unpaid consultant. It would be Farley's job to select the referees. And King had designated *Ring* magazine, the so-called "Bible of Boxing," as the standard source of boxers' ratings and rankings. In January of 1977, the circus began.

Within weeks the rumors, the whisperings started to surface. Boxers were paying kickbacks to be allowed into the tournament. Referees were on the take. Certain won-lost records had been wildly falsified. On February 13, heavyweight Scott LeDoux lost what appeared to be a highly unjust decision to a fighter named Johnny Bourdreaux in a quarterfinal bout. As the ABC cameras and microphones remained live, LeDoux flew into a tirade, storming about the ring and shrieking, "Fix! Fix!"

LeDoux's outburst brought on a grand jury investigation. Now newspaper columnists were beginning to focus on the possibility of corruption. Arledge tried to contain the firestorm. He sent out word that any fighter who had firsthand knowledge of deceit or improper payments should contact his office. The results were shocking. Writing in *Newsweek,* Pete Bonventre reported one of the more damning revelations: a manager named Doug Lord claimed that lightweight Kenny Weldon paid a kickback to get into the tournament. Weldon confessed to ABC, Bonventre wrote, that he had paid one-third of his seventy-five-hundred-dollar purse to George Kanter, a booking agent who had dealt with King—and who claimed that the payment from Weldon was nothing more than a "booking fee."

More confessions and disclosures tumbled in. By the seventh week of the telecasts, in late April of 1977, Arledge had heard enough. He pulled the tarnished tournament off ABC and announced his own investigation. For once, the magic of timing seemed to have failed Arledge. His impending appointment as head of ABC News was public knowledge, and now that appointment appeared gravely threatened.

What perhaps saved him was his will to act, to acknowledge disaster and take his losses. (Wussler's apparent paralysis in a similar situation was what sealed his doom at CBS.) By transforming his network into the role of investigator of the debacle—he hired crime investigator Michael Armstrong to probe the affair—Arledge was able to put some crucial distance between ABC and the grotesque charade that it had transmitted to the American sports-watching public.

"We uncovered every lead that got uncovered," Arledge insisted a few years afterward. And in fact no one was ever convicted. Armstrong released a 327-page report that suggested unethical conduct at several levels. King himself escaped implication in wrongdoing, and after a while, the focus of everyone's wrath became *Ring* magazine and its hopelessly unreliable records.

As for the other networks, they had of course learned a valuable lesson. It was literally weeks before NBC, in September of 1977, aired a prime-time event called "A Night With the Heavyweights." The event was promoted by a man in a tuxedo with electric hair, a man named Don King. "We thought it over very carefully," an NBC Sports executive explained.

CBS Sports' scandal and ABC Sports' scandal were tawdry enough— as domestic scandals went. But the spirit of the hustler's decade in TV sports seemed to call for something more: some really grand abomination that would ring out the epoch on a superbly sour note. American television was equal to the summons. It took all three networks *and* the Union of Soviet Socialist Republics to carry things off with the requisite geopolitical burst of flatulence, but the 1970s did indeed end in a highly appropriate tangle of wheezing network sports executives, blustering vice commissars, grasping middlemen, dollar bills, tureens of caviar, letters of agreement, more dollar bills, spools of "upbeat" reports on Soviet life, more network functionaries—all suddenly arrested in mid-wallow by the rumble of Soviet tanks across the border of Afghanistan. If the three major networks could find one scrap of satisfaction in the way they performed in contending for the rights to the 1980 Olympics in Moscow, it was this: they managed to make the communist bureaucracy of Mother Russia itself behave like a bunch of groveling capitalists.

Before the tragicomedy had reached its climax, and a surprised NBC found itself clutching $85 million worth of what proved to be phantom rights, the following indignities—among others—had played themselves out:

ABC's *A.M. America* (the precursor to *Good Morning America*) aired a week of euphoric glimpses into life in the Soviet Union—which were reviewed by Soviet officials before they were aired—CBS's Mary Tyler Moore narrated a prime-time special from Moscow on the Bolshoi Ballet, and NBC shelled out $1.2 million for a show called "The Russian Festival of Music and Dance" (CBS and NBC admitted that their programs were a deliberate ploy to ingratiate themselves with the Soviets; ABC denied it); the Russians openly informed the networks that favorable political coverage would be one price for winning the contract (each network red-bloodedly denied that it would bend to such terms, but there was a lot of whispering that the other guys made all sorts of secret promises); and the man who could claim the distinction of being the world's most august elder statesman of telecommunications, CBS's founder and board chairman William Paley, made a personal visit to Moscow to plead his network's case.

There is even a photograph that nicely captures the degree of trust and esteem that the three networks earned for themselves in the eyes of the United States Congress for their deportment in the Moscow Olympic quest. The photograph appeared in the October 10, 1977, issue of *Broadcasting*, the special-interest voice of the radio-TV industry. The photograph shows a lineup of senior executives from all three networks. The men are standing solemnly shoulder to shoulder, each with his right hand raised. The senior executives are being sworn in to testify before another House communications subcommittee, convened to examine the extent to which the networks guaranteed concessions to the Soviets during their competition for rights.

This is the way the saga unraveled:

The quest for the Moscow Olympics had started as early as 1974, when the International Olympics Committee designated the U.S.S.R. as the host country for 1980. Each network sent several delegations to visit informally with Soviet Olympic officials. It was in 1975 that the spate of Soviet valentines began to air on American TV.

The Americans and the Soviets started to toss actual dollar figures back and forth at the Montreal Olympics of 1976. The initial Soviet demand was a shocking $210 million, but after a period of ceremonial stalking out of rooms, the networks submitted counter-offers that clustered in the low seventies. In the autumn of that year, CBS signed as a mediator the man who would ultimately play the decisive role for NBC—a small-time West German entrepreneur named Lothar Bock, who had good contacts among the Soviets.

Within weeks, Lothar Bock convinced CBS that he had firmed up an Olympic contract for them with the Soviets. And then CBS's Paley made a corporate move that inadvertently put the Russians on their guard: he dismissed Arthur Taylor as president of CBS, Inc. The Russians apparently interpreted the firing as a rebuke to Taylor for his efforts in securing the Games. Suddenly, Lothar Bock detected an imperious chill. He telephoned Robert Wussler, then CBS Sports president, and suggested that Wussler talk Paley himself into visiting Moscow as a show of good faith. The CBS founder wasted no time in complying. His meeting with the Olympic Organizing Committee chairman, Ignati Novikov, was cordial, and once again CBS allowed itself to believe that it had a deal.

It was not to be. The Soviets' next move was to issue a document to all three networks outlining procedures for final bidding. It was as though Paley had never made his pilgrimage. Obediently, leaders of CBS, NBC and ABC hurried off to Moscow. There, they learned some more shocking news. It seemed that the winning network would be required to pay $50 million "for equipment and facilities"—a sum to be assessed on top of the winning bid. The Russians were very quickly perfecting their sardonic imitation of degenerate capitalist greed.

But there was yet more. The lucky network that would qualify to pay this usurious "equipment and facilities" fee would first have to survive a brutal bidding duel that would reduce them to the aspect, as Roone Arledge later remarked, of three scorpions fighting in a bottle. There was to be a new sealed bid every twenty-four hours; after each new high bid was announced, the two lesser bidders would be given the chance to increase the figure by a minimum five percent.

Greed plays strange tricks on one's ideology. Just as the Russians were behaving more like capitalists with each twist of the screw, the American network capitalists now began to grasp the historic inevitability of socialism. On December 16, 1976, the representatives of CBS, NBC and ABC in Moscow linked arms, swore solidarity before the yoke of the imperialist oppressor—and went on strike. They walked out of a meeting with Novikov and left Russia. Back in the United States, these newly enlightened comrades vowed not to have any dealings with the Soviets until the Justice Department ruled on their collectivist proposal for pooled coverage.

But they forgot about Lothar Bock. The small entrepreneur stayed on in Russia, and continued to wheel and deal with the Soviets as if he were a representative of CBS, which, technically, he still was. Once again, astoundingly, Bock brought the Russian Olympic Committee around to the brink of a deal with CBS. And then, just as stunningly, CBS threw up its hands and announced it was dropping out of the pool; CBS was just too disgusted, it seemed, with the base materialism of Ivan the Bear.

Now Bock stood alone. CBS released him from his contract, and he returned to the United States to seek a connection with NBC. Bock and Carl Lindemann, the head of NBC Sports, met for breakfast at a Manhattan hotel, and by the time the meal was over—very little of it was actually consumed—Lindemann came to the realization that Bock could deliver the Olympics to NBC. It was done—after one last-ditch effort by Arledge and ABC, involving one last eleventh-hour dash back to Moscow.

The price was $85 million—plus a $1-million commission to Lothar Bock, plus the commitment to purchase fifteen TV programs that Bock would produce, plus a four-year consultancy deal for Bock (his harvest from NBC eventually amounted to more than $7 million), not to mention some $36 million NBC spent in equipment and training and its all-out promotional campaign on its own airwaves, including the creation of NBC *SportsWorld*. NBC also sold about $150 million in commercial time—a phantom sale, as it turned out, to cap a phantom crusade. The Soviets' adventure in Afghanistan prompted the United States to withdraw from the Moscow Olympics, and NBC Sports plunged into a tailspin from which it had not completely recovered in 1983.

XX

PAY TV

The 1980s opened with a rush of obituary notices memorializing the late, great era of network television sports.

Dead at thirty-six. Bumped off by a squad of video gunsels known variously as cable TV, pay TV, pay-cable TV, pay-per-view TV, direct broadcast satellite, super stations and even video games. Deceased after a decade-long slide from its glory days, a slide marked by hypertension, erratic spending, associating with known fast-buck artists and known gamblers.

Sure, the heart and lungs were still working (as long as Cosell was around, the lungs were still working), but it was just a question of when to throw the switch and cut the life-support system. Already the new cable and pay-cable systems such as PRISM in Philadelphia and Sportschannel in New York were slashing their way through obsolescent over-the-air telecasts in local urban markets: local NBA basketball, major-league baseball and professional hockey telecasts were disappearing from the airwaves and showing up on the wired screen. In Seattle, the NBA Supersonics leased their own channels and sold home games directly to subscribers for $125 the season, take it or leave it.

But local-station systems were not the end of cable's encroachment into major sports. Championship boxing, a closed-circuit theater attraction in the sixties, became an early selling point of Home Box Office, the massive Time, Inc., cable system launched in 1972. It carried several Muhammad Ali bouts in the seventies. As the eighties began, HBO was outbidding the networks for such superstar names as Sugar Ray Leonard, Larry Holmes, Gerry Cooney, Thomas Hearns, Aaron Pryor and Alexis Arguello. HBO also carried tape-delay of top tennis events such as Wimbledon and the U.S. Open.

At about the same time, the NBA negotiated contracts with two cable networks, USA and ESPN, that allowed each system the national rights to forty regular-season and ten playoff games. Major-league baseball had a contract with USA for a series of national Thursday night cablecasts. All of these contracts included blackout clauses within the home team's market area, and none precluded telecast deals with over-air networks.

Cable television was not a technology new to the 1980s, of course. Its history dates almost as far back as over-air television itself—to 1948, when remote communities in the United States developed collective antenna systems designed to bolster signals that were weakened by hills or by sheer distance. Through the fifties, cable grew slowly, and always as a technical service; people bought it for no other reason than to improve their reception of network shows. But certain shrewd observers were beginning to see greater potential. They noted that coaxial cables could generate one thousand times the capacity of a telephone wire and at least four times the capacity of standard over-air TV transmission. By 1965, some cable entrepreneurs were talking openly about a coming "Age of Cable" in which wired households would be absorbing original programming from a vast spectrum of sources, competing with the over-air barons instead of merely enhancing the barons' signals.

But that age was deferred and deferred. The prospect of cable terrorized the vested interests in broadcasting; those interests relied on the Federal Communications Commission, seldom a revolutionary force, to protect the status quo. The FCC obliged with a system of rules and prohibitions that effectively kept cable operators from unleashing the full power of their system.

All this started to change in 1976, when the FCC approved a copyright law that, on its face, seemed to strengthen the broadcast establishment's position still further. It required over-air stations to license the programs they beamed out, and allowed them to charge "just and reasonable" copyright fees for their use.

License? Charge a fee? The National Cable Television Association gleefully pounced on that law with a "please-don't-throw-me-in-that-briar-patch" yelp that should have put the broadcasters on alert. Clearly, now it was legal for a cable operator to pick up a station's signals, as long as he paid a price. Now cable operators could offer their subscribers that promised smorgasbord of finished, network-quality programing. The floodgates were finally open.

The following year, HBO claimed a major victory in the United States Supreme Court. The Court, responding to an HBO suit, reversed the FCC's so-called "antisiphoning" rules. This opened the way for cable and pay-TV operators to bid for rights to sports leagues that already retained agreements with over-air networks. For example, USA Network could now cablecast some Thursday major-league baseball games although NBC held the rights to weekend telecasts.

The final barrier to unlimited cable activity fell in 1980. The FCC repealed the rules that had kept cable systems from importing unlimited programs from distant TV stations. Sports programing in particular benefited from this development, as it had, in particular, from the others. Now the growth of cable homes began to escalate rapidly: from 13 million subscribers in 1977, it had reached nearly 24 million by 1982, which represented nearly thirty-five percent of the total United States households owning television.

Another form of the cable invasion surfaced with the advent of Atlanta's Ted Turner and his "Super Station," WTBS. In January 1982, Turner—whose station beamed its signal via satellite into cable homes throughout the United States—completed a deal to pay the NCAA $17.5 million for rights to thirty-eight Saturday night college football games over a two-year period. The deal marked one of the first, and certainly the largest, rights agreements by a cable dealer for major live sports events other than boxing.

Turner's impact upon television sports, like his impact upon all of television, was original and profound. The man who gave America its first national twenty-four-hour TV news service, Cable News Network, in 1980, used his Super Station to make his entree onto the national scene, and shrewdly used the 1976 copyright rule to forge his Super Station. The rule, of course, stipulated merely that a satellite (or microwave) distributor did not have to ask a station's permission to carry its program, as long as he paid the fee. But as the station owner and satellite distributor, Turner thrust himself far beyond this passive role. He acted as a forceful salesman for WTBS's offerings to cable systems nationwide; and his spectacular success—21 million customers by 1982—enabled him to claim yet another offbeat achievement: he made *national* teams, in effect, out of the baseball Atlanta Braves and the basketball Atlanta Hawks, both of which he also owned, by sprinkling those teams' video images into all corners of the country. While sociologists pondered the curious cultural impact of a child reared in, say, Peculiar, Missouri, growing up with an image of the Atlanta Braves as her "home" team, Turner puffed his cigars and sailed his yachts and watched the millions pile up.

It was only a matter of time, people predicted, before a mammoth cable entrepreneur, his wealth bloated on profits gleaned from earlier conquests, would deliver the networks a finishing blow: snatch up a truly irreplaceable jewel, a World Series or a Super Bowl. And then the game would be over, the networks finally stripped of their remaining claim on exclusive inventory. Howard Cosell himself predicted it. "Pay television," he told a columnist in April 1982, "in some form, cable or otherwise, is the economic imperative of major sports from now on."

Indeed, for a few wild months it seemed that the networks themselves were rushing to join the enemy. CBS formed a working alliance with USA. ABC and ESPN signed a contract for the joint creation of a pay-per-view cable network, and later cooperated in sharing the telecasts and the rights revenues of the new United States Football League.

And just in case anyone was demanding statistical confirmation of the crisis, a report released on November 30, 1981, by N. W. Ayer, Inc., a prestigious advertising agency, provided it. "For years, there seemed to be no end to the proliferation of sports programs (on network television). . . . The trend could now be reversing. While the networks continue to program as much sports as ever, viewership has dropped for virtually all sports. . . . Even the seemingly invincible Super Bowl has not been spared as it has dropped from a forty-seven rating in 1978 to forty-six in 1980 to forty-four in 1981."

The Ayer report then offered a sport-by-sport breakdown of the decline, including summaries of auto racing ("achieves only a minor degree of success on network television"), baseball ("ratings were slightly lower than . . . 1980"), bowling ("the increase in viewers observed in the late seventies seems to have leveled off"), college bowl games ("an off season in 1981 with unusual ratings declines"), Super Bowl ("faltered slightly in 1981") and tennis ("consistently fails to produce competitive audience viewing levels"). Golf and horseracing were up somewhat. The agency did not rate boxing.

And yet by the early months of 1983, it was still far from certain that the new technologies of cable and microwave would soon overwhelm the established networks and drive them out of sports programing. The competitors were having problems of their own. ESPN, the twenty-four-hour all-sports cable network launched in 1979 with a $10-million investment by Getty Oil, ran up deficits of $30 million each in 1980 and 1981, and lost another $20 million in 1982. Part of the explanation was that so many cable competitors had flooded the field—WTBS, USA, and the Christian Broadcasting Network in addition to the established HBO—that ESPN's rights costs shot up far higher than expected.

Perhaps the most measured prediction for the future fortunes of TV sports—networks versus cable systems—was tendered early in 1982 by the National Economic Research Associates, Inc., a leading firm of consulting economists. "The impact of pay TV on the value of league network contracts, and on the number of network sports broadcasts," the NERA concluded, "will be significant but small . . . the total number of broadcasts (free and pay) will increase. In short, pay TV seems to be a method of extracting more profit from the television audience—which, as a form of price discrimination, it could be expected to do."

Other experts were withholding any final predictions about network TV's long-term viability in sports coverage until 1987. In that year, the networks' famous $2-billion combined contract with the National Football League would be up for renewal. Whether commissioner Pete Rozelle elects to honor his historic relationship with the networks or whether he will at long last make good on his repeated threats to originate NFL programing within the NFL could very well determine the continuance or the end of significant sports programing on network TV. It is not beyond the scope of possibility that some NFL owners, following the lead of maverick Al Davis, who transferred his team from Oakland to video-rich Los Angeles against Rozelle's virulent opposition, will bolt from the collective system and try to forge lucrative cable and pay-per-view contracts within their own markets.

In the meantime, CBS Sports, NBC Sports and ABC Sports entered the 1980s at a peak of efficiency and competitive sophistication. To look inside the system of a functioning network sports contingent of the eighties was to glimpse an extremely dense, complex accumulation of video intelligence that was at once heavily dependent upon the most immediate nuances of technology and cultural modes and derivative of the great evolving style that Roone Arledge established at ABC Sports back in the early 1960s.

And although observation of an Olympics telecast might yield more sense of sweep and grandeur, the true essence of TV sports competition could be found on an ordinary weekend in which no overriding exclusive event made one network the focus of sports attention—that is, a weekend in which each network was competing on an equal basis for the same audience pool.

The weekend of May 22 and 23, 1982, was typical in that regard. On that Sunday the three network sports "magazines"—CBS *SportsSunday,* NBC's *SportsWorld* and ABC's *Wide World of Sports*—would divide most of America's TV audience for sports. Although the magazines would take the air at staggered times, there would come an hour or so in the late afternoon when all three would overlap. In that span of time, the frenzied intensity of competition for a common viewership would reveal each network sports division in its most elemental values, assumptions and techniques.

On that weekend, I joined the NBC Sports contingent that traveled from New York to Atlantic City, New Jersey, to televise several boxing events for *SportsWorld.*

NBC's may have been the most compelling sports division of the early 1980s. Savaged first by the aborted Moscow Olympics and then by the baseball players' strike of 1981 (NBC owned weekend network telecast rights to big-league ball games), and further destabilized by the departure of several talented program executives, including Chet Simmons for ESPN, NBC Sports was in the process of reinventing itself.

On the other hand, NBC Sports was a division that still operated out of a programing strategy that was umbilically connected to Arledge's great, early coterie. That strategy had been implanted and refined by Don Ohlmeyer, until his departure from NBC a few months previously to form a production company.

Ohlmeyer, a hulking, explosive and ferociously competitive man, had spent several years as part of the same talented group of Arledge protégés that produced Dick Ebersol. Ohlmeyer directed auto racing, Olympics events and aspects of *Monday Night Football* over a ten-year period. A hell-raising Notre Dame graduate in 1967, Ohlmeyer had worked variously as a TV station gofer and a bouncer in a Chicago singles bar before he was "discovered," playing pool in a South Bend bar, by a couple of ABC Sports producers in town to telecast a Notre Dame football game. Ohlmeyer taught the ABC men something about pool, and they agreed to teach him something about television.

Like Dick Ebersol, Ohlmeyer formed a close and emotional relationship with Arledge. "If I had a father in this business, it was Roone," he said. And then, like Ebersol, he ultimately fled: "It was like leaving the womb. It was difficult as hell to leave. But I had to answer the question—was I any good on my own, or was I just an extension of Roone?"

As an executive producer at NBC Sports, Ohlmeyer found out that he was pretty good, although his hypertense, bellowing style infuriated many NBC veterans. "When I got over there I said, 'You guys aren't worth a shit,'"Ohlmeyer recalled with a smile of satisfaction. "It was my way of challenging them."

Ohlmeyer created NBC *SportsWorld*. He made several key advances in the use of sports audio, often pushing crowd noise up above the announcer's voice and experimenting with highly sensitive ground-level directional microphones. But his most lasting legacy was in the NBC Sports production staff itself. He handpicked and organized the nucleus of a young, ambitious and highly experimental staff that soon became known in the industry for a new-wave sensibility in its programing.

It was out of curiosity about how a high-gloss sensibility was affecting sporting events, athletes and audiences that I journeyed on that March weekend to Atlantic City.

XXI

THE ICEMAN CLOWNETH

n Saturday, Atlantic City is plastered by fog. But nobody has come here for the weather. Atlantic City was never what you'd call a weather type of town. Atlantic City's idea of weather is a thermostat. Inside the Atlantic Room, on the mezzanine level of the Tropicana Hotel, the weather remains the same as it always is: under control.

But even the visibility inside the Atlantic Room is limited today. Its Kiwanis-luncheon dimensions are choked with men and women who have come to see what the television lights are all about. Shouldering their way around the center of the room are half a dozen NBC Sports production people dressed in their official network windbreakers, one famous network sportscaster, a few cosmeticky women whose stiletto heels suggest a kind of festivity but whose faces seem stunned, and finally, the men: some of them young and lean and mustachioed, most of them middle-aged and short and thick. All the men are clad in nylon warmup suits with personal monograms ("Lou") stitched on the front. All the men are as expressionless as the fog. These people are the media chroniclers, the wives and girlfriends, the managers and trainers of professional boxers, and a few actual boxers—the inner circle of the fight crowd.

But this is not a Fight Crowd as Norman Mailer or Budd Schulberg would understand fight crowds. These people lack the suppressed eroticism that has always elevated fight people into folk myth. This, it strikes me, is the *made-for-television* fight crowd.

NBC Sports has come to telecast boxing matches from the Tropicana. On Friday, three white Freuhauf semi-trailer trucks with the NBC Peacock painted on the sides rolled down to Atlantic Avenue from Rockefeller Center in New York. The three Freuhauf trucks (Mobile

Unit N-2, as they were collectively known) have brought with them three RCA TK-760 "hard" color cameras; one RCA TK-76 minicam; three videotape machines; two hand-held "shotgun" microphones; several small lavalier mikes; a Chryon character-generator for creating names, statistics and other captioned information on-screen; a "video control area" complete with power supplies to feed voltage through Triaz cables and then to the cameras inside the hotel; a transmission area where technicians will monitor the visual signal as it leaves the truck and flashes first to New York and then over the NBC network; a maintenance bench area; and a miniaturized but self-contained control room, complete with some twenty television monitor screens on the forward wall, seats and desk space for five production staffers, a brace of headset phones for communicating with NBC people inside the hotel, as well as in New York, five wall telephones, innumerable clipboards, and, most important, the control room's nerve center, a sprawling panel of levers and square plastic buttons that glow in color-keyed hues of yellow, red and green. This instrument, known as a Grass Valley Switcher and operated by the crew's technical director, will translate the verbal commands of the director, as he selects from possible camera shots displayed on the various monitor screens, into the "line" picture seen by NBC viewers across the country.

In addition to the equipment, the NBC Sports contingent also includes a manpower force of twenty-one staff technicians, five production assistants, a unit manager, a floor director, a "compliance and practice" supervisor, a public relations man, and a pro forma representative from NBC's executive management—in this case, the manager of technical sports operations.

Marv Albert, the most prominent of the three announcing Albert brothers, has come down from New York to handle the blow-by-blow duties for the telecast. Flying in to join Albert, from his residence in Tampa, Florida, is Dr. Ferdie Pacheco, the celebrated "Fight Doctor," who will provide color commentaries and feature interviews.

The fight people step back when Pacheco struts into the room. He is one of them; he is the surrogate TV star for all the hard, aging hipsters in the gyms and in the casinos who know the fight game and like the lights. Pacheco is a practicing medical doctor, but he talks in the fast impersonal patter of a good lounge comic, and he wears his collars open, the points as long as Sammy Davis's. Pacheco was once Muhammad Ali's personal physician, a fact he is not exactly shy about mentioning. His curious compulsion for one-line gags, and a certain shrewdness about the fight world, attracted the network peoples' attention, and Pacheco found himself, suddenly, in fleshy middle age, a TV celebrity. Now Pacheco has consolidated an impressive amount of power inside NBC Sports: besides his on-air commentator role, Pacheco is the man who approves—and sometimes informally arranges—every bout telecast on NBC.

What this means is that Dr. Ferdie Pacheco controls the destiny of every fight person in the Atlantic Room. In the 1980s, each television network has assembled what amounts to a repertory cast of fighters. Each network has its own version of Pacheco, a sort of impresario on the lookout for fresh talent. But this is television. Boxing talent isn't enough. A certain panache is also necessary; a knack for projecting warmth and sincerity—a way of relating to people. To have a chance at landing a spot in a network repertory, a professional American fighter— typically a young man, black or ethnic, trying to pummel his way out of poverty—is expected to be at the same time charming and articulate and clever: if not another Ali, then at least a Donny Osmond with eight-ounce gloves.

In the crowded Atlantic Room now, a small young man has taken a seat on one of the two wooden chairs positioned in front of some red velvet drapes that reflect the glare of the television lights. The young man has a peaceful Hispanic face. He is wearing a brown velour warmup suit. Except for the faint beginnings of scar-tissue crescents on his forehead and cheekbones, he might be mistaken for one of the Tropicana's bellhops, or a car-park attendant.

This is the featherweight boxer José Nieto. Nieto is one of fourteen children in a family so poor that its idea of upward mobility was to flee the Bronx for Honduras. That happened when José was four. He learned the trade of fighting as a child in Honduran slums. An aunt brought him back to New York when he was ten. He spent his teenage years in and out of detention homes. But José Nieto had his eye on the American middle class. He harnessed his brutality; made it respectable: he learned to box. He won the New York Golden Gloves, fought in the Marines. He got married, enrolled in a community college. Now, at age twenty-seven, José Nieto is one day away from boxing on television. His appearance on NBC will bring him about seventy-five hundred dollars.

Nieto will earn every cent: his opponent will be a former United States Boxing Association featherweight champion named Rocky Lock-ridge, whose 24–2 pro record included nineteen knockouts. Rocky

Lockridge is the number-two ranked featherweight in the world. As an amateur he fought 218 matches, winning 210.

But before he can climb into the ring with Lockridge, José Nieto must endure a trial for which his childhood of back-street violence hardly prepared him: he must record a television interview that will be put on the NBC airwaves just before his fight. The interview will establish to the American public what a charming, articulate and clever guy José Nieto is; what a *cuddly* sort of guy. If Nieto performs well in the interview, his value as a promotable personality will soar. Of course, it will help if he wins the fight. But in TV boxing, winning is not necessarily everything. "I want to put on the air the kind of folks I'd like to see when I'm sitting at home," Pacheco told me earlier. "I want to see *real people* fighting."

But even before Ferdie Pacheco can commence the interview with Nieto, there is one additional layer of preparation.

Towering over Nieto now is a figure who might have stepped from the bosom of a highly affluent, rather suburban rock band. This figure is lean and flat-bellied like a lead guitarist, and his razored mane of red hair and beard sparkle when he glides into the field of TV lights. But his clothes are about power. In a roomful of people for whom "casual" is a sort of sacred ordeal, his own casualness seems almost catatonic: pale brown hopsack jacket over an open-collar dress shirt of rich blue with white pinstripes. The gray suede slippers are by Gucci.

This is Mike Weisman, one of network television's hottest young sports producers. Weisman, who is thirty-two years old, earns five hundred thousand dollars a year for producing NBC Sports programs. His authority in the room is tacit but unquestioned: "What we're gonna do is, we'll do what we call 'word association,'" Weisman is explaining in a slightly overmodulated voice to Nieto's upturned face. Some of the aimless shifting around in the Atlantic room stops. People begin to peer toward the TV lights. A cameraman is adjusting the focus of the minicam aimed at Nieto.

"Which means," continues Weisman, "that if we give you a word, you say the first thing that comes into your mind." Weisman pauses. He gazes down at José Nieto. José Nieto stares upward at Weisman. "Sometimes funny things come out of it," Weisman informs Nieto. Another pause. "Sometimes serious things come out." Yet another silence.

Weisman brings his hands together in a clap of finality that sounds just a shade forced. "Whatever comes to your mind," he repeats. "It's just as if we opened your mind, and whatever came out." Nieto listens. "We've done it with several fighters," Weisman assures him. "Trust us," he tells Nieto. "Believe me," he says. He hesitates for a moment, his hands still clasped. "Don't think about it," he suggests.

Ferdie Pacheco is now moving briskly through the onlookers and into the pool of television lights. He carries a clipboard in one hand. Nieto's body gives up some of its tension as Pacheco replaces Weisman under the lights and sits down on a chair opposite the fighter. Here, at last, is a known quantity.

Mike Weisman plunges from the pool of TV lights into the larger dimness of the Atlantic Room; it is as though someone suddenly switched his hair and beard off. He seems thankful that his conversation with Nieto is over.

I ask Weisman to explain the reason behind the word-association game with Nieto.

"My feeling is, I'm bored with just talking heads," Weisman whispers as Pacheco waits for his cue to begin. "Plus, the important thing is, we're learning something important about these kids. You get some really revealing responses on this game. We threw the word 'KO' at Alex Ramos a few weeks ago. You know what his comeback was? *'I hope to get up and finish strong.'* Revealing. He went on and lost the fight."

A few days later, in New York, I would ask another young NBC Sports programer why he thought this sort of interview was in vogue. His answer was more blunt. "American television is always trying to advance the myth of a classless society," he said. "There isn't supposed to be any underclass in TV's view of the world. Americans associate boxing with a seamy, sort of barbaric segment of society. So naturally the impulse would be to make these guys cuddly and lovable. They're coming into our living rooms."

In the Atlantic Room, Mike Weisman checks his wristwatch and decides to get the Nieto interview going. He nods to the director. The director calls for quiet in the room. The minicam goes hot, the videotape rolls, and Dr. Ferdie Pacheco begins throwing words at José Nieto.

"Goal," is the first word on Pacheco's clipboard.

Nieto's face creases in thought. The dark brows draw together. He is silent for so long that one begins to suspect he may not have heard the question.

"Uh—*to win*," he murmurs, finally.

Pacheco is ready with another one. "Hero."

Again, Nieto sinks into some private abyss. Moments pass. Throats are cleared. Will someone offer a clue from the sidelines?

"*Uh—I'm one.*" Nieto steals a glance at Pacheco. The doctor's face is noncommittal; the answer apparently stands.

"Family."

Another pause, but not quite so vast this time; Nieto is getting the hang of it. *"Reunion."*

"Fear."

"None." At last, an easy question.

"Pain."

"Defeat." Nieto is looser now, faster; he is perhaps beginning to sense that he can go the distance.

"Dream." *"Crown."*

"KO." *"Finish quick."*

"The greatest. *"Duran."*

"Hate." *"In the ring."*

"Food stamps."

Nieto does a take. The whole *room* does a take. *Food stamps?* What the hell kind of—? José Nieto is suddenly in trouble; that one came out of nowhere. *Food stamps.* You can almost see him trying to mentally cover up, wait for the bell . . .

Then Ferdie Pacheco bangs his clipboard on the top of Nieto's head and lets out a horselaugh. "Food stamps" was his little way of ending the session. A *joke.* The entire room chuckles. Once. José Nieto looks relieved. He has endured his "audition." Or so he thinks.

"Let's do it again," calls out Weisman.

Boxing once again found its way back to mainstream respectability on television. Just as Muhammad Ali single-handedly revived the sport in the sixties following the trauma of racketeering investigations and the demise of James Norris, another savior emerged to erase the taint of corruption that settled over ABC's 1977 "United States Boxing Championships." Sugar Ray Leonard.

Like Ali, Leonard restored to boxing a needed cachet of glamour, sexuality and human charm. Unlike Ali, who became an antihero in a political age, Leonard was a hero in a new, apolitical disco age. When he fought Thomas (Hit Man) Hearns for the welterweight championship on September 16, 1981, the various closed-circuit telecasts of the bout reached 250 million human beings—one-sixteenth of the earth's population. Boxing was indeed back in style.

But in 1982, boxing was in style for another reason that had to do with network television's own interests. Already convinced that the threatened NFL players' strike would become a reality in the fall, the three networks were moving quickly to orchestrate large-scale viewer interests in "backup" sports that they could move into Sunday afternoons in the absence of football games. Boxing was the most logical backup sport. There were those in network TV, in fact, who believed that boxing, and not football, was the real TV game. The affinity between the sport and the medium was primal: boxing was drama compressed to an intensity perfectly expressed within the charged energy of the small flat screen. It was drama shorn of all complexities and qualifications—force against force, played out violently upon a bright, stark, claustrophobic landscape. It was the ultimate content of television—simplistic, random, morally neutral, pure sensation without past or future.

The matches in Atlantic City were a part of the first phases of this buildup. They took place several months before the new revival in boxing culminated in yet another dark, grotesque series of episodes: the fatal beating, televised on CBS, of the Korean Duk Koo Kim by the fists of Ray (Boom Boom) Mancini in November 1982; the shocking and prolonged pounding administered to Randy (Tex) Cobb by heavyweight champion Larry Holmes on ABC a couple of weeks later—a fight that inspired Howard Cosell to swear angrily that he would never again call a professional boxing match on TV.

In the Atlantic Room, Mike Weisman is back inside the pool of TV lights. Now he is going over some interview ground rules with another fighter: a middleweight named Bobby Coolidge, a twenty-nine-year-old lefthanded boxer from Foley, Minnesota. Coolidge, whose professional record stands at 20–2–1, is nicknamed "The Iceman." Tomorrow, the Iceman will make his television debut; as with Nieto, the price will be high. Coolidge is scheduled to meet an Eastern seaboard legend on the rise: the babyfaced twenty-year-old Bobby Czyz, an unlikely mixture of brutality and intellect. Czyz graduated sixth in his high-school class of 330 and secured an appointment to West Point military academy. He decided to box instead. He has knocked out twelve of his first seventeen professional opponents, and no one has beaten him.

For the Iceman interview, Weisman has hit on a different premise. Now the crew is dragging its lights, cameras, cables and microphones to the other end of the Atlantic Room and is reassembling this equipment directly in front of a large potted palm.

At first glance, Iceman appears to be the sort of personality who might make José Nieto look, by contrast, like Richard Pryor. Tall and rangy, his blonde hair cropped close to his skull, Iceman peers at Weisman through flat blue eyes, over a nose whose cartilege has already been reshaped to a simulation of Dick Tracy's. He does not particularly strike one as a natural choice for cockamamie TV boxing hijinks. Nevertheless, Weisman is giving it a try.

". . . When he says *that,*" Weisman is telling Iceman, "we're gonna turn on the *fan.*" As he did with Nieto, Weisman pauses expectantly. There is not a great deal of visible reaction from Iceman.

"It's gonna be funny," continues Weisman. "It really is. You're gonna think he's gonna be *yelling* at you—and he *is* gonna be yelling at you. Then *you* say, 'Would you excuse me, Dr. Pacheco?' And you walk off the set, and . . . we're gonna do this a few times. Trust us. Don't worry."

Iceman studies Weisman for a long moment. He strokes his chin. It seems as though everyone in the Atlantic Room is hypnotically fixed on Iceman's moving fingers.

Then Iceman grins.

The effect on Weisman is electric. He all but springs into the air. *"He likes it!"* screams Weisman. *"We got it!"*

Ferdie Pacheco materializes beside Iceman. At the same instant, an NBC technician begins to hurry toward them through the crowd. The technician is delicately cradling a Galaxy twelve-inch oscillating fan with bright blue blades. The technician abruptly flops down to the floor, on his back. He plugs the fan into a socket, flips the switch to "on," and aims the fan upward, so that its breeze hits Iceman and Pacheco.

Back out of camera range, Mike Weisman is whispering again. "Here's the bit," he says. "What we try to do at NBC is entertain as well as inform. Here, we're playing off Iceman's nickname. The bit's gonna be that Ferdie starts off telling the viewer that 'we're awaiting the arrival of Iceman Coolidge.' He's playing it very straight. Then he says, 'I think I hear Iceman now,' and the fan starts blowing Ferdie's hair. You won't actually *hear* any wind; they'll dub it in New York. But Ferdie's gonna raise his voice. He conducts a normal interview with Iceman, but all the time this terrific wind is blowing. Halfway through it, Iceman leaves the set for a minute. The wind stops blowing. When he comes back again, the wind starts up. So we can see it's the Iceman's wind. You got it?"

In the interviewing area, another NBC technician has now dropped crosslegged to the floor. He is gripping the potted palm by its base. He begins to shake it, so that the branches move as if in a gale. Someone notices that the Galaxy twelve-inch oscillating fan is not having much of an effect on Pacheco's thinning hair. Weisman orders a search for a larger fan. Pacheco calls across the room to Marv Albert, "Hey, Marv, loan me your hair a minute, will you?" After several minutes, a second fan—a square window model—is produced and trained on the two men.

Iceman is now getting deeply absorbed in the mood of the moment. "Can you hear me all right?" he calls professionally to the sound men in a high, reedy voice.

Weisman orders a couple of takes. Iceman performs his role with a certain rakish abandon, but something is missing from the heart of the scene.

"Is there any *intrinsic motivation* for Iceman to leave the set?" wonders an assistant producer.

"I got it," says Weisman. "It'll be: 'Iceman—*telephone!'*"

There is still not enough wind to unsettle Pacheco's hair. Mike Weisman begins to prowl the Atlantic Room. He snatches up a large cardboard rectangle—it is a billboard announcing a Tropicana nightclub act—and thrusts it at a stagehand. "Wave this," Weisman commands.

The crew tries another take.

"Cut," yells Weisman. "Shiver, Doc, shiver! You're dyin', Doc! Shiver."

Another take.

"I understand you do roadwork with a goat," Pacheco shouts at Iceman. "I understand you live in an earth shelter."

"No, no, no, no," calls Weisman. "He starts to walk off when you say 'southpaw.'"

Another take. Perhaps forty minutes have gone by now.

"I don't know how much longer I can do this," says the stagehand who has been waving the cardboard. "My thumbs are killing me."

"Get him out after 'southpaw,'" calls Weisman.

"I thought all I had to do was box," quips Iceman Coolidge. Everyone laughs. Once.

NBC Sports is scheduled to originate live from the Tropicana at 3:00 P.M. Sunday, May 23. NBC Sports' broadcast day at the Tropicana gets underway at 3:00 A.M. It is at this hour that Howard Strawbridge begins his prowl. The last floor show from the Tropicana's main showroom has ended ninety minutes ago. The sequined chorus girls and the tuxedoed comics are gone now, and the only sound in the vast, draped hall is the grinding clatter of a huge elevated cubicle that the hotel's black-shirted stagehands are dragging out to the center of the floor. This is the boxing ring.

The ring will come to rest beneath a square perimeter of forty quartz lights suspended from the room's ceiling. These lights will blaze into the eyes of customers at ringside as they peer up at the fighters, turning what was historically a privileged section for the loftiest of high-status spectators into a test of the will, a migraine zone for the stars. Can't be helped; these are television lights—Howard Strawbridge's lights—and the ringsiders are used to it by now: More than a few of these customers, the women as well as the men, look as if they'd like to see the light that can make them blink.

(Veteran TV cameramen like to reminisce about the early days of telecasting fights from Madison Square Garden, in the mid-1940s. After the first few weeks of television's invasion, there began to appear vacant seats where once had reposed New York's crème de la crème of politics, show business and the underworld. It wasn't the bright lights that drove these diamond-pinkied dignitaries away, however—it was the realization that their faces were appearing on television. Right alongside their mistresses'.)

From 3:30 to 8:30 A.M., Howard Strawbridge will tinker with the forty quartz lights, standing on a stepladder, twisting each just so with his long, slender fingers, into the wee hours, until each individual beam is precisely focused and coordinated with the chroma level of the three RCA TK 760s mounted on scaffolding at the edges of the room. Then Strawbridge will turn his attention to the half-dozen smaller lights, each coated with a color gel (three orange, three blue) that hang among the quartz lights. "I like to have a little something on one shot that we can 'refer to,'" says Strawbridge, "and in this case, that happens to be the star filter that we use on our wide shots. You'll see the ring from a distance, and above it what look like these long daggers of light—orange and blue. That's done by a mesh filter we put over one of the lenses; it reflects these color gels like a prism. If you'll notice on your screen, the whole shot is darker when the star filter is in use. That's because it filters out a lot of the light that we've keyed for our normal shots."

When Strawbridge comes down off his stepladder, he will still have work to do. He must next attend to the several "foot candles" beaming upward from below the level of the ring. Without these lights, the fighters would appear to be wallowing in a waist-deep fog.

By the time he is finally finished, Strawbridge will be wallowing in a fog of his own. He will try to force himself to sleep for four or five hours in his hotel room before he must report to the truck and supervise the lighting quality for the actual telecast.

At around ten o'clock in the morning Jimmy Nottingham wanders down from his own hotel suite into the boxing area. That is Nottingham's job: to wander around. To put it bluntly, Nottingham is a snoop. His official title is "supervisor of compliance and practice." What that means is that Nottingham must maintain eternal vigilance against ushers who wear straw hats with "Tropicana" printed on the crown; for cornermen in the ring who have "Tropicana" stitched on the backs of their shirts; for large posters placed casually in the main camera's line of sight that say "Tropicana," even for the name "Tropicana" on the ring's canvas itself. Nottingham doesn't have anything in particular against the hotel Tropicana. He must ferret out similar subtle gambits of commercialism wherever the NBC Sports cameras go. It seems that while television has no inhibitions about bending sports to its own needs, television is grievously offended at the thought of being similarly used.

"It's a constant dogfight," Nottingham says with the cheerful air of a man who loves a good contest—any good contest. Not too many years ago, Nottingham was punting footballs for Yale, and he still keeps himself in athletic trim—although he says he has never *forcibly* removed anybody's Tropicana hat.

"I have to look at everything," Nottingham continues. "Here I'll check out the boxing ring's cornerpost pads, the ring mat, the fighters' *trunks* . . . Yesterday we taped a fight at another hotel in town; we wanted to have something in the can in case today's fights run short. This place, if you can believe it, had a *neon sign* spelling out the hotel name right above the main exit door. It was directly in the main camera's field of view. The hotel people told us it was a fire law requirement; it pointed out the exit. Well, I called up the fire marshal. He said it was a lie. But the sign was up, and we couldn't unhook it without short-circuiting the room's entire power supply."

So what did NBC do? Swallow its moral sense and telecast the neon sign?

Nottingham looks extremely bored. "Naw," he says. "We made an adjustment. What the hotel people don't understand is that we can make a fight look as though it is being held inside a barn in the Midwest if we want to. Plus, we instructed the announcers to not even mention the hotel name once, like we usually do."

"Compliance and practice" people are relatively new components of TV sports crews. They began cropping up not long after CBS embarrassed itself with the winner-take-all tennis series fiasco.

"But the commercialism thing is all over," says Nottingham. "Sometimes it's hard to control. Take auto racing. You've seen those cars with their oil-company stickers, their tire labels on the side, the works. How is a TV network gonna control *that*? Well, luckily for us, I guess, that problem sort of solved itself. The advertising guys at the agencies started to get smart. They realized those stickers were kind of hard to read when a car was going about 180 mph. So instead of stickers and signs, they'd just start painting the *whole car* in the color of a brand-name oil can. They counted on the public to recognize the design and make the connection, based on the TV commercials. Sort of subliminal, you know."

Shortly before 2:00 P.M. on Sunday, Mike Weisman concludes a production staff meeting in the Atlantic Room. He returns to his hotel suite and changes into a fresh pair of slacks and a clean shirt. He takes an elevator to the lobby, pushes his way through the crowds of gray-haired gamblers and through the revolving glass doors that lead to the limousine arcade. He climbs the four iron steps up to the NBC mobile van, opens the heavy cream-colored door, ducks his head and enters a small, unventilated, harshly lighted metal-gray enclave, already acrid with cigarette smoke.

This is Mobile Unit N-2's self-contained control room with its twenty TV monitor screens, its battery of telephones and its master switching unit. Seven men, sitting in three rows and facing the monitor screens, will compose the live boxing telecast from Atlantic City. They include, besides producer Weisman, a director, a technical director (who punches the buttons on the switcher an instant after being ordered to do so by the director), an associate director (who keeps track of elapsed time, down to tenths of seconds), a production assistant, a manager of sports operations and the lighting director.

It is here that Mike Weisman, no longer the whimsical, half-cajoling young impresario of the day before, will rule like Captain Bligh for the next four hours.

Back at Rockefeller Center in New York, a functionally identical but much larger control room is filling up with its own technical crew. This is Studio 6A, the nerve center of NBC *SportsWorld*. With its shag carpeting, its spotless white walls and panel surfaces, its three gradu-ated tiers of desks facing a wall of large monitor screens; with micro-phones twisting up like steel cobras on their adjustable metallic coils, and with square yards of dark audio knobs and colored video buttons, Studio 6A looks like the bunker that will someday decide the fate of the earth.

The commander-in-chief of Studio 6A is Linda Jonsson, a tall and decisive blonde woman of thirty-two. Jonsson is the coordinating pro-ducer of NBC *SportsWorld*. Connected by a direct phone line to Mike Weisman in his truck, Jonsson will exercise final authority over the product that Weisman beams in from Atlantic City. It is her job to integrate these images with commercial breaks, videotaped material and other programing elements that will compose the finished look of *SportsWorld*.

Because of time considerations, NBC has decided to telecast the Nieto–Lockridge bout an hour before *SportsWorld* goes on the air, under the improvised title of "Ringside." The Iceman Coolidge–Bobby Czyz fight will be telecast within *SportsWorld,* because Czyz is one of NBC Sports' designated stars. The network has promoted him heavily, and is counting on him to draw a large audience to *SportsWorld.* A taped interview of Czyz will also air before the fight. But unlike the Iceman Coolidge interview, this one will show Dr. Ferdie Pacheco as serious, even respectful.

At twenty seconds before 3:00 P.M. on Sunday, May 23, the associate director inside Mobile Unit N-2 calls out, "Here we go, everybody. Have a good one." This will be the last clearly audible remark anyone utters for the rest of the telecast.

"Ten seconds to time," says the associated director, as Mike Weisman commands, "Cue the theme."

At 3:00 P.M., the NBC "Ringside" graphics flash across TV screens around the United States. There is a commercial followed by Ferdie Pacheco's whimsical word-association game with José Nieto from the day before.

Marv Albert appears live on-screen to introduce the Nieto–Rocky Lockridge fight *("in what should be a brawl . . .")* but Weisman isn't listening. He is intent upon an off-air monitor screen, a pan of faces at ringside.

"That's her," he shouts suddenly. "That's Rocky's wife!"

"Rocky Lockridge's wife," the director echoes into his headset microphone. The cameraman inside the Tropicana freezes the shot, zooms in close. If Lockridge, the heavy favorite, begins to assume control of the fight, Weisman will order a "Quantel" of Mrs. Lockridge: a facial close-up, electronically compressed and then superimposed, in a corner, over the principal fight shot.

There is a commercial break ("Wait for local! Wait for local!"), and then a long shot of the fighters at center ring, hearing the referee's instructions under the blue-and-gold dagger points of Harold Strawbridge's star filter.

And then the bell sounds and the Nieto–Lockridge fight begins.

"Ready trunks," calls out the director, and the associate director positions his fingers above a colored switcher button.

"Trunks." On-screen, a logo appears, linking the name of each boxer to the color of his trunks.

"Lose the trunks."

The early rounds are not a howling success for José Nieto, of word-association fame. "There he stands," comes Pacheco's voice. "He's been rocked in almost every round, there he stands—he certainly hasn't taken a step backward, has he?"

"Oh, a *combination by Lockridge,*" groans Albert, who sounds almost pained at the sight. Weisman leans to his right and issues a terse order to the director, who passes it along into Albert's earpiece. Weisman has decided that NBC will stay live, rather than cut to a commercial break, before round four begins.

Albert says, "Let's listen in on the corner of José Nieto between rounds." Simultaneously, in the noisy truck, the associate director is counting off the seconds to a videotape replay from the minicam at ringside. The home viewer can see Nieto, his face turned upward and his open mouth sucking air, while the clearly audible voice of his trainer screams: "How come you're gettin' hit, Joe? You gotta move to your right; as you move in, you gotta keep on movin' to your right . . ."

"I like to get audio from the losing fighter's corner," Weisman had remarked earlier in the day. "It's always more interesting."

During round four, Weisman orders the Quantel shot of Rocky Lockridge's wife. Her voice can be heard screaming, "Get that *jab* out there!" In round five, a cameraman locates Nieto's wife, Chi Chi. The closeup of her face reminds one of the women in the Atlantic Room the day before: stunned.

"And a *right* by Lockridge," Albert yells. "And an *uppercut* by Lockridge!"

In round six, Albert—with prodding from Weisman—reminds the viewers that in the word-association test, Nieto's response to the word "fear" was "none."

In round seven, NBC's ringside sound man picks up Nieto's trainer screaming, "I know you can do it! *Don't let me down!* Don't give him no space. Don't give him no damn space, Joe!"

With twenty-six seconds remaining in the eighth round, it is suddenly over. Nieto is still on his feet, but he has collapsed against the referee's chest. "Nieto had *no idea* where he was," Marv Albert bawls. Inside the Mobile Unit N-2, there is suddenly a bedlam of shouting voices. But the commotion has nothing to do with the fortunes of José Nieto, yesterday's Atlantic-Room darling.

"Think about the clock!" comes Weisman's voice, rising above the others. He orders several videotape replays of Rocky Lockridge's decisive flurry against Nieto. The associate director begins counting down to the videotape as Weisman continues to scream commands.

Weisman changes his mind. "We don't need any videotape!" he shouts. The associate director reflexively continues count a beat or two.

"Lissen to me!" Weisman screams. *"Gimme a freeze-frame!"* His voice lowers. "Just trust us," he says. Then another impulse seizes him. "Get a closeup of Carolyn Lockridge!" A cameraman isolates the winner's wife. She looks pleased.

The associate director, John Filippelli, looks at his stopwatch and recommends a thirteen-second summation of the fight from Marv Albert, to be heard under the freeze-frame, and the director orders it. Outside, Albert at once begins to improvise remarks covering exactly thirteen seconds, while voices from the truck ring in his earpiece.

"No commercial," Weisman barks, over the voice of the director. "Think about the clock! Think about time!" As Weisman shouts, his voice mingles with that of the director, who is shouting for Pacheco to begin his interview with Lockridge. "We'll go directly to the undercard!" shouts Weisman. The assistant director begins to compute the time lengths of various subsidiary bouts that had been videotaped earlier for use in just such an emergency.

Inside the ring, the victorious Rocky Lockridge babbles happily away to Ferdie Pacheco's questions. José Nieto is nowhere in sight. Lockridge never mentions him by name; neither does Pacheco. It is as though Nieto already belongs to another time.

Back in Studio 6A in NBC Rockefeller Center, Linda Jonsson is dividing her attention between the monitor screens and the clock. She is thinking about time. Her own exercise in anxiety will commence at four o'clock. Exactly two hours later, with complete indifference to her best or worst timing efforts, *Weekend News* will replace *SportsWorld* on the NBC airwaves. If every one of Jonsson's programing decisions in those two hours is correct, *SportsWorld*'s final credit will fall from the screen within a tenth of a second of 5:58 P.M., leaving exactly two minutes for commercials before the news.

Iceman Coolidge's test against Bobby Czyz will be the featured event in this day's *SportsWorld*. But while the fight represents a seminal event in the life of Coolidge, and perhaps in that of Czyz as well, for Linda Jonsson it represents only irritation.

The fight will be the only live event on *SportsWorld*. It could last ten rounds, or it could last ten seconds. What that means is that Jonsson and her staff will have to add or delete videotaped segments according to the fight's length. That is, they will edit *SportsWorld* even as the show unfolds, constantly subtracting elapsed time and trimming the videotaped events to fit the remaining time. This harrowing skill is known as "collapsing." Among the components on Linda Jonsson's videotape reels are the interviews with Iceman Coolidge and Bobby Czyz, some sumo wrestling bouts from Tokyo, and highlights from the World Invitational Mixed Pairs Body Building Championships from Las Vegas.

But the fight will be irritating for Jonsson in still another way. After every three-minute round, she must decide whether to cut to a commercial or stay live at ringside. Commercial breaks are moments of crisis in network strategy. Viewers use them as opportunities to flick from channel to channel with their remote-control switches. Every three minutes, Jonsson must risk losing most of her audience to CBS *Sports Sunday* or to ABC's *Wide World of Sports*. To minimize this risk, she must monitor the programing developments on those competing programs, as well as keep abreast of the ticking clock—trying to time her own breaks to coincide with flat moments on the competing channels. And to add the final measure of irritation that Linda Jonsson must deal with during the Iceman–Czyz match, she knows that even as she monitors CBS and ABC, CBS and ABC are monitoring her.

At 4:30 P.M., the ring announcer in Atlantic City announces the featured Czyz–Coolidge fight. The core of tension, both in Mobile Unit N-2 and in Studio 6A, is about to be plumbed. The opening bell sounds. Iceman Coolidge, NBC's remaining aspirant to star status in boxing, dances out to center ring—to be met by the shattering right hand of Bobby Czyz.

"Iceman Coolidge apparently stunned by that right hand of Czyz," comes Pacheco's voice.

A moment later: "Already a nick under the eye of Iceman . . ."

A moment later: "Oh, Iceman is *rocked* . . ."

With less than a minute remaining in the first round, Marv Albert screams that "Coolidge is just looking to last the round." It is sadly true. The Iceman's face is a sponge of blood and welts. A few seconds later, Pacheco's voice exclaims: "Coolidge is fighting back, but boy, what punishment he is taking—"

In the truck, Mike Weisman stiffens. He grabs a headset phone.

"Don't be afraid to criticize if Iceman looks bad, Ferdie, you gotta do it!" Weisman shouts. Later, Weisman would explain that he wanted to restrain the Fight Doctor from pretending that the fight was even. No amount of euphemism, however, can conceal the fact that something horrible is happening here. As the bell ending round one sounds, Czyz has battered Coolidge so badly that the Iceman wobbles off toward the wrong corner. The assistant director has already begun counting down to commercial.

In New York, Linda Jonsson makes an instant decision.

"I said no goddamn way we go to commercial," Jonsson recalled later. (On CBS, the basketball game was approaching halftime.) "The fight may not last any longer. Why throw away a commercial? We refused to allow the truck to count down."

Instead, Weisman—who is communicating with Jonsson by phone— now screams at the director: *"Go to the corner!"*

Out at ringside the minicam crew rushes to a vantage point below Coolidge's stool. As Iceman's bloodstreaked face fills the screen, America hears the following exchange:

"You know who you are?"

"Yeah."

"Who am I?"

"You're Morgan."

"Get the name up! Get the name up!" Weisman is shouting inside the truck. An associate finally locates the graphic of Jim Morgan, Coolidge's trainer. A moment later it flashes on-screen.

"How do you feel?"

"I feel fine."

"You wanna continue?"

"Yeah."

Round two begins.

"And they did nothing for him!" Ferdie Pacheco is declaring. "The corner did nothing for Iceman. There was only one man working on his eye, there was no ice—nothing to revive him!"

No ice for the Iceman. There is the stuff of poetry here, or at least one of those four-alarm ironic allusions that television seems to treasure so dearly. Twenty-four hours earlier, Mike Weisman might even have built a sketch around the idea. But now, Weisman doesn't even indicate that he heard Pacheco; he is talking into his headset mike. The time for conferring identity upon the boxers is past. Now, at least to the NBC Sports production crew in the truck, the boxers are merely expressions of digital time.

The second round ends, and the third, and the fourth. Coolidge's face is a mat of blood. Weisman instructs Pacheco to be ready to rush up into the ring for the postfight interview. "Be very, very fast," he advises.

In New York, Linda Jonsson faces a hard choice. She is already one commercial break behind, but she can see that this fight might end at any moment. She takes a chance and orders a commercial. Her misjudgment provides the one moment of grace that Iceman Coolidge, the cooperative straight man, receives from NBC television: it is under the cover of an ad for Old Spice aftershave that his corner throws in the towel.

In New York, a week or so after the fights, I visited Mike Weisman in his office at NBC Rockefeller Center. I asked him whether, in all honesty, he didn't think that José Nieto and Iceman Coolidge had been used as props—spear-carriers in the service of NBC's competitive needs vis-à-vis CBS and ABC. I was not assuming deliberate *mismatches*. Nieto, after all, did last nearly eight rounds with Lockridge, and Coolidge's record coming into the Czyz fight was a respectable 20–2–1. Still—

"Yes," said Weisman after a long moment's thought. "They *were* spear-carriers." I waited for more. "But once the telecast started," Weisman continued, "I couldn't even think of them as spear-carriers. In my telephone conversations with Linda, we weren't even thinking of subject matter. We were thinking of time."

"What will happen to Nieto and Lockridge?" I asked. I was curious to learn something about the career decisions faced by fighters who have been soundly outclassed in their weight divisions.

Mike Weisman shrugged. His telephone was ringing and he wanted to pick it up. "They'll never box on NBC again," he said.

XXII

THE PRIMAL PLAYING FIELD

N *ever box on NBC again."* That doleful sentence tolls in the mind's ear like some Shakespearean banishment—" *The hopeless word of 'never to return' breathe I against thee, upon pain of life . . ."*

All the accumulated logic of television sports' four decades is weighted in those five words. The imperial assumption is unmistakable. Television rules American sports utterly; there is almost no contemplation of sports that is not bounded by an imaginary frame, the soft-cornered rectangle that contains the flat cathode field, the true playing field of sports now.

By March of 1983, Iceman Coolidge and José Nieto were nonpersons inside that primal playing field. Mike Weisman was the number two man inside NBC Sports, and climbing. Now television seemed not only to rule sports, but to *generate* sports according to its needs. A group of multimillionaire businessmen led by David F. Dixon, a New Orleans art dealer, commissioned a market research firm to find out whether Americans—TV viewers, not grandstand fans—would watch professional football in the spring and summer. They found that seventy-six percent of the sample said they would, and signed television contracts with ABC and with ESPN. Thus assured that the nation's premier sports network and a leading cable network would carry their pro football league, the group *then* set about assembling the league's remaining necessities—players, coaches, host cities, stadiums. This was the cathode genesis of the United States Football League.

Quite typically of the disembodied way in which things work in this new cathode sports universe, the USFL registered its most glorious victory some ten days before any USFL team actually took the field. Blandly ignoring its own rules against signing a college player before his college eligibility had expired—rules that were themselves modeled on guidelines established by the National Football League—the USFL handed the nation's top collegiate player, the All-American Herschel Walker, a $3.9-million contract to run at halfback for the New Jersey Generals. Walker's first act as a television football professional was also weirdly consistent with the cathode universe's self-authenticating power: he told what he later admitted was an untruth; that he had not signed as a professional. And then the next day Herschel Walker blandly recanted this untruth and admitted that he *had* signed, and asked God's forgiveness, and Herschel Walker's agent, who had led Walker to the USFL, explained that Walker "felt" that he had not signed a contract (although Walker had, in fact, signed a contract) and that the owner of the New Jersey Generals, who tendered the contract, had "no working knowledge" of NCAA rules and regulations.

And Chet Simmons, the commissioner of the United States Football League—the same Chet Simmons who had entered the charmed universe of television sports so many years before as an aide to Edgar J. Scherick at the advertising agency of Dancer, Fitzgerald & Sample, and who had been a charter member of the legendary ABC Sports coterie that formed first around Scherick and, later, around Roone Arledge; the same Chet Simmons who had lost the ABC power struggle to Arledge and fled with his business acumen and comprehension of television sports esthetics to a middling good career at NBC, and then later at ESPN, from whence he ascended virtually without noticeable transition to the commissionership of this new television-generated professional football league, thereby completing some recondite loop—Chet Simmons produced a supremely cathodic rationale for all of the secrecy and violated rules and manipulations that had buffeted the confused young Walker into lying in his first public act as a television football professional. Simmons explained that it was a "special circumstance."

Just so. And in the ensuing days, it was widely explained that the chain of events just described, this forced and dissembling propulsion of Herschel Walker into the United States Football League, had given the league an "instant credibility." Just exactly so.

And Iceman Coolidge and José Nieto, in return for their own full measure of complicity in the new cathode sports universe's self-authenticating requirements, could never box on NBC again. The operative difference in these vastly differing consequences of submitting to the new universe, apparently, was not that Coolidge and Nieto abandoned their natural behavior and attempted to act out contrived roles that were handed them by the lords of this universe. The operative difference was that Coolidge and Nieto—lost.

As for the USFL, knowledgeable people soon began to explain that the league could not survive on television revenues alone, that it must attract paying fans to the stadiums where the games were being played if its "credibility" were to continue. But even this declaration on behalf of live attendance ("the fan to the game, not the game to the fan") only served to underscore how absolutely disconnected was the USFL from any sustaining system other than television.

For the live fans were not directly necessary to the financial survival of the league. The fans were necessary to cover the otherwise empty seats in the giant stadiums, seats that would inevitably appear, from time to time, in camera range. The fans were necessary as *props*—as a kind of extended studio audience, to strengthen the illusion of the television viewer at home that he was watching a credible sporting event.

Such a complicated interplay between illusion and reality calls forth poetry. And the poetic incantation that summed up, more or less, the unity of the new universe was spoken in the appropriate crucible of Howard Cosell's *SportsBeat* by an entrepreneur working in the metier of pay-per-view, a branch of cable that decodes a scrambled signal if the viewer has paid a price in advance.

"All of us that are involved in pay-per-view in the United States," this sonneteer began, "are real excited about the USFL. That's a group of very strong businessmen who have some very innovative ideas about bringing football back to the people and bringing down ticket prices, offering it to people over ABC, over ESPN, and ultimately into the pay-per-view ranks. And what they will ultimately do, I feel, and many do, that they will use pay-per-view as a logical extension of the stadiums. So that we'll see season tickets being sold in the home in the given city. And if you can't make it out to the stadium that day, you'll be able to buy a hundred-dollar season ticket to the USFL, your team, and watch all the home games on your television set, while the games are broadcast away, to the city away. It's very exciting—"

So it would seem, for a nation with a numeraled football jersey on its back and time on its hands. The prospects are for a long season of sports beyond counting, an endless season. And perhaps that is a good thing. For the primal playing field of the cathode screen, unlike the obsolete stadiums that appeared—fleetingly, at times, in camera range—the primal playing field contains no exits.

BIBLIOGRAPHY

Adams, Russell B. *King C. Gillette*. New York: Little, Brown & Company, 1978.

Barber, Red. *The Broadcasters*. New York: Dial Press, 1970.

Barnouw, Eric. *Tube of Plenty: The Evolution of American Television*. New York: Oxford University Press, 1975.

Cosell, Howard. *Cosell*. New York: Playboy Press, 1973.

———. *Like It Is*. New York: Playboy Press, 1974.

Hess, Gary Newton. *An Historical Study of the DuMont Television Network* (unpublished dissertation). Northwestern University, 1960.

Johnson, William O., Jr. *Super Spectator and the Electric Lilliputians*. New York: Little, Brown & Company, 1971.

Lipsyte, Robert. *SportsWorld*. New York: Quadrangle, 1975.

McNeil, Alex. *Total Television*. New York: Penguin Books, 1980.

Metz, Robert. *CBS: Reflections in a Bloodshot Eye*. New York: Playboy Press, 1975.

Percy, Walker. *The Message in the Bottle*. New York: Farrar, Straus and Giroux, 1975.

Quinlan, Sterling. *Inside ABC*. New York: Hastings House, 1979.

Schwartz, Tony. *The Responsive Chord*. California: Anchor Press, 1973.

INDEX